Great Books About Things Kids Love

ALSO BY KATHLEEN ODEAN

Great Books for Girls:
More than 600 Books to Inspire Today's Girls
and Tomorrow's Women

Great Books for Boys:
More than 600 Books for Boys 2 to 14

Great Books About Things Kids Love

More Than 750 Recommended
Books for Children 3 to 14

Kathleen Odean

Ballantine Books
New York

To Ross

A Ballantine Book
Published by The Ballantine Publishing Group

www.randomhouse.com/BB/

LIBRARY OF CONGRESS CATALOGING-IN-PUBLICATION DATA
Odean, Kathleen.
Great books about things kids love : more than 750 recommended books for
children 3 to 14 / Kathleen Odean.—1st ed.
p.   cm.
ISBN 0-345-44131-1
1. Children—Books and reading—United States—Bibliography.
2. Children's literature, English—Bibliography.   3. Children—Books and
reading—United States.   4. Best books.   I. Title.

Z1037 .O23 2001
011.62—dc21
00-068072

Cover design by Barbara Leff

Manufactured in the United States of America

First Edition: May 2001

10 9 8 7 6 5 4 3 2 1

Contents

CONTENTS

CONTENTS

CONTENTS

Acknowledgments

I want to thank the following people who helped make this book happen: the many children I've worked with over the years in schools and public libraries, who inspired this guide; my wonderful nieces and nephews, for their enthusiasm about all kinds of books; my fellow librarians and other friends in the children's book world, for their thoughts about what children like to read and their dedication to children and books; the staff at the Barrington Public Library, for filling so many interlibrary loan requests; my agent, Lisa Ross, for her ideas and support; my friends Martha Wellbaum, Elizabeth Overmyer, Mary Lee Griffin, Donna Good, Debby Neely, Pam Jenkins, Virginia Smith, Carol Entin, Nancy Cottrill, Melody Allen, Karen Breen, Kerri Ullucci, and David Kitts, for sharing their ideas and excitement about children's books; and my husband, Ross Cheit, who would have loved to have had a book like this when he was young.

Introduction

"I like stories about children and wild animals and explorers."
Garnet in *Thimble Summer* by Elizabeth Enright

"Would you like me to read to you?"
"Yeah. About airplanes."
So Anastasia climbed up on the high hospital bed and read to Sam from one of the library books she had brought him.
Anastasia at Your Service by Lois Lowry

Annie put the dinosaur book back with the other books. Then she gasped.
"Wow," she whispered. "Look at *this*."
She held up a book about Egypt.
Mummies in the Morning by Mary Pope Osborne

INTRODUCTION

"What sayeth he?" asked the red-cross knight's friend.

"Methinks they know of us," whispered the tall one.

"Sure," I said. "I've read all about you guys—the sword in the stone, Lancelot and Guenevere, Merlin the Magician."

Knights of the Kitchen Table by Jon Scieszka

"The best kind of book," said Barnaby, "is a magic book. . . . The best kind of magic book . . . is when it's about ordinary people like us, and then something happens and it's magic."

Seven-Day Magic by Edward Eager

"What is the use of a book," thought Alice, "without pictures or conversations?"

Alice's Adventures in Wonderland by Lewis Carroll

Wild animals, explorers, airplanes, ancient Egypt, knights and wizards, and stories about magic in everyday life—these are just a few of the things children love to read about. The speakers quoted above are all fictional characters, but they speak for real children, too, who have so many interests they want to explore, often starting when they are young.

When I think about what motivates a child to pick up a book and read, or prompts a young child to ask a parent to read aloud, the answer often has to do with the subject of the book. True, some avid readers have an inner drive to read, but most children choose a book because it is about *something they love*. In my seventeen years as a children's librarian, I have seen child after child check out a book not just because I said it was a good story but because it was about dragons, dinosaurs, or dolls. Children who ordinarily wouldn't pick up a book unless they had to changed their minds when offered a collection of brain teasers, a photo-essay with great shots of snakes, or books about baseball, ballet, trucks, horses, monsters, or drawing. Most children don't realize what a rich array of books exists on so many fascinating subjects. Parents can take advantage of their children's excitement about different subjects as a way to get them excited about reading. This guide will help parents and children find books to satisfy their curiosity and their thirst for "pictures or conversations."

The larger goal of this guide is to help your child learn to love reading and to make sure that books mean more to him or her than just a school assignment. (For ways to incorporate reading into your child's everyday routine, see the sections of the book under the heading "Encouraging Your Child to Read.") If a child isn't enthusiastic about reading in school but loves soccer, a book on soccer technique may suddenly make reading worthwhile. A novel with a lot of soccer action or a biography about a favorite player may capture his or her interest. The child's devotion to soccer will spill over to books on the subject, giving books and reading a new and positive status. Learning can take on a practical purpose—such as understanding soccer better—that hooks a child into reading.

Oftentimes, children don't understand why they are taught certain things in school, particularly when they have to study things they don't enjoy. Why do they have to study geography? What is the point of learning math? Outside of school, parents can encourage their child's individual interests and help make learning an active process that arises from the child, not from a set curriculum. Many children who can't see the relevance of reading in school feel differently if they are calling the shots and deciding what they learn about. Frequently these are subjects that never surface in a classroom, like figure skating, detective work, magic tricks, or marbles.

INTRODUCTION

Sometimes children want to learn more about what they've studied in school, after the teacher has gone on to the next subject. For example, children who develop their love of poetry thanks to an enthusiastic teacher may want to make it part of their lives at home. Children who have learned origami in school while studying Japan often want to do more origami outside of school. Or they might listen to a novel about knights and castles in school and want to read other books like it on their own. These are great opportunities for parents to promote books at home and this guide is a great resource for these times.

Parents can also use this book to nudge children who already enjoy reading to widen their horizons. Readers who have been immersed in fiction sometimes extend their enthusiasm to nonfiction if the topic is right. Biographies offer an effective segue into nonfiction thanks to the strong narrative line biographies use to tie the facts together. Historical novels pair naturally with books about history. Children who read *Number the Stars*, a novel about the Danish resistance during World War II, will readily pick up *Tell Them We Remember*, an informational book about the Holocaust.

Conversely, readers who prefer nonfiction may be drawn to novels related to a topic they love. Children who like the outdoors and treasure their field guides often relish wilderness survival books like *My Side of the Mountain*, or fiction about wild animals like *Swimming with Sharks*.

Children who have not developed strong interests or an affinity for books can be steered toward both with help from adults. All too often, children assume that the books assigned in class represent all books, and their experience tells them that reading leads to worksheets or book reports. These children are delighted to hear about books that require no worksheets, on topics they never thought books would address, like secret codes or roller coasters. Even television and movie fans can find tie-ins that lead them to reading, as more children's books are made into movies and television shows. Interest in a popular movie can spill over to books, too; for a while, any book with the word *Titanic* in its title snagged even the most reluctant readers.

Adults need to remember that there's a lot children don't know about the world of books. Children don't automatically ask if a novel they like has a sequel or if the nonfiction book they just read is one in a series, yet if they knew, it would extend their enthusiasm about one book to the next. Most children don't realize that they can find directions for building forts, making pop-ups, or knitting finger-puppets in a book. And they have to be introduced to different types of books like field guides and shown how to use them. But with help from caring adults and with access to the growing number of wonderful books, children can move smoothly along the path to becoming lifelong readers.

How I Made the Choices

To choose the books in this guide, I read or reread every one, and read many of the shorter ones and some of the novels aloud to children. A number of the novels have also been read aloud by classroom teachers I know, with great success. Still others I've given to older children to read and tell me their reactions.

The guide is a *selection* from the many good children's books in print and is far from exhaustive. I had to make choices among the relevant books available, trying to achieve a balanced whole, so inevitably many fine books are omitted, which should not be interpreted as rejection. For most of the subject categories, many other books are available. In the back of the guide, I list resources to help parents find more books if their child wants to pursue a topic further.

The subjects I've included do not exhaust the topics that interest children. You will not find entries on fads such as Pokémon or Beanie Babies, or music and movie stars, simply because their popularity can wane so quickly. Plenty of books are available on these topics, and they might be a good choice for the child who doesn't usually enjoy books but is caught up in the fad.

I drew on my extensive experience as a children's librarian in choosing the topics, but I know that individual children will have serious interests I didn't cover. In my work, I've had children ask for books on fencing, specific military battles, how to perform magic spells, and much more. Children who have immigrated from other countries often want to pore over photographs of their countries of origin. I couldn't cover every topic, on account of space limitations, but I urge parents to pursue their children's specific needs for information at a library, through the public library interlibrary loan system, or at a large bookstore. Again, a section at the back of this guide gives useful information about locating more books.

In the area of picture-story books, I looked for different art styles as well as strong writing, since these books often provide the main way many children see art. I looked for novels with good prose, fully developed characters, and strong plots. Not all topics lend themselves to novels, so in some areas, the list of novels is shorter than in others. The nonfiction varies the most, from nearly wordless books of visual puzzles to photo-essays to long, well-documented texts on serious subjects. In areas where information changes quickly like geography and science, I tried to find the most recent good books whenever possible.

In all the categories, my goal was to include a diversity of cultural groups, to reflect the many backgrounds of children in this country. I also tried to include a balance of books in which the main characters are girls and others where they are boys. This effort is most obvious in the sports fiction lists, although it was not always possible to find enough books on girls to create a balance. My annotations reflect the strengths and weaknesses of each book to make it easier for parents and children to make decisions on what to try.

How to Use the Guide

Each book entry gives the author, title, illustrator, publishing information, number of pages, an age range, and a description. The publishing information includes the original year of publication and the name of the publisher of the hardcover, paperback, or both, depending on which are in print. I have only included books that are in print as this guide is going to press, in order to make it easier for parents to buy them if they want.

I mention in the annotation if a book won a Newbery or Caldecott Medal. These are annual awards given by the American Library Association to the most distinguished children's books of the year. The Newbery Medal is for writing, and the Caldecott for illustration. Each year several other outstanding books are named Newbery or Caldecott Honor Books. (Parents of older children will want to keep their eye out in bookstores and libraries for winners of a new award, the Michael L. Printz Award, first given in 2000. It is for outstanding books for readers ages 12 to 18, and is also bestowed by the American Library Association.)

The books are arranged under eight large categories: Animals, Animals, Animals; Arts and Crafts; Folklore and Fantasy; History and Adventure; Games, Puzzles, Hobbies, and Holidays; Science, Math, and Technology; Sports for Everyone; and Transportation and Engineering. Within the large categories are more specific topics. Within each topic, the books appear by age range, starting with the youngest. Also indicated is whether the book is a picture book, which is a short fictional book with lots of pictures; picture book nonfiction or picture book biography; fiction; nonfiction; folklore collection; biography; or collective biography, a book about a number of people.

For picture books of any sort and folklore, the age levels indicate ages of children who would like to listen to it but who cannot necessarily read the book on their own. For the other categories, the age range suggests reading ability, although this is an estimate and won't apply to all children. In these categories, the phrase "Of interest to younger children" after the age range means that the books are suitable for younger children interested in the topic. In the case of a novel, it means the book would make a good read-aloud for younger children. With nonfiction, the phrase suggests that the younger kids would enjoy looking at the photographs or illustrations on their own, or that they would like to listen to some of the text. For example, many younger children are fascinated with animals. They might not want to listen to sixty pages on a certain animal, but might enjoy highlights from the text and looking at the photographs. The phrase "and up" in an age listing, as in "9 and up," means I think this book would interest anyone older than nine, even adults, often because of its usefulness, like a field guide, or because of spectacular photographs.

For older children who are most interested in novels and biographies, parents may also like to consult my earlier guides *Great Books for Girls* and *Great Books for Boys*, which have a higher percentage of fiction and biographies than this guide does. Generally I tried to avoid listing books from the earlier two guides in this one, in order to give parents the maximum coverage of good books available. About 15 percent of the books in *Great Books About Things Kids Love* appear in the other two books. This guide provides the most nonfiction choices of the three.

INTRODUCTION

In using this guide, parents will probably want to browse through the subjects of interest to their child, read book descriptions, and decide what sounds good. The book also suggests new interests that may hook your child into reading. Older children may want to look through the guide themselves, reading the annotations and choosing books that sound appealing. Voracious readers are always looking for new ideas and less enthusiastic readers may find a new topic that takes their fancy.

Near the back of the book, after the subject listings, you will find suggestions for magazines and reference books. Magazines are perfect for children who feel intimidated by long books or children who have special interests that magazines address, like science and history. Since many children love to receive mail, having a magazine arrive just for them makes reading more exciting.

The suggestions for reference books include basics like recommended almanacs, dictionaries, and atlases, some of which you may want to acquire to have for easy reference at home. I also list field guides, another wonderful kind of book to own. For some children, reference books such as the *Guinness Book of World Records* have an enormous appeal. Children often learn how to use indexes and tables of contents through reference books, a useful side effect.

I have also put together some ideas for extending the excitement about books into different aspects of daily life and tips on reading aloud. This chapter includes suggestions for starting book clubs, linking books and travel, using movies and television to promote books, hosting parties around books, and more.

The last chapter gives information about locating books through bookstores and libraries. Since this guide cannot possibly cover all subjects or books on a subject, I give advice on

HOW TO USE THE GUIDE

finding more and include a list of Dewey Decimal numbers for popular nonfiction topics, which will help children who like to browse for books in public and school libraries. I have also put together a short list of children's books that provide information and emotional support on serious issues that children encounter.

Helping Your Children Discover Their Wings

My goal in this guide is to help children enjoy books and reading. Books were one of the best things about my own childhood and I want to pass on that joy. I also want to honor the interests of children. From my years as a librarian, I know that kids can have intensely strong interests and real information needs. I take that seriously and respect that their interests might not be the same as my own. Parents will notice that many of the subjects in this guide are not at the top of the list of what parents think children *should* learn. True, I've included science, ecology, history, poetry, and other "serious" topics that plenty of children love to read about, but also have sections with the headings Ghosts, Aliens, and UFOs; Pirates and Buried Treasure; and Brain Teasers and Riddles. There are lots of sports books and other topics that might be considered "light," but for many children, these are exactly the topics that will light up their faces and get them reading.

With all the best intentions in the world, parents sometimes have set ideas about what children should read. They want their children to acquire useful knowledge or be exposed to the best literature. This leads parents to ask librarians for the "classics," despite the fact that children typically find the older classics tedious. To these parents, reading about magic tricks or enjoying a science fiction novel may seem to be a waste of time. But, in fact, those readers are still getting benefits, like learning to translate directions into actions with the magic tricks, or encountering vocabulary in the science fiction book that is undoubtedly more sophisticated than what they hear on the playground. And, of course, they are enjoying the books. In an age when literacy and acquiring information are increasingly linked to success, a positive attitude toward reading goes a long way.

Not all books have to be classics, and not all reading has to be directed toward a goal. Books and reading have multiple purposes: the joy of wonderful language, visual pleasure, sustained learning, sources of quick information, escapism, providing directions for projects, and much more. Magazines, newspaper sports pages, Internet sites, e-mail, computer manuals, and baseball cards are other forms of reading that you should encourage if they appeal to your child. Keep an open mind as to the topics, purposes, and formats that capture your child's attention—you may be surprised by what they choose. Reading about things that interest them brings children pleasure, takes them to new places, and may very well turn them into lifelong readers.

As the actress Helen Hayes said about children blessed with good parents and good books, "From your parents you learn love and laughter and how to put one foot before the other. But when books are opened you discover that you have wings."

Great Books
About Things
Kids Love

Animals, Animals, Animals

Birds

Ehlert, Lois. *Feathers for Lunch*. 1990. Hardcover and paperback: Harcourt. 32 pages. Ages 3–8. PICTURE BOOK.

This tall, thin book brims with color and creativity as it introduces twelve common North American birds. Bright collage illustrations show a cat prowling a yard with a bell around its neck to warn the birds of its presence. Discreet labels identify the life-size birds and the many colorful plants near them, while the large typeface conveys the minimal text. This feast for the eyes ends with more details about each bird, its size, food, and home range. A fine melding of outstanding graphics and solid information.

Erdrich, Louise. *Grandmother's Pigeon.* **Illustrated by Jim LaMarche. 1996. Hardcover and paperback: Hyperion. 32 pages. Ages 3–8. PICTURE BOOK.**

A magical grandmother rides off on the back of a porpoise, leaving her grandchildren a nest of eggs. When the eggs hatch, the family cannot identify the birds. An ornithologist who comes to see them announces in shock that they are extinct passenger pigeons. Now the children need to decide if they will release the birds to the wild or turn them over to scientists. Expansive, light-filled illustrations add mystery and charm to the tale.

McMillan, Bruce. *Wild Flamingos.* **1998. Hardcover: Houghton. 32 pages. Ages 3–8. NONFICTION.**

Page after page of stunning photographs of flamingos make this a captivating book. Taken on a visit to the island of Bonaire, in the West Indies, the photos show the brilliantly colored birds in a variety of activities—seeking food, twisted into strange poses for grooming, flying, and interacting in groups. A straightforward text supplies information about the flamingos and their habits. A visual celebration.

Yolen, Jane. *Owl Moon.* **Illustrated by John Schoenherr. 1987. Hardcover: Philomel. 32 pages. Ages 3–8. PICTURE BOOK.**

Pen-and-watercolor illustrations suffuse this Caldecott Medal winner with the magic of going out on a winter night to look for owls. A father and child venture from their farmhouse across snowy fields to woods. In a snowy clearing, the father calls like an owl and a huge owl finally appears in several stunning pictures. This poetic combination of words and watercolors will cast a spell on readers that lasts even when the story is finished.

BIRDS

Guiberson, Brenda Z. *Spoonbill Swamp*. Illustrated by Megan Lloyd. 1992. Hardcover and paperback: Henry Holt. 32 pages. Ages 4–8. PICTURE BOOK NONFICTION.

Watercolors brimming with lush natural pinks, oranges, and greens make this an unusually lovely informational book. It describes life in the swamp for spoonbill parents and their nest of chicks as well as for an alligator and its young. Scenes switch back and forth between the animals until a spoonbill and alligator dangerously cross paths. Water seems to splatter across the page thanks to the artist's brush technique, drawing the reader into the swamp environment. All ends well with glowing scenes as evening falls over the water in this outstanding book.

Morrison, Gordon. *Bald Eagle*. 1998. Hardcover: Houghton. 32 pages. Ages 4–8. NONFICTION.

This unusually elegant book follows the life cycle of a bald eagle from one spring to another, starting with the egg hatching. Large pen-and-ink color drawings show each detail of the birds and life in the nest, then depict flying and hunting for food. Smaller black-and-white drawings give additional information. The gracefully written main text can be read aloud as a story. A stunning combination of art and fact.

Fleming, Candace. When Agnes Caws. Illustrated by Giselle Potter. 1999. Hardcover: Atheneum. 32 pages. Ages 4–9. PICTURE BOOK.

In this tongue-in-cheek tale, eight-year-old Agnes and her mother, Professor Octavia Peregrine, an ornithologist, travel to the Himalayas to find the rare pink-headed duck. Thanks to Agnes's uncanny ability to imitate birdcalls, they succeed, but then must outwit the villainous bird hunter Colonel Edwin Pittsnap. The fresh illustrations provide a sense of time and place, and add visual humor about birds. Full of bird lore and birdcalls, this is a treat.

Hill, Elizabeth Starr. *Bird Boy.* **Illustrated by Lesley Liu. 1999. Hardcover: Farrar, Straus & Giroux. 64 pages. Ages 7–10. FICTION.**

Although Chang cannot talk, he communicates better with birds than other people do. He lives with his parents on a houseboat on China's Li River, where the family's cormorants help Chang's father fish. Chang is thrilled to be old enough to help with night fishing and raising a baby cormorant. A neighborhood bully threatens Chang's new responsibilities until Chang refuses to be bullied any longer. Children will relate to this simple story, even though it is set far away.

Peterson, Roger Tory. *Peterson First Guide to Birds of North America.* **1986. Paperback: Houghton. 128 pages. Ages 8 and up. Of interest to younger children. NONFICTION.**

Beginning birdwatchers will find this handy pocket guide the perfect place to start learning about familiar birds. The first fifteen pages provide a thoughtful introduction to identifying birds by size, wing patterns and shape, and much more. Birds are grouped in eight visual categories to facilitate identification. Two to seven birds appear on a page, with short descriptive paragraphs on the facing page. Although children may prefer photographs, the colored drawings highlight certain features in ways photographs can't. For more advanced guides try *A Field Guide to the Birds* and *A Field Guide to Western Birds*.

Brown, Mary Barrett. *Wings Along the Waterway*. 1992. Hardcover and paperback: Orchard. 80 pages. Ages 9–12. NONFICTION.

In this beautiful nonfiction book, large watercolors complement the well-written introduction to twenty-one waterbirds. Two to four pages describe birds that live in wetlands such as egrets, herons, ospreys, and loons. The information briefly covers habitat, nests and reproduction, eating habits, camouflage, and environmental concerns. Delicately colored illustrations, well-integrated with the text, appear on every page and occasionally fill wordless double-page spreads. This outstanding informational book, notable for its artwork and design, is a pleasure in every way.

Sattler, Helen Rooney. *The Book of North American Owls*. Illustrated by Jean Day Zallinger. 1994. Hardcover: Clarion. 64 pages. Ages 9–12. NONFICTION.

All informational books should be this beautiful, informative, and well-written. Five chapters describe types of North American owls, their habits and habitats, courtship, baby owls, and threats to their well-being. The lovely illustrations, which combine watercolor and colored pencil, provide details such as close-ups of feathers, eyes, bones, and more. The second half of the large book comprises a "Glossary of Owls," with pictures, descriptions, and territory maps of specific owls on each page. An excellent way to learn more about a familiar bird.

Blatchford, Claire H. *Nick's Mission*. 1995. Hardcover: Lerner. 148 pages. Ages 9–13. FICTION.

Nick, who plans to spend all summer swimming, objects to daily therapy to improve his poor speech, the result of being deaf. When a stranger asks Nick to take photographs from a raft in order to save the local lake, Nick skips therapy and heads out on his inflatable boat. On the lake's opposite side, he sneaks into a boathouse where he discovers smuggled scarlet macaws, spectacular parrots from South America, and endangers himself to save the birds. A lively mystery about bird smuggling, with interesting insights into one boy's feelings about being deaf.

Patent, Dorothy Hinshaw. *Pigeons*. Photographs by William Muñoz. 1997. Hardcover: Clarion. 78 pages. Ages 9–13. NONFICTION.

This fine overview of pigeons, illustrated with many color photographs, reveals how remarkable these wild birds are. Patent describes their origin in the United States, their habitat and life cycle, and related birds. She reviews scientific experiments that show how intelligent pigeons are, able to learn quickly and grasp surprising visual concepts. Also amazing is the pigeon's ability to find its way home from a long distance. One chapter relates impressive exploits of homing pigeons in wartime. Readers will come away with a changed view of this adaptable, intelligent bird.

George, Jean Craighead. *My Side of the Mountain*. 1988. Hardcover and paperback: Dutton. 178 pages. Ages 10–14. FICTION.

Teenager Sam runs away from New York City to his family's land in the Catskill Mountains, where he teaches himself to live off the land with nothing but an ax and a flint and steel. He befriends a raccoon and weasel, and trains a baby falcon, whom he names Frightful, to catch small game for him. Sketches of his hard-earned knowledge show plants that are good for eating and how to devise a snare for game. An absorbing survival story with a timeless quality, this is a Newbery

Honor Book. Followed by *On the Far Side of the Mountain* and *Frightful's Mountain*.

Hobbs, Valerie. *Carolina Crow Girl*. 1999. Hardcover: Farrar, Straus & Giroux. Paperback: Puffin. 144 pages. Ages 10–14. FICTION.

Eleven-year-old Carolina lives in an old school bus with her mother and baby sister. While parked illegally on land near the California coast, Carolina rescues a newborn crow fallen from its nest and begins to raise it. Stefan, a boy in a wheelchair who plans to be a naturalist, befriends Carolina and Crow. When his family, who own the land, invites Carolina to stay with them while her mother moves on, Carolina must decide what matters in life and what to do with Crow. A thoughtful, beautifully written short novel.

Cats

Harper, Isabelle. *My Cats Nick and Nora*. Illustrated by Barry Moser. 1995. Hardcover: Scholastic. 32 pages. Ages 2–7. PICTURE BOOK.

Barry Moser has directed his considerable talents as a watercolorist to a simple story written by his young granddaughter. In it, she describes a visit from her cousin and how they play with her two cats. The simple words are perfect for reading to preschoolers or for beginning readers to read themselves. The highlights of the book are the large, wonderful illustrations of the two girls and the cats.

Voake, Charlotte. *Ginger*. 1997. Hardcover and paperback: Candlewick. 40 pages. Ages 3–7. PICTURE BOOK.

The bright-eyed cat named Ginger has a fine life, with good food and a beautiful basket. Large, humorous watercolors show Ginger's shock when his young owner gets a kitten. "He'll be a nice friend for you, Ginger," she says, but Ginger doesn't agree. Frustrated when the kitten follows him everywhere, Ginger escapes into the rainy outdoors. Luckily, the girl comes up with an idea that leads to a surprisingly happy conclusion. A wonderful read-aloud.

Calhoun, Mary. *Blue-Ribbon Henry*. Illustrated by Erick Ingraham. 1999. Hardcover: Morrow. 40 pages. Ages 3–8. PICTURE BOOK.

The adventurous cat Henry is spending the day at the county fair where he will be in a pet show. Put in a cage while his human family enjoys the fair, Henry escapes and tries to save The Kid, the boy in the family, who has entered a greased pig contest. Later, wandering on his own, Henry takes a Ferris wheel ride and saves a lost child. Soft, realistic illustrations contrast nicely with the less realistic but always intriguing escapades of the cat. One in a delightful series.

Choi, Yangsook. *New Cat*. 1998. Hardcover: Farrar, Straus & Giroux. 32 pages. Ages 3–8. PICTURE BOOK.

Large, rounded pictures introduce New Cat, who lives at the tofu factory of her loving owner, Mr. Kim. Everything seems great to New Cat except that she is not allowed in the production room, where she can see a mouse resides. The night that she finally gets into the room, her presence keeps a disaster from occurring. A beautifully designed book with wonderful illustrations, a brave cat, and a happy ending.

Darling, Kathy. *ABC Cats*. Photographs by Tara Darling. 1998. Hardcover: Walker. 32 pages. Ages 3–8. NONFICTION.

Here is a wonderful collection of cat photographs. For each letter of the alphabet, a different cat breed takes the stage, each with a large photograph, a smaller photo of a kitten, and a paragraph of description. The clean layout provides a fine setting for these appealing creatures. Many children will be surprised at so many breeds and how different they can look from each other. A pleasure to read and especially to look at.

Moore, Inga. *Six-Dinner Sid*. 1991. Hardcover: Simon & Schuster. Paperback: Aladdin. 32 pages. Ages 3–8. PICTURE BOOK.

Sid, a cunning cat, has figured out how to get six dinners a day, one each from six residents of Aristotle Street who all believe he is their cat. He has to work for the dinners by remembering how to behave differently with each owner. The jig is up when he gets sick and each of the owners brings him to the same vet. But Sid works out his own solution when the owners band together to limit his meals. Charming colored pencil illustrations convey Sid's personality and his surroundings.

Bonners, Susan. *Why Does the Cat Do That?* 1998. Hardcover: Henry Holt. 32 pages. Ages 4–9. PICTURE BOOK NONFICTION.
Anyone interested in cats will enjoy this clever book. A character called Bob, who is unfamiliar with cats but has taken a cat-sitting job, is constantly puzzled by the cat Molly's behavior. After each puzzling incident, illustrated in soft pen-and-watercolor, the author provides a page of explanation for the cat's actions. Many relate to how cats live and hunt in the wild, and how cats treat humans as fellow cats. Readers will look at house cats in a new, more appreciative light after reading this excellent short book.

Scott, Carey. *Kittens: An Ideal Introduction to the World of Kittens.* 1997. Hardcover: DK. 40 pages. Ages 4–9. NONFICTION.
Cat lovers will purr with pleasure over this book, which features several photographs of cuddly kittens on every page. Each double-page spread focuses on a type of kitten or a topic relating to kittens such as newborn kittens, Persian longhairs, marmalade kittens, tortoiseshell kittens, and so on. A main paragraph discusses each topic with more information in the captions. The last three topics are "Choosing Your Kitten," "Caring for Kittens," and "Kitten Comforts" like toys and baskets. Delightful for browsing.

Miller, Sara Swan. *Three Stories You Can Read to Your Cat.* Illustrated by True Kelley. 1997. Hardcover and paperback: Houghton. 48 pages. Ages 6–8. Of interest to younger children. EASY READER.

Readers will laugh at the cat's facial expressions in this easy-to-read book that has three stories addressed to a cat. The first opens, "One day you woke up early," and proceeds to describe a rainy day in the life of the listening cat. The second story concerns a bug that the cat tracks but doesn't eat. In the final chapter, the cat's owner tells the cat not to do anything bad, and the cat responds in an unexpected way. Cheerful pictures add humor to this enjoyable book.

Petersen-Fleming, Judy, and Bill Fleming. *Kitten Training and Critters, Too!* Photographs by Darryl Bush. 1996. Hardcover: Tambourine. 40 pages. Ages 7–10. Of interest to younger children. NONFICTION.

This photo-essay offers simple ways to train kittens and shows professional animal trainers working with different animals. Each double-page spread has advice for young owners on the left-hand page and scenes of training exotic animals on the right. The instructions on training, accompanied by clear photographs, address how to approach the responsibility of training and to use specific commands such as "No" and "Come." A useful beginning guide to kitten training. Also see the authors' book *Kitten Care and Critters, Too.*

Mayerson, Evelyn Wilde. *The Cat Who Escaped from Steerage: A Bubbemeiser.* 1990. Hardcover: Atheneum. 66 pages. Ages 8–11. FICTION.

Nine-year-old Chanah secretly makes room in her basket for Pitsel, a stray cat, as her Polish family boards a ship for Ellis Island. Chanah works hard to hide the cat, even though she knows immigration officers will send it back if they spot it when they land. When Pitsel gets loose on the ship, Chanah and her loyal cousin sneak into forbidden ship areas to find her. A short, lively novel about love of family and pets in the face of hardship.

Namioka, Lensey. *Yang the Third and Her Impossible Family*. Illustrated by Kees de Kiefte. 1995. Hardcover: Little, Brown. Paperback: Yearling. 144 pages. Ages 8–11. FICTION.

New to the United States, all Yingmei wants is to fit in and not have her family embarrass her. She hopes to be friends with the popular girl Holly, who gives her a kitten that Yingmei has to hide from her family. She knows the kitten will create chaos in their house, but she loves it and successfully hides it in the basement for a while. Yingmei struggles with the differences between China and America, and learns to appreciate her family members for who they are. One in a perceptive, sometimes hilarious series.

Le Guin, Ursula K. *Catwings*. Illustrated by S. D. Schindler. 1988. Hardcover: Orchard. Paperback: Scholastic. 40 pages. Ages 8–11. Of interest to younger children. FICTION.

Mrs. Jane Tabby takes it in stride when her four kittens are born with wings. She raises them, then sends them off into the world. Two girls and two boys, the winged cats make their home in a wooded area, only to find they have enemies they hadn't expected. Charming pen-and-ink drawings with washes of pastel color help bring the kittens to life in this small book, good for reading aloud to younger children as well as for independent readers. First in a series.

Neville, Emily. *It's Like This, Cat*. 1963. Hardcover and paperback: Harper. 180 pages. Ages 9–13. FICTION.

"My father is always talking about how a dog can be very educational for a boy. This is one reason I got a cat,"—so begins this timeless novel about an adolescent named Dave and his cat Tom. Set in Manhattan in the 1960s, it deals with the life of a fighting tomcat in a big city, a boy's conflicts with his dictatorial father, and unexpected new friendships. The voice of Dave rings true as someone in the stage between childhood and being an adult, whose well-loved pet helps the transition.

Fogle, Bruce. *Know Your Cat: An Owner's Guide to Cat Behavior*. Photographs by Jane Burton. 1991. Hardcover: DK. 128 pages. Ages 11–14. Of interest to younger children. NONFICTION.

This attractive book full of sharp photographs explains why cats do what they do, but not how to train them or care for them. The first chapter, "Understanding Your Pet," covers such topics as "Cat Talk" and "Marking Territory." Other chapters look at how cats relate to humans, other animals, and other cats; birth and kittenhood; stages in growth; adult cat behavior; and the history of domestic cats. Interesting and fun for browsing.

Dinosaurs

Wahl, Jan. *I Met a Dinosaur.* **Illustrated by Chris Sheban. 1997. Hardcover: Creative Editions/Harcourt. 32 pages. Ages 2–7. PICTURE BOOK.**

Spacious, sometimes haunting illustrations show the different kinds of dinosaurs that appear in a girl's life after she visits a natural history museum. Her parents always offer a mundane explanation—it's a moose or a cow—but the girl knows better. The story, told in few words, ends in her bedroom, which happens to be filled with dinosaur-shaped furniture. An afterword gives more information on dinosaurs. The book's elegant design sets it above most dinosaur stories for young children.

Most, Bernard. *How Big Were the Dinosaurs?* **1994. Hardcover and paperback: Harcourt. 32 pages. Ages 2–8. PICTURE BOOK NONFICTION.**

Although the illustrations are cartoonlike, this short introduction to dinosaurs offers facts in its text as well as humor. Most of the double-page spreads discuss two dinosaurs, giving pronunciation, a fact about its size, and a quip, such as, "With all those protective plates, Stegosaurus would be a perfect crossing guard." The pictures convey size by depicting the dinosaurs in modern settings like a basketball court and a bowling alley. One of several popular dinosaurs books by this author.

O'Brien, Patrick. *Gigantic! How Big Were the Dinosaurs?* **1999. Hardcover: Henry Holt. 32 pages. Ages 2–8. NONFICTION.**

Each wide double-page spread features a colorful painting of a dinosaur or other ancient beast juxtaposed against a more modern object. For example, the triceratops looms over a knight in armor on horseback, with the simple text, "This mighty giant's massive head was a dangerous weapon." The pictures carry most of the information, while an appendix adds a bit more about each creature. Informational and amusing.

Carrick, Carol. *Patrick's Dinosaurs.* **Illustrated by Donald Carrick. 1983. Hardcover: Clarion. Paperback: Houghton. 32 pages. Ages 3–7. PICTURE BOOK.**

At the zoo, Patrick's older brother Hank points out that a brontosaurus was heavier than ten elephants. Suddenly Patrick sees a brontosaurus looking straight at him. When they canoe on the zoo lake and Hank mentions that a diplodocus could stay underwater like a submarine, Patrick spots a huge shadow under the water: Could it be a diplodocus? Only Hank's final reassurance that dinosaurs are extinct makes the imaginary creatures disappear. Followed by *What Happened to Patrick's Dinosaurs?* and *Patrick's Dinosaurs on the Internet.*

Whybrow, Ian. *Sammy and the Dinosaurs.* **Illustrated by Adrian Reynolds. 1999. Hardcover: Orchard. 32 pages. Ages 3–7. PICTURE BOOK.**

When Sammy finds a box of dinosaurs in his grandmother's attic, he washes them and keeps them in a bucket. He reads books about dinosaurs, then names each one. They go everywhere with him and sometimes talk to him in quiet voices that no one else can hear. Clever, appealing pictures show the toys moving as if they were alive, appearing especially happy when they see Sammy after an absence. A wish fulfillment fantasy for young dinosaur devotees.

Pringle, Laurence. *Dinosaurs! Strange and Wonderful.* Illustrated by Carol Heyer. 1995. Hardcover: Boyds Mills. Paperback: Puffin. 32 pages. Ages 3–9. PICTURE BOOK NONFICTION.

This colorful book enthusiastically introduces dinosaurs of many kinds, describing them and giving pronunciations of their names. It briefly discusses the work of paleontologists in discovering dinosaur bones and other fossils that constantly reveal new information. Slick pictures in appropriately lurid colors suggest what the dinosaurs might have looked like. Large print, ample white space, and an effective design combine with thoughtful writing to make a fine beginning book for dinosaur fans.

Lessem, Don. *Supergiants! The Biggest Dinosaurs.* Illustrated by David Peters. 1997. Hardcover: Little, Brown. 32 pages. Ages 4–8. NONFICTION.

This appropriately large-sized book concentrates on huge dinosaurs. Each double-page spread shows a different dinosaur, describes where paleontologists found its bones, and explains how much we know about it. A sidebar lists the dinosaur's length, estimated weight, where it lived and when, diet, and distinguishing features. Color acrylic paintings place the gigantic creatures in their settings, sometimes juxtaposed against familiar objects to demonstrate their size. Certain to be a hit with those who love dinosaurs.

Gillette, J. Lynett. *Dinosaur Ghosts: The Mystery of Coelophysis*. Illustrated by Douglas Henderson. 1997. Hardcover: Dial. 32 pages. Ages 5–9. NONFICTION.

Young paleontologists will love this book. It supplies information about the small dinosaur, the coelophysis, and its discovery, and offers several possibilities of how the coelophysis at a certain site in New Mexico might have died. After describing the dig where dozens of these dinosaur skeletons were found, the author presents one possible scenario of death after another, giving the strengths and weaknesses of each argument, thus replicating a scientific discussion in an accessible way. A fascinating scientific journey, with useful photographs and excellent paintings.

Osborne, Mary Pope. *Dinosaurs Before Dark*. 1992. Hardcover and paperback: Random House. 64 pages. Ages 6–9. FICTION.

One day Jack and Annie climb up to a mysterious tree house filled with books. Looking at one about dinosaurs, Jack says, "I wish I could see a Pteranodon for real," and suddenly he does. The tree house spins wildly and they land in the time of dinosaurs. Annie makes friends with some dinosaurs, but when Tyrannosaurus Rex appears, the children know they must somehow leave. The first in the popular "Magic Tree House" series. A companion volume, *Dinosaurs Research Guide*, provides information about dinosaurs.

Griffith, Helen V. *Dinosaur Habitat*. Illustrated by Sonja Lamut. 1998. Hardcover: Greenwillow. Paperback: Avon. 96 pages. Ages 8–12. Of interest to younger children. FICTION.

Ryan, who loves dinosaurs, treasures the terrarium he made to house his brightly painted plastic dinosaurs. Now that he is sharing a room with his older brother Nathan, Ryan worries that Nathan will harm his things. When Nathan throws across the room a fossil that Ryan found, they are both in for a huge surprise. The room fills with mist and when it clears, they are in a land of dinosaurs. Each time a new dinosaur appears, an adventure follows, some scary, some enjoyable. A lively short novel about a popular subject.

Butterworth, Oliver. *The Enormous Egg*. Illustrated by Louis Darling. 1956. Paperback: Little, Brown. 188 pages. Ages 9–13. FICTION.

Twelve-year-old Nate Twitchell is surprised to find one of the family hens sitting on a huge, leathery egg, and more surprised when a tiny triceratops hatches out. A congenial visiting paleontologist helps Nate figure out how to feed and take care of Uncle Beazley, as he names the dinosaur. Word spreads quickly about the extraordinary event, and soon politics and commerce threaten to interfere with Uncle Beazley's quiet existence. A wonderful read-aloud that combines humor, gentle satire, and plenty about dinosaurs.

Tanaka, Shelley. *Graveyards of the Dinosaurs: What It's Like to Discover Prehistoric Creatures*. Illustrated by Alan Barnard. 1998. Hardcover: Hyperion. 48 pages. Ages 9–13. Of interest to younger children. NONFICTION.

Imagine leading an expedition to the Gobi Desert in Mongolia and uncovering a nest of dinosaur eggs, or going to Argentina as a young professor and finding the rare skull of a *Herrerasaurus*. Each year scientists learn more about dinosaurs thanks to expeditions like the ones described in this exciting book. Photographs show the desolate places that paleontologists search for dinosaurs and the remarkable discoveries they have made. Sidebars offer imagined scenes of each dinosaur's final hours. Dinosaur devotees shouldn't miss this fine book.

Hill, Pamela Smith. *Ghost Horses*. 1996. Hardcover: Holiday House. Paperback: Avon. 224 pages. Ages 10–13. FICTION.

Sixteen-year-old Tabitha is fascinated by the dinosaur bones in the Black Hills near her South Dakota home. But it's 1899, and young ladies are discouraged from studying science. Tabitha's father, a fire-and-brimstone preacher, loathes all mention of Darwin, dinosaurs, and women's rights. Nevertheless, Tabitha resolves to work for the dinosaur hunter from Yale who is coming to dig for bones. She comes up with a plan and, despite obstacles, starts to follow her dream. An exciting story about the early days of paleontology.

Cohen, Daniel, and Susan Cohen. *Where to Find Dinosaurs Today*. 1992. Hardcover: Cobblehill. 210 pages. Ages 10–14. NONFICTION.

This is a regional guide with state listings for museums, parks, fossil quarries, and commercial enterprises that have to do with dinosaurs. Each entry gives from one paragraph to several pages of description, as well as location, hours, admission fees, and phone numbers. Because the book was published in 1992, it is best to call and confirm the information. A valuable resource with more than a hundred listings for travelers who love dinosaurs.

Zindel, Paul. *Raptor*. 1998. Hardcover and paperback: Hyperion. 176 pages. Ages 11–14. FICTION.

Gruesome descriptions of rapacious raptors dominate this thriller. Teenager Zach and his friend Uta, a member of the

Ute tribe, venture into the caves near a Utah paleontological dig and find a dinosaur egg. Zach takes it home and when it hatches, the mother dinosaur attacks his house. The teenagers return to the caves where a nightmare exploration hurdles them from one danger to another, with vivid scenes involving huge mutant dinosaurs. Not for readers with weak stomachs, this is a wild, grizzly adventure.

Dogs

Feiffer, Jules. *Bark, George.* **1999. Hardcover: Harper. 32 pages. Ages 2–6. PICTURE BOOK.**

When his mother tells George, a lanky puppy, to bark, he answers with a meow and then a series of other animal noises. So his mother takes him to a vet, and the man pulls animal after animal out of George's throat. The problem seems to be solved until a surprising twist at the end shows that George has a new but similar problem. On clean, wide pages, the cartoon-like illustrations show funny facial expressions and priceless body language. A clever catchy story from a master cartoonist.

Keats, Ezra Jack. *Whistle for Willie.* **1964. Hardcover: Viking. Paperback: Puffin. 32 pages. Ages 2–6. PICTURE BOOK.**

How Peter wishes he could whistle! If he could, he knows that his dog, Willie, would run straight to him. While he practices, the two of them hang around their urban neighborhood, twirling around and making chalk drawings. No listener can resist practicing along with Peter as he tries to whistle and all will rejoice when, to his surprise, he finally succeeds and Willie responds. This longtime favorite with outstanding collage illustrations makes a perfect read-aloud. Other books about Peter include *Peter's Chair* and *The Snowy Day*.

Wells, Rosemary. *McDuff Comes Home*. Illustrated by Susan Jeffers. 1997. Hardcover: Hyperion. Paperback: Little, Brown. 32 pages. Ages 2–7. PICTURE BOOK.

McDuff, a small, white dog, gets lost one day while chasing a rabbit and finally falls asleep in a vegetable garden. The older woman who finds him and says she'll drive him to the police station puts McDuff in the sidecar of her big red motorcycle. In response to McDuff's barking, she ends up at his owners' house to everyone's delight. The old-fashioned pictures strike just the right note. One in a series.

Day, Alexandra. *Good Dog, Carl*. 1985. Hardcover: Green Tiger. Paperback: Aladdin. 40 pages. Ages 3–6. PICTURE BOOK.

In this nearly wordless book, Carl, a huge black dog, is left in charge of the baby one day and they proceed to create enjoyable messes together. They bounce on the bed, try on jewelry in front of the mirror, get into the fish tank, and more. But before the mother comes home, Carl cleans up all traces of the mischief, with no harm done. The first in a very entertaining series.

Rylant, Cynthia. *Henry and Mudge Take the Big Test*. Illustrated by Suçie Stevenson. 1991. Hardcover: Bradbury. Paperback: Aladdin. 42 pages. Ages 3–8. EASY READER.

Henry's big dog, Mudge, is completely lovable but not well trained, so he and Henry enroll in dog behavior school. At first, Mudge is oblivious to the training, but Henry keeps practicing and the huge dog starts to improve. But has he learned enough to pass the test and graduate? Illustrated with sunny pictures, this is an entry in a long, satisfying series perfect for beginning readers but also good for reading aloud.

Pomerantz, Charlotte. *The Outside Dog.* Illustrated by Jennifer Plecas. 1993. Hardcover and paperback: Harper. 64 pages. Ages 4–8. EASY READER.

When a stray keeps coming back to the small home she shares with her grandfather in Puerto Rico, Marisol wants to keep it. Her grandfather refuses but Marisol's persistence slowly pays off. First Grandfather lets her feed the dog, which she calls Pancho, then he lets her buy Pancho a flea collar. When Pancho disappears for a few days, Grandfather is as worried as Marisol and as happy when the dog returns. Charming childlike pictures create a rural setting, and the inclusion of Spanish words and glossary adds a nice touch.

Evans, Mark. *Puppy.* 1992. Hardcover: DK. 48 pages. Ages 4–9. NONFICTION.

This short entry in the ASPCA "Pet Care for Kids" series is full of photographs of charming puppies and children caring for them. Written in a way children can understand, the book gives advice for first-time dog owners on basics like food, sleep, grooming, playing, and more. Even those children who don't have a dog but wish they did will enjoy the photographs. An attractive introduction to a popular topic.

Petersen-Fleming, Judy, and Bill Fleming. *Puppy Training and Critters, Too!* Photographs by Darryl Bush. 1996. Hardcover: Tambourine. 39 pages. Ages 7–10. NONFICTION.

This useful photo-essay offers ways for children to do simple puppy training. Each double-page spread gives advice to young owners on one page, while the facing page shows scenes of trainers with exotic animals and gives interesting bits of information. The instructions on training, accompanied by clear photographs, explain how to use specific commands and gestures. A fine beginning guide that provides an intriguing glimpse of professional animal trainers.

Gardiner, John Reynolds. *Stone Fox*. Illustrated by Marcia Sewall. 1980. Hardcover and paperback: Harper. 85 pages. Ages 8–12. FICTION.

In this short novel based on a legend, ten-year-old Willie is determined to save his grandfather's Wyoming farm. They need five hundred dollars to pay back taxes, and Willie's grandfather has given up all hope. When Willie learns of a dog race with a five-hundred-dollar prize, he is sure that he and his dog, Searchlight, can win, until the undefeated Arapaho Indian Stone Fox enters the race. Excitement, courage, and generosity mark the heart-wrenching climax that will leave many readers in tears.

Naylor, Phyllis Reynolds. *Shiloh*. 1991. Hardcover: Atheneum. Paperback: Bantam. 144 pages. Ages 8–12. FICTION.

When eleven-year-old Marty befriends Judd Travers's dog, the boy realizes that Travers has been hurting the dog and denying it food. Marty's family is too poor to afford pets, but Marty nevertheless builds a pen in the woods for the dog he names Shiloh. When Marty's parents learn about his dilemma with Shiloh, they understand his feelings and concerns but have no easy answers. Marty struggles with questions of law and ownership, and treatment of animals in this compelling book, which won the Newbery Medal. Followed by *Shiloh Season* and *Saving Shiloh*.

Rodowsky, Colby. *Not My Dog.* **Illustrated by Thomas F. Yezerski. 1999. Hardcover: Farrar, Straus & Giroux. 80 pages. Ages 8–12. FICTION.**

Ellie desperately wants a puppy. She checks out library books about puppies and learns all she can. But instead of a puppy, her parents adopt a full-grown dog that an older relative can no longer keep. At first stubborn eight-year-old Ellie refuses to accept Preston as her dog, but his loyalty and intelligence gradually win her over. Readers will sympathize with Ellie but also with Preston in this realistic and satisfying short novel.

Byars, Betsy. *Wanted—Mud Blossom.* **1991. Hardcover: Delacorte. Paperback: Yearling. 148 pages. Ages 8–13. FICTION.**

One in a terrific series about the Blossom family, this enjoyable novel focuses on the family dog, Mud. When the irrepressible Junior, youngest of the three children, brings home the school hamster and it disappears, he believes Mud is responsible. So Mud goes on trial, accused of murder, with the Blossom children and their hilarious friend Ralphie as lawyers and jury. Funny and serious by turns, this is another winner—and a great read-aloud—by an outstanding writer.

Rock, Maxine. *Totally Fun Things to Do with Your Dog.* **1998. Paperback: Wiley. 128 pages. Ages 9–12. Of interest to younger children. NONFICTION.**

This large paperback is brimming over with ideas for playing with dogs. It includes some training tips, advice about walking and running with dogs, and games with balls and Frisbee. It also suggests ideas for partying with dogs, photographing them, putting on unofficial dog shows, and more. The tone is enthusiastic and the book is easy to use. Young dog owners will love it.

Lowry, Lois. *Stay! Keeper's Story*. Illustrated by True Kelley. 1997. Hardcover: Houghton. Paperback: Yearling. 160 pages. Ages 9–13. Of interest to younger children. FICTION.

What is life like from a dog's point of view? An articulate dog tells his story from his youth spent near the back door of a French restaurant, to his time with a homeless man, on to his fame as a photographer's model, and finally his home with an adoring girl and her mother. True to a dog's nature, the narrator focuses on food and smells but also offers wry insights into human behavior. With plenty of humor for adults, this makes a good read-aloud for younger children, too.

Henkes, Kevin. *Protecting Marie*. 1995. Hardcover: Greenwillow. Paperback: Puffin. 195 pages. Ages 10–13. FICTION.

Fanny doesn't feel complete without having a dog around, but her volatile artist father hates any disturbances, especially when his painting isn't going well. He once gave her a puppy, only to take it away again. Now he has given her another dog, but she is torn between her love for her new pet and her fear that her father will betray her again. The well-rounded characters and their real emotions will hold the attention and sympathy of pet lovers.

Kehret, Peg. *Shelter Dogs: Amazing Stories of Adopted Strays*. Photographs by Greg Farrar. 1999. Hardcover: Albert Whitman. 144 pages. Ages 10–14. NONFICTION.

Dog lovers will be fascinated by these eight stories about dogs that proved their worth after being left at animal shelters.

One trained as a service dog to pick up dropped items and open doors and cupboards for an owner with multiple sclerosis. Another, adopted by an animal trainer, has acted on television and in movies. Each one is amazing in its own way. The book includes sidebars of additional information and black-and-white photos.

Fogle, Bruce. *The Encyclopedia of the Dog*. 1995. Hardcover: DK. 312 pages. Ages 12 and up. Of interest to younger children. NONFICTION.

Although this huge volume was not published as a children's book, kids love it. Its expansive pages are packed with excellent photographs of dogs and information about them. The first few chapters give the history of dogs, their role in different cultures, and an overview of their behavior. The book goes on to describe more than four hundred breeds grouped in categories, giving each breed's strengths and weaknesses as pets. It ends with advice on choosing and taking care of dogs. A splendid book, helpful and perfect for browsing.

Horses and Horseback Riding

Baker, Karen Lee. *Seneca.* **1997. Hardcover: Greenwillow. 32 pages. Ages 3–7. PICTURE BOOK.**

The narrator loves everything about her horse, Seneca. No aspect of taking care of her pet daunts her: cleaning the stall, feeding him, fetching water, taking stones from his hooves, grooming him. She rides him through the woods, where she sometimes falls as the horse jumps over logs. She and Seneca like galloping best, as an exuberant picture conveys. Expressive watercolors in fall tones show a jeans-clad girl and her large white horse enjoying their time together. Sure to appeal to young animal lovers.

McMillan, Bruce. *My Horse of the North.* **1997. Hardcover: Scholastic. 32 pages. Ages 3–8. NONFICTION.**

In this delightful photo-essay, the Icelandic girl Margret has her own horse and important tasks to accomplish while riding. The large, vibrant photographs show Margret and her two friends on horseback, herding cattle and helping with the big sheep round-up. Sweeping shots of the countryside give a flavor of Iceland, and an author's note adds more information about the country and its unique horses. A pleasure for horse lovers, who will want to plan a trip to Margret's homeland.

Rounds, Glen. *Once We Had a Horse*. 1996. Hardcover and paperback: Holiday House. 32 pages. Ages 3–8. PICTURE BOOK.

Scratchy vibrant illustrations show a small brother and sister and the old horse they grow to love. The children live on a ranch where one day a cowboy brings them a gentle old horse. Humorous scenes show how they learn to climb on its back and eventually manage to stay on. The children are persistent and take setbacks in stride, just as the horse takes their attempts to ride him without fuss. Readers will be envious of the children's summer with the old horse. Altogether wonderful.

Locker, Thomas. *The Mare on the Hill*. 1985. Hardcover: Dial. Paperback: Puffin. 32 pages. Ages 5–9. PICTURE BOOK.

Sweeping vistas show a horse racing through green pastures, grazing under glorious autumn trees, and standing near a red barn under stormy skies. Two boys slowly win the trust of the mare, which was mistreated by a previous owner. Finally, after a year, a storm brings the mare down close to the barn where she soon gives birth to a foal. Children's books rarely feature magnificent, formal artwork such as these paintings, which glow with a love of nature through the seasons.

Polacco, Patricia. *Mrs. Mack*. 1999. Hardcover: Philomel. 40 pages. Ages 8–11. PICTURE BOOK.

This sentimental picture-story book, based on the author's childhood, will have young riders cheering and crying. Ten-year-old Patricia, who longs to ride horses, is disappointed when her father takes her to a rundown stable. She soon realizes that the manager, Mrs. Mack, knows all there is to know about horses, and with her help, Patricia learns to ride through trial and error. She also learns how to make friends with a variety of people as the summer progresses. Polacco's warm illustrations, many of horses, add color and drama to the unusually long text.

Ryan, Pam Muñoz. *Riding Freedom*. Illustrated by Brian Selznick. 1998. Hardcover and paperback: Scholastic. 144 pages. Ages 8–11. FICTION.

Charlotte Parkhurst may have been the first woman to vote in the United States, long before women were legally allowed to. She spent much of her adolescence and adult life disguised as a male and voted under a male name. This short novel draws from incidents in her intriguing life, including her stint as a stagecoach driver. Her love of horses and her talent for handling them kept her going through hard times and provided her greatest satisfactions. A compelling read for horse enthusiasts.

Lauber, Patricia. *The True-and-False Book of Horses*. Illustrated by Rosalyn Schanzer. 2000. Hardcover: Harper. 32 pages. Ages 8–11. Of interest to younger children. PICTURE BOOK NONFICTION.

Do horses walk on tiptoe? Can some horses count? What do the noises that horses make mean? These questions and more are answered in this entertaining book that starts with a short introduction on the history of horses. One or two illustrated pages address each of fourteen questions in a clear, readable manner. Diagrams add more information, showing bone structure and how a horse moves. Good for browsing or reading from start to finish, this will interest animal lovers and clear up some mysteries and misconceptions.

Henry, Marguerite. *Misty of Chincoteague*. 1947. Hardcover: Simon & Schuster. Paperback: Aladdin. 145 pages. Ages 8–12. FICTION.

Paul and Maureen are staying on Chincoteague Island near Assateague Island, where wild horses run free. Every year the local men drive some of the wild horses to Chincoteague and sell them. The siblings are determined to buy the Phantom, a legendary wild mare that is captured with her foal, Misty. The children have saved their money, but at the last minute it's uncertain if they'll get the horse of their dreams. Although somewhat marred by its old-fashioned attitude toward females, this novel is still likely to please horse lovers.

Ryden, Hope. *Wild Horses I Have Known*. 1999. Hardcover: Clarion. 96 pages. Ages 8–13. Of interest to younger children. NONFICTION.

Spectacular photographs fill this exceptional book about wild horses that live in the mountains on the Wyoming-Montana border. Ryden, an expert on wild horses, compresses a lot of information and enthusiasm into her lucid text about wild horses and their behavior. But her stunning photography is the book's highlight. Horse admirers will want to look at the horse pictures again and again, and will also enjoy the twenty smaller photographs in the back that show specific horse colors. Outstanding.

Lester, Alison. *The Quicksand Pony*. 1997. Hardcover: Houghton. 162 pages. Ages 9–12. FICTION.

Biddy and Joe, who both love ponies, have never met although they live near each other in Australia. Biddy lives on a farm with her family, while Joe has lived in the wild with his mother since he was a baby. But when Joe is nine, their paths cross in a way that will change Joe's life forever. They meet because of a horse that gets stuck in the quicksand while herding cattle. This short, lyrical novel vividly paints the picture of two engaging children, the horse they both love, and how their very different lives come together.

Haas, Jessie. *Unbroken: A Novel.* **1999. Hardcover: Greenwillow. 192 pages. Ages 9–13. FICTION.**

After her mother dies in a horse-riding accident, Harriet's only hope for the future is her unbroken Morgan colt. The thirteen-year-old orphan must live with her mild uncle Clayton and her aunt Sarah, a woman with a powerful personality who despised Harriet's mother. Harriet's dream to continue her education depends on training the colt, a task she has never tried before. Despite her hardships, she copes with her fate in a realistic way that will win the reader's sympathy. Set in 1910 in rural Vermont, this is a beautifully written novel.

Platt, Chris. *Willow King.* **1998. Hardcover and paperback: Random House. 194 pages. Ages 9–13. FICTION.**

When her neighbor is going to have his newborn foal killed because the horse has crooked legs, thirteen-year-old Katie intervenes and ends up raising Willow King. She struggles to break and train the horse, tasks far more difficult than she expected. She gets help from Jason, an attractive fellow student. Will his attention lead to a romance? Can Willow King overcome his problems and become a winning racehorse? Written by a former jockey and based on a real horse, this story will capture the hearts of horse lovers.

Pritchard, Louise. *My Pony Book.* **1998. Hardcover: DK. 64 pages. Ages 9–14. NONFICTION.**

Each double-page spread in this attractive volume provides considerable information about one aspect of ponies:

grooming, feeding, tack, jumping, and much more. It will be extremely helpful to pony owners, but will also appeal to those children unlikely to own a horse but who love reading and dreaming about them. One page shows colors and markings, with examples of palominos, duns, dapple grays, and other horse colors, while another shows twenty-two different breeds. A wonderful compendium of facts and photographs.

Rodenas, Paula. *The Random House Book of Horses and Horsemanship.* **Illustrated by Jean Cassels. 1997 Revised Edition. Hardcover and paperback: Random House. 180 pages. Ages 9–14. NONFICTION.**

This large book full of glossy photographs gives detailed information about horses and their riders. It covers the history of horses, different breeds, horse care, training and riding, workhorses, horses in competitions, and horse activities such as Pony Club, 4–H, fox hunting, merit badges, and riding for the handicapped. The knowledgeable author treats each topic thoroughly, accompanied by many large and small photographs, mostly of horses. Sidebars provide interviews with a groom, a veterinarian, a jockey, a stunt rider, and many more horse people. A treasure house for young riders.

Insects and Spiders

James, Betsy. *Mary Ann.* 1994. Hardcover: Dutton. 32 pages. Ages 3–7. PICTURE BOOK.

Amy is sad that her friend Mary Ann is moving away. In her friend's honor, Amy names her new praying mantis "Mary Ann," but is devastated when the insect dies after laying eggs. The girl's parents assure her that baby praying mantises will hatch, then cheer her up by taking her to visit her human friend Mary Ann. When the family returns, the eggs have hatched without the lid on the terrarium. To Amy's pleasure, the house is filled with hundreds of young insects. Great fun.

McDonald, Megan. *Insects Are My Life.* Illustrated by Paul Brett Johnson. 1995. Hardcover and paperback: Orchard. 32 pages. Ages 3–7. PICTURE BOOK.

"Insects are fascinating. Insects are my life!" proclaims Amanda Frankenstein, a girl who devotes herself to the study and care of insects. She argues with her brother, who loves dinosaurs, and trades insults with a schoolmate who disparages her interest. But, luckily, she finds a kindred spirit at school, a girl who has a similar passion about reptiles. Amanda is unwavering in her intent to be an entomologist, even though her mother won't allow bugs in the house. A thoroughly engaging book with pictures that capture Amanda's spirit.

Carle, Eric. *The Very Quiet Cricket.* 1990. Hardcover: Philomel. 32 pages. Ages 3–8. PICTURE BOOK.

Vibrant collages of hand-painted paper sweep across the pages of this wide book. Under a huge sun, a cricket hatches from an egg. A bigger cricket chirps a welcome by rubbing its wings together to chirp, but when the little cricket imitates the action, nothing happens. Different insects including a locust, praying mantis, spittlebug, cicada, and dragonfly greet the little cricket who still cannot answer. Finally, to the delight of young listeners, the cricket chirps (a microchip embedded in the book makes the noise). Expect to read this again and again.

French, Vivian. *Spider Watching*. **Illustrated by Alison Wisenfeld. 1995. Hardcover: Candlewick. 32 pages. Ages 3–8. PICTURE BOOK.**

This charming book combines information with a story about spiders. "My brother loved spiders, and so did I," it opens. The girl who tells the story hopes to share her enthusiasm about the spiders living in their shed with her visiting cousin Helen. At first, Helen finds spiders scary. But when she watches one repair a web, she changes her mind. The illustrated story appears on the right-hand pages of the book, while the left-hand pages supply more information about spiders. The old-fashioned-looking watercolors suit the story and visually convey spider facts.

Van Allsburg, Chris. *Two Bad Ants*. **1988. Hardcover: Houghton. 32 pages. Ages 3–8. PICTURE BOOK.**

When two ants break ranks with fellow workers and stay in a kitchen to eat sugar, they begin a strange and dangerous series of adventures. First, a large silver scoop lifts them up and stirs them into hot brown liquid. After that, they nearly get toasted and then nearly drowned. Superb illustrations show the ants' perspective, so readers have to interpret the pictures and figure out what causes each new danger. Highly recommended.

Facklam, Margery. *The Big Bug Book.* **Illustrated by Paul Facklam. 1994. Hardcover and paperback: Little, Brown. 32 pages. Ages 4–9. PICTURE BOOK NONFICTION.**

The Madagascar hissing cockroach, the giant wetapunga, and the tarantula hawk wasp—these are some of the thirteen large insects in this entertaining book. Life-size color pictures of the insects accompany three or four paragraphs on their habits and habitats. The pictures place the creatures near everyday objects such as a baseball bat and a plate of cookies, so children can get a good sense of their size. A topic with a lot of appeal, well-executed.

Parsons, Alexandra. *Amazing Spiders.* **Photographs by Jerry Young. 1990. Hardcover and paperback: Knopf. 32 pages. Ages 4–10. NONFICTION.**

In this "Eyewitness Junior" book, each double-page spread features a large photograph of a spider surrounded by small drawings and photographs. Information is conveyed in the many captions, on subjects including "Giant, Hairy Spiders," "Black and Deadly," and "Jumpers and Spitters." The book highlights unusual spiders such as those that can walk on water and others that capture prey in unusual ways. This eye-catching introduction to a popular topic is one in a series of appealing photography books about nature.

Sonenklar, Carol. *Bug Girl.* **Illustrated by Betsy Lewin. 1998. Hardcover: Henry Holt. Paperback: Yearling. 112 pages. Ages 8–11. FICTION.**

Fourth-grader Charlie has an Amazing Bug-A-View, a magical instrument that can turn a person into a bug. His friend Suzanne swears she will never use it after it temporarily turns her little brother into a slug. But on a class field trip, when Charlie becomes a beetle and is about to be killed,

Suzanne knows the only way to save him is to become a bug herself. A light read that relies on a suspenseful plot and broad humor.

Anderson, Margaret J. *Children of Summer: Henri Fabre's Insects.* **Illustrated by Marie Le Glatin Keis. 1997. Hardcover: Farrar, Straus & Giroux. 112 pages. Ages 8–12. FICTION.**

Based on a true story, this novel describes life with insect expert Henri Fabre, a French teacher and writer who lived from 1823 to 1915. The narrator, Fabre's ten-year-old son, enthusiastically shares his father's explorations and experiments. For example, together they collect burying beetles and watch them maneuver dead moles. Black-and-white drawings illustrate the insects and scientific activities. Although the narrative is low-key, readers who like insects will enjoy this short novel and be inspired to observe the insects around them more closely.

Dahl, Roald. *James and the Giant Peach.* **Illustrated by Nancy Ekholm Burkert. 1961. Hardcover: Knopf. Paperback: Puffin. 118 pages. Ages 8–12. Of interest to younger children. FICTION.**

Orphan James Henry Trotter, age seven, lives with his nasty aunts Sponge and Spiker, who soon get crushed by a giant peach. The peach, which grows larger than the tree it grows on, saves James, who crawls into it and finds himself among human-sized insects. With them, he finds the love he has missed since his parents died. When the peach starts rolling away, he becomes the leader of their extraordinary expedition through the air. A well-loved story and a popular read-aloud.

Holch, Gregory J. *The Things with Wings*. 1998. Hardcover and paperback: Scholastic. 240 pages. Ages 9–12. FICTION.

Every year thousands of emerald rainbow butterflies migrate through Angel Falls, eleven-year-old Newton's new hometown. When the outgoing Vanessa befriends him, Newton joins her adventures chasing the butterflies but shakes his head at her dream of flying. Newton finds increasingly mysterious things are happening. Who is the man in mirrored sunglasses? What is hidden in the walled garden? Where have all the other kids their age disappeared to? A highly enjoyable, magical story centered around butterflies.

James, Mary. *Shoebag*. 1990. Hardcover and paperback: Scholastic. 135 pages. Ages 9–12. FICTION.

When the cockroach Shoebag mysteriously changes into a boy, the human family in the house where Shoebag lives welcomes him into their lives. The daughter, whose nickname is Pretty Soft, has a tutor because she is a television commercial star, but Shoebag goes to the local school, where he encounters a bully. But he also makes a friend who changes his life and Pretty Soft's. Full of the contrasts between life as a cockroach and life as a human boy, with the cockroach ways sometimes coming out on top, this is an engaging story with a happy ending.

Fletcher, Ralph. *Spider Boy*. 1997. Hardcover: Clarion. Paperback: Yearling. 184 pages. Ages 9–13. FICTION.

Bobby loves spiders so much that he keeps a journal about them, with amazing facts from it given in italics throughout this novel. His pet tarantula, Thelma, is his best friend now that his family has moved from Illinois, where he had lots of friends, to New York State. At his new school, Bobby has to deal with a bully but also makes a friend. Eventually he feels more at home, although only after some hard moments. A compelling story full of spider facts.

Dewey, Jennifer Owings. *Bedbugs in Our House: True Tales of Insect, Bug, and Spider Discovery.* **1997. Hardcover: Marshall Cavendish. 64 pages. Ages 9–13. Of interest to younger children. NONFICTION.**

In this entertaining memoir about her childhood in New Mexico, the author describes adventures involving insects and spiders, at school and with her friends, including one about a black widow bite. She liked to take stink bugs for walks with kite string around their middles, and filled her room with jars of insects and spiders. Factual sections at the end of each chapter, combined with the beautifully rendered drawings, provide a lot of information in a readable manner.

Pringle, Laurence. *An Extraordinary Life: The Story of a Monarch Butterfly.* **1997. Hardcover and paperback: Orchard. 64 pages. Ages 9–13. Of interest to younger children. NONFICTION.**

By focusing on the life of one monarch butterfly, this book takes the reader on an amazing journey from Massachusetts to Mexico. The butterfly, called Danaus, starts as an egg on a milkweed plant. The lovely, informative paintings show each stage as Danaus moves from egg to caterpillar to chrysalis. Finally she emerges as a butterfly and embarks on a dangerous three-thousand-mile journey to her Mexican wintering ground. Readers learn all about monarchs, their habits, and their instinctual journey through a lively narrative.

Fischer-Nagel, Heiderose, and Andreas Fischer-Nagel. *An Ant Colony*. 1985. Hardcover: Carolrhoda. 48 pages. Ages 9–14. NONFICTION.

Ant colonies follow intricate rules laid out in this informational book. It focuses on a red ant colony, describing the different kinds of ants and the roles they play. Photographs and diagrams show body parts as well as parts of the well-organized anthill. The book examines the life cycle of the ants, their food sources, their enemies, and more. Color photographs supplement the text in this straightforward look at a remarkable insect.

Zim, Herbert S., and Clarence Cottam. *Insects: A Guide to Familiar American Insects*. Illustrated by James Gordon Irving. 1987 Revised Edition. Paperback: Golden. 160 pages. Ages 9 and up. Of interest to younger children. NONFICTION.

"By dealing only with common, important, and showy insects, this book will help the novice begin a fascinating study," reads the first line of the instructions for using this field guide. The introduction then gives practical suggestions for children interested in learning more about insects. The clear organization and a good index make it possible for the reader to locate the pages on insects they want to identify. Each page has a range map, a description, and a color picture of the insect with useful details. Butterflies and moth larva are shown, too. An inexpensive little guide packed with information.

More Pets

Keats, Ezra Jack. *Pet Show!* **1972. Paperback: Aladdin. 32 pages. Ages 3–7. PICTURE BOOK.**

In this old favorite, the neighborhood children are talking about a pet show. Archie plans to bring a cat, but on the day of the show, he can't find it even with the help of his friends. The other children head for the show, where each wins a prize such as "noisiest parrot" and "handsomest frog." When Archie finally arrives without the cat, he offers the judges a most unusual pet. Vividly colored collage illustrations show a rundown urban neighborhood with a strong sense of community. A warmhearted story that celebrates all kinds of pets.

King-Smith, Dick. *I Love Guinea Pigs.* **Illustrated by Anita Jeram. 1994. Hardcover and paperback: Candlewick. 32 pages. Ages 3–8. PICTURE BOOK NONFICTION.**

King-Smith's love of guinea pigs suffuses this charming book. In simple words with a personal touch, the text gives the history and characteristics of guinea pigs, with an emphasis on why they are so lovable. It also includes tips for keeping guinea pigs as pets and how to make them happy. Irresistible illustrations show the bright-eyed animals eating, exploring, and being cuddled. Likely to make the reader rush out to get a guinea pig.

Rylant, Cynthia. *Henry and Mudge and Annie's Perfect Pet*. Illustrated by Suçie Stevenson. 2000. Hardcover: Simon & Schuster. Paperback: Aladdin. 42 pages. Ages 3–8. EASY READER.

When Henry's cousin and next-door neighbor Annie wishes she had a pet, Henry recalls getting his much-loved, enormous dog, Mudge, who was little at first. Henry can understand why Annie wants a pet, and he enlists his parents' help. In a series of funny pictures, Henry and his parents think about Annie's personality and the pets she wouldn't like. A trip to the pet store with Annie produces the perfect solution: a bunny. A delightful entry in a delightful series.

Park, Barbara. *Junie B. Jones Smells Something Fishy*. 1998. Hardcover and paperback: Random House. 66 pages. Ages 6–9. FICTION.

It's going to be Pet Day in Junie B. Jones's classroom, but cats and dogs are not allowed. Junie B. feels "real gloomy" until her grandmother mentions raccoons. Unfortunately, her mother forbids that idea and suggests a worm. Junie B. enjoys the worm but gets truly excited when her grandmother brings home a dead fish she caught. Why won't her parents let her take that to school on a leash? No one is funnier than Junie B. Jones. Younger readers who laugh their way through this entry in the series will want to read all the books about her.

Landau, Elaine. *Minibeasts as Pets*. 1997. Hardcover and paperback: Children's Press. 48 pages. Ages 7–11. Of interest to younger children. NONFICTION.

Minibeasts such as ladybugs, millipedes, ants, and crickets offer pet owners the advantage of being small and free. This short book, illustrated with color photographs, explains how to find these small pets and how to take care of them. It discusses what to feed them and how to create an appropriate habitat. The unusually large print makes this a good book for younger readers, even if they aren't looking for a pet. It concludes with suggested books, useful Web sites, a glossary, and an index.

Cox, Judy. *Third Grade Pet.* **Illustrated by Cynthia Fisher. 1998. Hardcover: Holiday House. Paperback: Yearling. 112 pages. Ages 8–11. FICTION.**

At first, Rosemary objects to getting a rat as the third-grade class pet because she thinks rats are dirty and flea-bitten. But when the class gets a little white and gray rat, Rosemary is the one who names it Cheese. Then the teacher appoints her one of the two rat keepers for the week, and she starts to like Cheese. In fact, to protect him she secretly takes him home, the start of more excitement than she wants. An enjoyable story that includes tips on caring for rats.

King-Smith, Dick. *Sophie's Snail.* **Illustrated by Claire Minter-Kemp. 1991. Paperback: Candlewick. 96 pages. Ages 8–11. Of interest to younger children. FICTION.**

Sophie announces that she plans to be a farmer and surprises her family by listing the animals she will have. Though only six, she immediately starts saving money for her farm. Meanwhile, she has to settle for small pets like a snail, then wood lice, centipedes, earthworms, earwigs, and a slug in the potting shed. Her single-mindedness gets Sophie into trouble, but it doesn't stop her from doing just what she wants. The first in a fine series all of which involve plenty of pets, this is good for reading aloud to younger children.

Hurwitz, Johanna. *A Llama in the Family*. Illustrated by Mark Graham. 1994. Hardcover: Morrow. Paperback: Scholastic. 98 pages. Ages 8–12. FICTION.

When his mother promises a surprise, Adam hopes it will be a new bike. Instead, she brings home a llama in order to open a trekking business out of their Vermont farm. After a slow start, Adam learns to love Ethan Allen, as the llama is named. Meanwhile, Adam is saving money for a bicycle, a goal that changes when he has a chance to make the llama's life better. An agreeable story about an unusual pet, followed by *Llama in the Library*.

Mowat, Farley. *Owls in the Family*. Illustrated by Robert Frankenberg. 1962. Paperback: Bantam. 92 pages. Ages 8–12. FICTION.

The narrator, Billy, lives in Saskatoon, where he spends his free time on the nearby prairie. One day he comes home with Wol, a young great-horned owl so personable that eventually he's welcome in the house. In fact, Wol seems to think he's human, and keeps the family laughing with his escapades. A sunny atmosphere characterizes this story of a boyhood spent outdoors and in the company of many well-loved pets. Based on Farley Mowat's childhood, this is beautifully written and great for reading aloud.

Gutman, Bill. *Becoming Best Friends with Your Hamster, Guinea Pig, or Rabbit*. Illustrated by Anne Canevari Green. 1997. Hardcover: Millbrook. 64 pages. Ages 8–12. Of interest to younger children. NONFICTION.

In this helpful book, readers learn about the advantages and drawbacks of hamsters, guinea pigs, and rabbits as pets, along with details of how to care for them. Divided into sections for each animal, the text describes their characteristics, physical needs, breeding, and health problems. Anyone trying to choose among the three types of pets will find this guide especially useful. Many readers will enjoy the cartoonlike pictures, packed with silly humor, in this entry in the "Pet Friends" series.

Maze, Stephanie. *I Want to Be a Veterinarian.* **1997. Hardcover and paperback: Harcourt. 48 pages. Ages 8–14. NONFICTION.**

In this terrific introduction to being a veterinarian, large and small color photographs show a wide variety of vets and other animal workers at their jobs: large animal vets, equine vets, zoo vets, surgeons, researchers, and everyday "companion animal" vets. The text describes the work and advises children on how to prepare for being a vet through 4–H, camps, caring for a pet, studying hard, and more. An appealing book full of helpful information about a profession that attracts many children.

Engfer, LeeAnne. *My Pet Lizards.* **Photographs by Andy King. 1999. Hardcover: Lerner. 64 pages. Ages 9–13. Of interest to younger children. NONFICTION.**

Jamal's family has a dog, rabbit, turtle, hamster, snake, fish, birds, chameleons, and bearded dragon lizards. In a conversational tone, Jamal focuses on the lizards, how he takes care of them, and why he likes them as pets. He also gives information on caring for chameleons. Color photographs, sidebars, and appendixes add more information. An attractive, useful book in the "All About Pets" series, which covers cats, fish, hamsters and gerbils, rabbits, and rats.

Nelson, Theresa. *The Empress of Elsewhere.* 1998. Hardcover: DK Ink. Paperback: Puffin. 278 pages. Ages 10–13. FICTION.

When Mrs. Monroe, a wealthy neighbor, asks Jim and his seven-year-old sister, Mary Al, to baby-sit her monkey, she really wants them to befriend J.D., her belligerent, foul-mouthed granddaughter. Eventually they do, and the three children draw together when they secretly rebuild a tree house on the lake on the Monroe estate. But that secret activity launches them and the monkey into reckless adventures that end in the Houston zoo. Jim's funny yet thoughtful narration conveys the strangeness of life in the Monroe mansion, the sad history of Mrs. Monroe and J.D., and the delight of becoming close to a monkey.

Silverstein, Alvin, Virginia Silverstein, and Laura Silverstein Nunn. *Snakes and Such.* 1999. Hardcover: Twenty-First Century Books. 48 pages. Ages 10–13. Of interest to younger children. NONFICTION.

What sort of pets do snakes, chameleons, iguanas, geckos, turtles, frogs, and salamanders make? This informative guide provides background information on these and other animals, then a clear assessment of their advantages and disadvantages as pets. A sidebar of "Fast Facts," accompanied by a snappy color photograph, sums up the cost, food, housing needs, and training possibilities for each, with special notes about problems. Each chapter gives several internet resources for more information. An entry in the "What a Pet!" series that includes books on small pets, exotic pets, and more.

Reptiles and Amphibians

Cowley, Joy. _Red-Eyed Tree Frog_. Photographs by Nic Bishop. 1999. Hardcover and paperback: Scholastic. 32 pages. Ages 2–6. PICTURE BOOK.

Spectacular color photographs show a tiny red-eyed tree frog at home in the rain forest. The book opens at sunset when many animals fall asleep and the frog awakens. A series of photographs show it hopping from branch to branch looking for food. A brief text, often just one sentence on a page, narrates the frog's action and identifies the other animals such as a boa, katydid, iguana, macaw, and toucan. Questions and exclamations spark up the narrative, but the book's highlight is the outstanding photography. An award-winning informational book for the young.

James, Betsy. _Tadpoles_. 1999. Hardcover: Dutton. 32 pages. Ages 3–7. PICTURE BOOK.

When Molly, her baby brother, and their mother go to the pond, Molly finds frog eggs and carefully takes some home. Over the summer, Molly and young Davey watch the eggs change into tadpoles and finally into little frogs. Meanwhile, Davey is changing, kicking like the tadpoles and taking his first steps. Molly hates the idea of returning the frogs to the pond, but the trip has some unexpected rewards. Cheerful pictures including close-ups of the tadpoles enhance this fresh story.

Johnson, Angela. *The Girl Who Wore Snakes.* **Illustrated by James E. Ransome. 1993. Hardcover: Orchard. 32 pages. Ages 3–7. PICTURE BOOK.**

When a zookeeper visits her school, Ali discovers that she loves snakes. She loves the way they look and loves to have a snake draped over her shoulders, despite what her classmates say. Radiant paintings show an African-American girl who revels in her new enthusiasm. She buys snakes but no one at home shares her interest until several of her aunts visit and one of them understands how Ali feels. Glorious illustrations in a book that breaks stereotypes about girls.

Mazer, Anne. *The Salamander Room.* **Illustrated by Steve Johnson. 1991. Hardcover: Knopf. Paperback: Dragonfly. 32 pages. Ages 3–7. PICTURE BOOK.**

When a boy named Brian finds a salamander, he invites it to live with him. For the rest of the book, Brian's mother asks him questions about how the salamander will live and Brian answers with his plans for his new pet. As they speak, Brian's bedroom becomes more and more like the kind of outdoor spot where a salamander would like to live. The large, striking pictures show more and more of this wonderful room, and children will wish that they, too, could transform their rooms with the same magic.

Arnosky, Jim. *All About Turtles.* **2000. Hardcover: Scholastic. 32 pages. Ages 3–8. PICTURE BOOK NONFICTION.**

The endpapers of this thoughtful book show turtle tracks in the sand, while the title and copyright pages show a full-sized alligator snapping turtle. The text describes turtles in general as well as specific land, sea, and freshwater turtles. Labeled pictures depict different types of turtles throughout the world. The paintings also show turtle body parts and eggs, and what different turtles feed on. Interesting details combine with the solid overview to make this a fine introduction to a familiar animal.

Wiesner, David. *Tuesday.* **1991. Hardcover and paperback: Clarion. 32 pages. Ages 3–8. PICTURE BOOK.**
This nearly wordless book depicts one wild night when frogs rise on their lily pads and fly around a neighborhood. Hundreds of them soar higher than telephone wires, diving at birds, and grinning with delight. They swoop low, straight into a clothesline, and several end up with capes made from laundry. Their beguiling adventure continues until dawn when the magic ends, catching them by surprise and leaving lily pads all over the town. Winner of the Caldecott Medal, this is guaranteed to make you smile.

Bunting, Eve. *Some Frog!* **Illustrated by Scott Medlock. 1998. Hardcover: Harcourt. 48 pages. Ages 5–9. PICTURE BOOK.**
Billy's class is having a frog-jumping contest, and his father has promised to visit and help Billy catch a frog. As usual, Billy's father doesn't show up, so his mother takes him to the pond and they come home with a huge frog. Energetic paintings show the two splashing through the pond, and later show Billy at school gearing up for the contest. Although Billy is disappointed that his father doesn't come, he appreciates the love of his mother and grandparents, who arrive in time to see his frog jump fifteen feet. "He's a bird! He's a plane! He's a superfrog!"

Martin, James. *Frogs.* **Photographs by Art Wolfe. 1997. Hardcover: Crown. 32 pages. Ages 5–9. NONFICTION.**

Stunning photographs of two dozen frogs grace the pages of this terrific book. The vivid greens, reds, blues, yellows, and oranges will grab the reader's attention as will some of the frogs' strange shapes. The text is just as fascinating. Besides basic frog facts, the reader learns about poison dart frogs, frogs that burrow in the desert, frogs that freeze solid for the winter, and much more. No animal lover will want to miss this top-notch combination of facts and superb photos.

Simon, Seymour. *Crocodiles and Alligators.* **1999. Hardcover: Harper. 32 pages. Ages 5–9. NONFICTION.**

Striking full-page photographs of crocodiles and alligators fill this fine photo-essay. Instead of using captions, the author works information about the photographs into the clearly written text. Readers learn about the differences and similarities of crocodiles and alligators, their long history, habits, and reproduction, and more. The book dispels myths by answering questions such as, "Could a crocodilian catch a running person?" This is a subject many children love, presented in a way they can understand and with pictures they'll enjoy.

Cutler, Jane. *'Gator Aid.* **Illustrated by Tracey Campbell Pearson. 1999. Hardcover: Farrar, Straus & Giroux. 144 pages. Ages 8–11. FICTION.**

Second-grader Edward spies a baby alligator in the lake at a local park, but no one else sees it, and those who know about Edward's vivid imagination doubt his word. But radio and television shows pick up the story and soon police, park rangers, broadcasters, and curious neighbors fill the park. Then an alligator "rescuer" comes from Louisiana. What has

Edward started? And what will happen to the alligator—if there really is one?

Montgomery, Sy. *The Snake Scientist*. Photographs by Nic Bishop. 1999. Hardcover: Houghton. 48 pages. Ages 8–13. NONFICTION.

In the spring, about eighteen thousand garter snakes travel twenty miles across Manitoba from their winter hibernation site to a marsh, then back again for the winter. This photo-essay explains how scientist Robert Mason studies the snakes and what he has learned over the years. The numerous color photographs focus mainly on snakes and show children, volunteers, and Mason's students handling the snakes and conducting experiments. The book will inspire future animal scientists while the terrific photos will delight those fascinated by snakes.

Snicket, Lemony. *The Reptile Room*. Illustrated by Brett Helquist. 1999. Hardcover: Harper. 190 pages. Ages 9–13. FICTION.

An entry in "A Series of Unfortunate Events," this tongue-in-cheek novel chronicles the terrible fate of the orphaned Baudelaire children. No matter how hopeful their circumstances, something terrible happens. They have gone to live with a congenial uncle who studies reptiles. He has a glassed-in reptile room where the siblings enjoy meeting the fictional reptiles such as the Dissonant Toad, Inky Newt, and Alaskan Cow Lizard. But soon dire events mar their happiness. Amusing and filled with cliff-hangers, this has a truly despicable villain.

Maruska, Edward J. *Amphibians: Creatures of the Land and Water*. 1994. Paperback: Watts. 64 pages. Ages 9–13. Of interest to younger children. NONFICTION.

An abundance of vibrant color photographs of frogs, toads, salamanders, and other amphibians will draw readers into this fine book written by the executive director of the Cincinnati Zoo. It opens with an overview of amphibians, then looks at three groups: tailless, which includes frogs and toads; tailed, which includes salamanders; and caecilians, wormlike burrowing creatures that live in tropical areas. It discusses life cycles, habitats, survival techniques, and much more, sometimes using examples from the Cincinnati Zoo's experiences. The final chapter examines the decline in number of amphibians and the reasons they are vanishing. A very appealing, useful book.

McCarthy, Colin. *Reptile*. 1991. Hardcover: Knopf. 64 pages. Ages 9–13. Of interest to younger children. NONFICTION.

This large "Eyewitness" book presents an appealing look at reptiles, with different topics on each double-page spread. Sharp color photographs, large and small, fill the pages, showing reptiles, how they move, their eggs, skeletons, and fossilized remains. Perfect for browsing, the book can be enjoyed just for the photographs or read cover to cover. Long captions in too small print convey much of the information. Animal lovers will also want to read other "Eyewitness" books such as *Amphibian*, *Fish*, *Mammal*, and more.

Zim, Herbert S., and Hobart Smith. *Reptiles and Amphibians: 212 Species in Full Color*. Illustrated by James Gordon Irving. 1987 Revised Edition. Paperback: Golden. 160 pages. Ages 9 and up. Of interest to younger children. NONFICTION.

This small field guide starts with turtles, then moves on to lizards, snakes, alligators, crocodiles, frogs, toads, and salamanders. The introduction gives an overview, then offers simple advice for learning more about reptiles and amphibians. Each page has color drawings with helpful details for identifying the animal, a range map, and a paragraph describing the reptile or amphibian, its size, habitat, and more. This is a very good tool for a beginning herpetologist. Experienced readers will enjoy Hobart Smith's more advanced guides from Golden Books.

Sea Animals

Mahy, Margaret. *The Great White Man-Eating Shark: A Cautionary Tale.* Illustrated by Jonathan Allen. 1989. Hardcover: Dial. Paperback: Puffin. 32 pages. Ages 3–7. PICTURE BOOK.

In this quirky crowd-pleaser, a boy named Norvin wishes he had the beach to himself so that he could "shoot through the water like a silver arrow." Oddly enough, Norvin looks a lot like a shark, so he makes a plastic dorsal fin, straps it on, and swims through the cove. Everyone runs screaming from the water, leaving the cove to Norvin for days—until he encounters a real shark who finds him very attractive. Exaggerated cartoonlike pictures will have readers laughing out loud.

Earle, Sylvia A. *Hello, Fish! Visiting the Coral Reef.* Photographs by Wolcott Henry. 1999. Hardcover: National Geographic. 32 pages. Ages 3–9. NONFICTION.

Vibrant photographs mostly of fish fill the pages of this oversized book. Simple text in a conversational tone gives a few facts as well as the impressions of marine biologist Sylvia Earle. Among the dozen close-up photographs are a bright orange, white, and black clownfish swimming in anemones; a strange golden frogfish; and a sparkling seahorse. A map shows where the reader can find coral reefs to see these creatures in person. A visual treat.

Foreman, Michael. *Seal Surfer*. **1997. Hardcover: Harcourt. 32 pages. Ages 4–9. PICTURE BOOK.**

Evocative watercolor paintings sweep across wide pages of this book about a boy and his grandfather. The two visit the sea together one spring and spot a seal and its pup on the rocks. As the seasons go by, they watch the pup grow. One summer the boy learns to surf and encounters the seal pup, now fully grown, on his surfing adventures. Observant readers will notice that the boy needs crutches or a wheelchair, although that fact isn't mentioned in the text and doesn't affect his love of the ocean and its animals in this magical book.

Schuch, Steve. *A Symphony of Whales*. **Illustrated by Peter Sylvada. 1999. Hardcover: Harcourt. 32 pages. Ages 4–9. PICTURE BOOK.**

Out on their dogsled, a Siberian girl named Glashka and her family see a bay where ice has trapped hundreds of beluga whales. They contact an icebreaking ship, which responds but can't come quickly. The people of Glashka's village keep the whales alive until the ship comes. At first, the whales refuse to follow the ship through the newly made passage to the sea, but then Glashka comes up with a surprising plan. Based loosely on a true story, this poetic tale with haunting oil paintings will grip those who love whales.

Arnold, Caroline. *Baby Whale Rescue: The True Story of J.J.* **Photographs by Richard Hewett. 1999. Hardcover and paperback: Bridgewater. 32 pages. Ages 7–11. NONFICTION.**

In January 1997, a baby whale estimated to be a week old was rescued from a beach in Southern California and taken to Sea World. Workers at the park cared for the exhausted, underfed whale for months. This fascinating photo-essay shows J.J., as they named her, in her new environment, where she gained nine hundred pounds in the first month. More than a year later, the park staff and Coast Guard carefully released J.J. back into the Pacific. The well-written true story incorporates many color photographs including underwater shots.

George, Twig C. *Swimming with Sharks*. Illustrated by Yong Chen. 1999. Hardcover: Harper. 128 pages. Ages 8–11. FICTION.

Would you like to slip into the ocean from a boat when sharks are swimming nearby? At the beginning of her summer visit to her grandparents, ten-year-old Sarah didn't want to. But as she gets used to snorkeling in the Florida waters and learns about sharks from her grandfather, Sarah becomes deeply interested in them. She joins forces with other shark advocates to trap some people who are killing sharks for their fins. An enjoyable story full of details about sharks and their place in ocean ecology.

Cerullo, Mary M. *Dolphins: What They Can Teach Us*. Photographs by Jeffrey L. Rotman. 1999. Hardcover: Dutton. 42 pages. Ages 8–12. NONFICTION.

The many sparkling color photographs in this book will delight dolphin enthusiasts. The well-organized text supplies facts and stories in a readable fashion with details that children will appreciate. Six chapters explore what we know about dolphins, how they survive in the sea, how they communicate, their family life, and how dolphins and humans help each other. A clear, appealing introduction to a fascinating sea mammal. Also see Cerullo's books on octopus, sharks, and other sea animals.

SEA ANIMALS

Markle, Sandra. *Outside and Inside Sharks*. 1996. Hardcover: Atheneum. Paperback: Aladdin. 40 pages. Ages 8–12. Of interest to younger children. NONFICTION.

Color photographs reveal the inside and outside of sharks in this absorbing photo-essay. The clearly written text amply describes the animal's physical features, while the captions and labels point out details in the photos. The close-ups of shark organs such as heart, eyes, and stomach will mesmerize some readers, while others might find them too graphic. A must-read for shark fans. One in a recommended series that includes snakes, bats, and other animals of great interest to children.

Hall, Elizabeth, and Scott O'Dell. *Venus Among the Fishes*. 1995. Hardcover: Houghton. Paperback: Yearling. 144 pages. Ages 9–12. FICTION.

When orcas invade the bay where the dolphin Venus and her family live, she and her brother leave Glacier Bay to seek help. They encounter many dangers on their journey, from other animals as well as humans. They also go out of their way to help fellow animals endangered by humans. In a surprising plot twist, Venus comes in close contact with humans in ways both good and harmful. Some readers will be distracted by how much the sea animals think and feel like humans, while others will enjoy Venus and her adventures.

Skurzynski, Gloria, and Alane Ferguson. *Deadly Waters*. 1999. Hardcover: National Geographic. 145 pages. Ages 9–13. FICTION.

Jack, Ashley, and their foster brother, Bridger, are in the Everglades with their mother, a wildlife veterinarian, who is trying to discover why manatees are dying there. When the kids are out fishing, they come across an injured manatee.

They also meet a man who steals Jack's camera and later tries to kidnap the boys. The police don't believe the kids but their parents do, and together they solve the mystery. The fourth book in the "National Parks Mystery" series, this will entertain readers while informing them about Everglades wildlife.

Kovacs, Deborah, and Kate Madin. *Beneath Blue Waters: Meetings with Remarkable Deep-Sea Creatures.* **Principal photography by Larry Madin. 1996. Hardcover: Viking. 64 pages. Ages 9 and up. Of interest to younger children. NONFICTION.**

Spectacular underwater photographs make this a beautiful book. The well-written narrative invites readers along on explorations of the three main zones in the ocean, reached by scuba diving and research submersibles. In each zone, research scientists photograph amazing creatures and catch some in jars. Graceful, transparent shapes and the lovely effects of bioluminescence turn the animals into works of art, set against dark backgrounds in the photos. The text weaves together many strands of information about the sea, animals, research, and the future of oceanography. Don't miss this one.

Zim, Herbert S., and Lester Ingle. *Seashores: A Guide to Animals and Plants Along the Beaches.* **Illustrated by Dorothea and Sy Barlowe. 1989 Revised Edition. Paperback: Golden. 160 pages. Ages 9 and up. Of interest to younger children. NONFICTION.**

Algae, sponges, worms, mollusks and their shells, birds, and other seashore plants and animals appear in this informative pocket-sized guide. An introduction suggests simple activities and equipment for amateurs, followed by short discussions of seashores, tides, waves, and more. Most of the small double-page spreads show several creatures or plants labeled with name and size, and discussed in a paragraph of text. Read the introduction, browse through the pages, then head for the seashore with this valuable guide in your pocket.

Hesse, Karen. *The Music of Dolphins*. 1996. Hardcover and paperback: Scholastic. 182 pages. Ages 10–14. FICTION.

What would it be like to be raised by dolphins? In this intriguing novel, Mila, a girl raised by dolphins since age four, and now, an adolescent, is found by humans. Scientists are thrilled to have the chance to study her, and at first the girl enjoys aspects of her strange, new life. But could it be that life with dolphins was better? Told through Mila's voice, the text moves from very simple to more sophisticated as she acquires human language. An unusual, thought-provoking novel.

MacQuitty, Miranda, and Vassili Papastavrou. *Sharks, Whales & Dolphins*. Illustrated by Frank Greenaway. 1997. Hardcover: DK. 128 pages. Ages 10 and up. Of interest to younger children. NONFICTION.

Despite the title, this "Eyewitness" anthology covers much more than the three animals named. It discusses the ocean itself, life in a coral reef, animals that move through jet propulsion, hot springs on the ocean floor, walruses, seals, and sea lions, among other topics. Two pages on each subject combine color photographs with a main paragraph and many long captions. It closes with several pages on deep-sea exploration and the equipment needed. A rich resource for browsing rather than reading cover to cover, this book is hard to put down.

Zoo Animals and Others

Jenkins, Steve. *What Do You Do When Something Wants to Eat You?* 1997. Hardcover: Houghton. 32 pages. Ages 3–8. PICTURE BOOK NONFICTION.

Extraordinary cut-paper illustrations delight the eye as readers learn how animals defend themselves from predators. Each defense mechanism is different and intriguing. The octopus shoots black ink to confuse attackers, the puffer fish swells up until it's too big to eat, and the pangolin rolls itself into an armor-plated ball. A brief text identifies the animals and actions. Few nonfiction books offer such exquisite illustrations, so don't miss this or Jenkins's other fine books.

King-Smith, Dick. *All Pigs Are Beautiful.* Illustrated by Anita Jeram. 1993. Hardcover and paperback: Candlewick. 32 pages. Ages 3–8. PICTURE BOOK NONFICTION.

"I don't care if they're little pigs or big pigs, with long snouts or short snouts, with ears that stick up or ears that flop down . . . I just love pigs." In this good-natured tribute to the pig, King-Smith talks about pigs he has owned in the past, such as six-hundred-pound Monty, who looked frightening but was a real "pushover." He also describes what pigs like to eat and how they like people to talk to them (and how they talk back). Humorous pen-and-watercolor illustrations show lots of farm scenes with pigs and the children and adults who love them.

Hanly, Sheila. *The Big Book of Animals.* **1997. Hardcover: DK. 48 pages. Ages 4–8. NONFICTION.**

This large volume is a browser's paradise of animals. Each double-page spread includes about seventeen photographs or drawings of animals. The book moves from one continent to another, with pages devoted to animals in habitats such as "South American Pampas" and "Asian Tropical Forests." A brief paragraph accompanies each animal. Although far from comprehensive, the book does show several hundred animals of different kinds, a tribute to the amazing wealth of animal life on the planet.

Aliki. *My Visit to the Zoo.* **1997. Hardcover and paperback: Harper. 40 pages. Ages 4–9. PICTURE BOOK.**

In this cheery book, two children visit a delightful zoo that includes an aviary and reptile house, primate house, rain forest structure, elephant house, and more. The lively illustrations incorporate many pictures of animals labeled with their names and places of origin. The text offers more facts about the animals and their habits. Aliki packs a lot into these pages in a way that celebrates the remarkable diversity of creatures and warns about the threats to their survival.

Bowen, Betsy. *Tracks in the Wild.* **1993. Paperback: Houghton. 32 pages. Ages 5–9. PICTURE BOOK NONFICTION.**

Bowen, who lives in the North Woods of Minnesota, uses animal tracks as a jumping off point for talking about the animals that live near her. Gorgeous woodcuts in natural colors show the tracks and each animal in its natural setting. Ermine, snowshoe hare, red fox, and river otter are among the animals she illustrates and discusses. Her conversational writing brings the animals to life while also supplying basic facts about them and how they cope with winter. An unusually attractive informational book with a personal touch.

Esbensen, Barbara Juster. *Swift as the Wind: The Cheetah.* Illustrated by Jean Cassels. 1996. Hardcover: Orchard. 32 pages. Ages 5–9. PICTURE BOOK NONFICTION.

Graceful, golden paintings show the cheetah in its natural habitat, running, hunting, and raising its young. The flowing text imparts much information about the fastest land animal, its life cycle, physical attributes, family life, and how it hunts. The pictures show it interacting with lions, Thomson's gazelles, zebras, impalas, elephants, and hyenas in Africa. The final pages discuss threats to its survival as its habitats disappear, as well as efforts to breed cheetahs. A wonderful introduction to an extraordinary creature.

Lewin, Ted, and Betsy Lewin. *Gorilla Walk.* 1999. Hardcover: Lothrop. 48 pages. Ages 5–9. NONFICTION.

In 1997, Ted and Betsy Lewin hiked for eleven hours through dense Ugandan forest to see a few of the six hundred mountain gorillas still in existence. Large, sun-dappled watercolors and smaller, often humorous, sketches combine with lively writing to pull the reader into the trip. The guided hikes, uphill and through mud, plagued by thirst and insects, culminate in the extraordinary experience of watching the huge gorillas from fifteen feet away. Full of information and inspiration, this is a treat for young adventurers and animal lovers.

King-Smith, Dick. *Dick King-Smith's Animal Friends: Thirty-One True Life Stories.* **Illustrated by Anita Jeram. 1996. Hardcover: Candlewick. 96 pages. Ages 8–11. Of interest to younger children. NONFICTION.**

The author of *Babe the Gallant Pig* and other wonderful novels, King-Smith has an amusing style that exudes gentle enthusiasm. Most of the stories in this collection are one to four pages, with expressive watercolors of animals on nearly every page. He starts with a story from his early childhood and goes on through pets he owned or other animals he encountered, including a dog he had for a short time while serving in Italy in the Second World War. A good read-aloud, this book will capture the heart of listeners and readers.

Bateman, Robert. *Safari.* **1998. Hardcover: Little, Brown. 32 pages. Ages 8–12. PICTURE BOOK NONFICTION.**

A personal tone characterizes this short book about African mammals. Painter and naturalist Bateman focuses on thirteen animals he has seen on safaris. For each, he provides several lifelike paintings, accompanied by a short text with facts, interesting details, and anecdotes from his own experiences. A small sidebar adds more information about each animal, which include the elephant, cape buffalo, rhinoceros, kudu, zebra, dik-dik, and more. An armchair safari children will enjoy.

Byars, Betsy. *Me Tarzan.* **Illustrated by Bill Cigliano. 2000. Hardcover: Harper. 88 pages. Ages 8–12. FICTION.**

When Dorothy's class auditions for a play about book characters, she tries out for Tarzan. Her yell, which sprawls across the page in bold type, is phenomenal. But every time Dorothy gives in to the urge to yell, more and more animals come running. This strange magnetic quality reaches a climax on the fateful night of the class play, which is also the night the circus is in town. Short chapters, occasional black-and-white pictures, and lots of humor enhance this top-notch story about a girl and the animals she attracts.

Lowry, Lois. *Zooman Sam.* **1999. Hardcover: Houghton. 156 pages. Ages 8–12. Of interest to younger children. FICTION.**

For Future Job Day at his nursery school, Sam decides to be a zookeeper. This launches him into giving explanations about animals to his fellow students as well as trying to train his own dog, who jumps around wildly whenever anyone mentions food. This book is the fourth in a series about Sam, the younger brother of Anastasia Krupnik, who is the central character of a related series. A very funny story, good for reading aloud to younger children, too

Rylant, Cynthia. *Every Living Thing.* **Illustrated by S. D. Schindler. 1985. Hardcover: Bradbury. Paperback: Aladdin. 82 pages. Ages 9–12. FICTION.**

Twelve stories explore the role that pets and wild animals play in the lives of children and adults. Dogs, cats, turtles, fish, a nest of robins, and even a hermit crab give characters the hope and love they need to get through hard times. Each story is short and beautifully written, with an effective mixture of happiness and sadness. Read aloud or alone, these thoughtful stories are certain to touch the reader.

Bishop, Nic. *The Secrets of Animal Flight.* **1997. Hardcover: Houghton. 32 pages. Ages 9–13. Of interest to younger children. NONFICTION.**

How do birds, insects, and bats fly? This outstanding photo-essay provides clear explanations to answer that question. Stunning high-speed photographs break flight down into its parts, showing close-ups of wings executing upstrokes and downstrokes. Thoughtfully conceived diagrams on many pages add useful information about topics like thermals, airfoils, and parts of feathers and wings. The clarity of the photographs, set in an elegant design, is extraordinary. This is nonfiction at its best.

Patent, Dorothy Hinshaw. *Back to the Wild.* **Photographs by George Muñoz. 1997. Hardcover: Harcourt. 80 pages. Ages 9–14. NONFICTION.**

This fine book describes four endangered animals that have been successfully bred in captivity and, in some cases, returned to the wild. The text starts with an overview of endangered animals and how captive breeding programs can help. Patent's evenhanded approach acknowledges the drawbacks and failures of such programs, then looks at instances of success: the red wolf, black-footed ferret, golden lion tamarin, and leaping lemurs. Each story, illustrated with crisp color photographs, explores the difficulties involved and how the zoologists overcame them.

Cross, Gillian. *The Great American Elephant Chase.* **1992. Hardcover: Holiday House. 194 pages. Ages 10–13. FICTION.**

Tad, a fifteen-year-old orphan, gets locked into a railroad car with a performing elephant named Khush and ends up far from home. His sure touch with Khush lands him a job, but then things go wrong again. He ends up fleeing from enemies with Khush and Cissie, the girl who owns the elephant. While trying to keep Khush a secret, Tad and Cissie head from Pennsylvania to the Nebraska frontier to find Cissie's friends. With help from unlikely sources, a wild ride on an ark, and a heartwarming climax, this adventure across late-nineteenth-century America will keep readers entranced.

Nirgiotis, Nicholas, and Theodore Nirgiotis. *No More Dodos: How Zoos Help Endangered Wildlife.* **1996. Hardcover: Lerner. 112 pages. Ages 11–14. NONFICTION.**

Zoos have transformed themselves over the last few decades, as this book so well describes. They have changed their focus and their design, now concentrating on what environment works best for the animals over what makes them easy for visitors to see. Their role in educating the public about preserving wildlife has also grown. Seven chapters, illustrated by color photographs, cover these topics and go into detail about zoos' efforts to breed animals in captivity, a complicated process entered into by a network of cooperating zoos. Readers will see behind the scenes at zoos and learn a lot about ecology in this well-written book.

Arts and Crafts

Art and Artists

de Paola, Tomie. *The Art Lesson*. 1989. Hardcover and paperback: Putnam. 32 pages. Ages 3–7. PICTURE BOOK.

Tommy loves to draw, and posts pictures all over his house. He follows his cousins' advice "not to copy and to practice, practice, practice." But in school, the teacher limits him to eight crayons, one sheet of paper, and directions to copy her drawing. Luckily, an understanding art teacher strikes a compromise with Tommy that gives him room for creativity. Young artists will enjoy reading about a child like themselves, while other children will relate to the frustration of too many rules.

Mayhew, James. *Katie Meets the Impressionists.* **1997. Hardcover: Orchard. 32 pages. Ages 4 and up. PICTURE BOOK.**

When young Katie and her grandmother go to an art museum on her grandmother's birthday, Katie magically enters paintings by Monet, Renoir, and Degas, trying to gather flowers for her grandmother. She meets Monet's son in the first painting and encounters him later in another. In each of the five paintings, she has a small adventure that gives meaning to the artwork. Children will want to enter paintings themselves, if only in their imagination, after reading this.

Geisert, Arthur. *The Etcher's Studio.* **1997. Hardcover: Houghton. 32 pages. Ages 5–9. PICTURE BOOK.**

In a simple story, a boy explains how he helps his grandfather, an etcher, prepare for a sale. The illustrations, which are themselves hand-tinted etchings, show the boy helping prepare paper and copper plates. Then the two use a press to produce prints. The boy paints each etching by hand, all the while imagining himself inside the pictures: on a ship, aloft in a hot-air balloon, and as a deep-sea diver. An afterword shows the step-by-step process and materials an etcher uses. A wonderful book about art.

Brown, Laurene Krasny, and Marc Brown. *Visiting the Art Museum.* **1986. Hardcover and paperback: Dutton. 32 pages. Ages 5–10. PICTURE BOOK.**

Three children and their parents wander through an art museum, looking at paintings, statues, mummies, armor, and more. As the children respond in different ways, their comments in cartoon balloons add humor and information. Photographs of real artwork appear alongside drawn reproductions set into cartoonlike illustrations. Useful appendixes give historical facts and details about the artwork as well as thoughtful tips on making the most of a museum visit.

Bulla, Clyde Robert. *The Chalk Box Kid.* **1987. Hardcover and paperback: Random House. 62 pages. Ages 6–9. FICTION.**

Gregory is having a hard time because his father has lost his job and the family has to move on Gregory's birthday. When everyone at his new school is given seeds to plant a home garden, Gregory doesn't take any because his new house has no yard. An artist at heart, Gregory uses chalk to draw for his own pleasure an elaborate garden on the walls of a nearby burnt-out building. When his classmates learn of it, the results help turn his life around and gain him new friends. A touching story about loneliness and art.

Venezia, Mike. *Alexander Calder.* **1998. Hardcover and paperback: Children's Press. 32 pages. Ages 6–10. BIOGRAPHY.**

One in an excellent series called "Getting to Know the World's Artists," this short biography makes learning about Calder a pleasure. Each page includes either a fine color reproduction of his art or a humorous cartoon based on the artist's life. The succinct text discusses his life and work, including his amazing wire circus, toys he made as a child, mobiles, stabiles, and wire sculptures. Large print set in generous white space makes this delightful biography accessible to younger readers.

Ames, Lee J. *Draw 50 Monsters, Creeps, Superheroes, Demons, Dragons, Nerds, Dirts, Ghouls, Giants, Vampires, Zombies and Other Curiosa.* **1983. Paperback: Doubleday. 64 pages. Ages 6–11. NONFICTION.**

In this nearly wordless book, each page demonstrates steps in drawing a particular person or monster. Starting with just a few lines, a series of the six or eight drawings per page adds lines and shading in a way that is easy to imitate. The drawings are mostly of famous characters from movies and literature such as Darth Vader, the Phantom of the Opera, Medusa, and Hercules, plus some creatures from the artist's imagination. Children will also enjoy *Draw 50 Animals, Draw 50 Athletes, Draw 50 Airplanes, Aircraft and Spacecraft,* and the many other popular drawing books by Ames.

Morrison, Taylor. *Antonio's Apprenticeship: Painting a Fresco in Renaissance Italy.* **1996. Hardcover: Holiday House. 32 pages. Ages 7–10. PICTURE BOOK.**

When Antonio is apprenticed to his uncle, a successful painter, he is disappointed at the tedious work making charcoal sticks and preparing paper. Luckily, his uncle has a commission to paint a large fresco in a chapel in Florence. They set up the scaffolding and prepare the walls with plaster; Antonio mixes the paints and enlarges his uncle's drawings to fit the expansive walls. Then the painting begins, culminating in an elegant finished room. An enjoyable, informative story about art set in 1478.

Walter, Mildred Pitts. *Suitcase.* **Illustrated by Teresa Flavin. 1999. Hardcover: Lothrop. 112 pages. Ages 8–11. FICTION.**

Alexander "Suitcase" Bingham is eleven years old, African-American, and over six feet tall. Everyone assumes he will love basketball and excel at it, but neither is true. What he does love is art. His art teacher and his mother encourage him, but his father wants Alexander to be an athlete like he is. A community center director patiently helps Alexander with his athletic training and supports his art ability. After a struggle to balance the two areas, Alexander realizes he can be both an athlete and an artist.

Maze, Stephanie. *I Want to Be a Fashion Designer.* **2000. Hardcover and paperback: Harcourt. 48 pages. Ages 9–14. NONFICTION.**

This appealing and useful book introduces the reader to famous designers as well as many different kinds of workers in the fashion industry. Each double-page spread uses concise text and color photographs to discuss topics like types of designers, fashion shows, use of technology, related careers, and more. Practical advice on pursuing a career in fashion is mixed in with more general information on fashion including history and international influences. Likely to appeal to fashion-conscious and artistic readers.

Ewing, Patrick, and Linda L. Louis. *In the Paint.* **1999. Hardcover: Abbeville Kids. 64 pages. Ages 9–14. Of interest to younger children. NONFICTION.**

Most fans probably do not realize that basketball star Patrick Ewing loves to paint. In this well-organized book, he teams up with an art educator to teach children his hobby. After checklists of supplies and painting basics come lots of tips on brushstrokes, mixing colors, and ideas on what to paint. The book is full of eye-catching examples of children's paintings. Throughout, small photographs of Ewing and quotations from him offer a special incentive for basketball fans to take up painting.

Björk, Christina. *Linnea in Monet's Garden.* **Illustrated by Lena Anderson. 1987. Hardcover: R&S. 52 pages. Ages 10–12. Of interest to younger children. FICTION.**

This charming short book combines watercolors of a Swedish girl's adventures with photographs of Monet and his family, and color reproductions of some of his paintings. Linnea travels to Paris with a friend, where they visit museums to see Monet's paintings, then visit his house and gardens at

Giverny. The first-person narrative presents a lot of background about Monet and his work, with more in sidebars about his personal life. An engaging blend of fiction and nonfiction.

Varriale, Jim. *Take a Look Around: Photography Activities for Young People*. **1999. Hardcover: Millbrook. 32 pages. Ages 10–13. Of interest to younger children. NONFICTION.**

This book's thoughtful approach reflects the author's experience teaching children photography. After an introduction about camera parts and film developing, the book is organized by principles of photography such as "Shadow and Light," "Camera Angle," "Composition," and more. Each topic covered has a brief general paragraph, then several specific activities for beginning photographers, illustrated with a black-and-white photograph taken by a child. The projects are right on target for kids. Highly recommended.

Mack, Tracy. *Drawing Lessons*. **2000. Hardcover: Scholastic. 168 pages. Ages 11–14. FICTION.**

Art means everything to seventh-grader Rory. Her artist father has given her drawing lessons for years, and she looks at the world through artist's eyes. But when her father becomes increasingly withdrawn and her parents' marriage flounders, Rory turns her back on art. She gets angry at her father, then feels responsible for his actions. But she finally turns to art again for solace and self-definition. Saturated in images of color and artistic views of the world, this novel creates a believable girl dealing with hard times.

Bauer, Joan. *Thwonk*. **1995. Paperback: Laurel Leaf. 215 pages. Ages 12–14. FICTION.**

A.J. wants to build her future around photography. A high school senior, she already has a darkroom and produces great shots for the student newspaper. Her father, a failed filmmaker, objects to her pursuing such an impractical dream. That's her biggest problem. Her other problem is a propensity to fall for handsome, self-centered guys. When a dry-witted cupid enters her life, A.J. makes some terrible decisions, which result in hilarious, if painful, consequences.

Partridge, Elizabeth. *Restless Spirit: The Life and Work of Dorothea Lange.* **1998. Hardcover: Viking. 128 pages. Ages 12–14. BIOGRAPHY.**

Many beautifully reproduced black-and-white photographs combine with a thoroughly researched text to convey the personal life and career of one of America's great photographers. The writing draws from oral histories; Lange's letters and journals; interviews; books and magazine articles; and the author's personal memories of Lange. Partridge's willingness to examine not just Lange's successes but also her problems, including those of balancing family and career, makes this an unusually vivid biography.

Hart, Christopher. *Drawing on the Funny Side of the Brain: How to Come Up with Jokes for Cartoons and Comic Strips.* **1998. Paperback: Watson-Guptill. 160 pages. Ages 12 and up. NONFICTION.**

For kids who dream about becoming a cartoonist or comic strip artist, this is a terrific place to start. Hart lays out step-by-step the skills that a cartoonist needs and how to acquire them. He teaches effective ways to draw comic strip characters, but the book has much more than that. It covers joke writing, layout and design, and serious advice about making a living as a cartoonist. The pages abound with concrete ideas and useful demonstrations. Look, too, for the author's other cartooning books.

Crafts

Klinting, Lars. *Bruno the Tailor*. 1996. Hardcover: Henry Holt. 32 pages. Ages 3–7. PICTURE BOOK.

When Bruno the beaver finds his apron in rags, he sets about making a new one in his sewing room. He chooses and washes fabric, irons it, makes a paper pattern, measures himself, and cuts out pieces. He bastes it together by hand, then sews it on a machine. The pictures show all the equipment including scissors, pincushion, measuring tape, thimble, and more. After a few setbacks, he has a perfect apron. A charming introduction to simple sewing, this includes an apron pattern. Also see *Bruno the Carpenter*.

Roche, Denis. *Loo-Loo, Boo, and Art You Can Do*. 1996. Hardcover: Houghton. 32 pages. Ages 3–10. NONFICTION.

Bright childlike pictures illustrate eleven simple, well-chosen crafts including potato prints, sculptures from odds and ends, paint mixed with sand, face masks, and more. The instructions for preparing materials are clear, but the execution is fairly open-ended, which will work well with children who are comfortable with crafts. Younger children will need adult help and so might older readers looking for detailed guidance. A good, enthusiastic starting point. Followed by *Art Around the World: Loo-Loo, Boo, and More Art You Can Do*.

Zweifel, Frances. *The Make-Something Club Is Back: More Fun with Crafts, Food, and Gifts.* Illustrated by Ann Schweninger. 1997. Hardcover: Viking. 32 pages. Ages 4–8. PICTURE BOOK NONFICTION.

This book offers a simple craft or cooking project for young children for each month of the year. The January craft is a light-catcher star picture made from aluminum foil, a pencil, and a felt-tip marker. Other projects are making cereal box puzzles, ant farms in glass jars, and simple kazoos. Cooking ideas include honey-butter toast and roll-up sandwiches. For each project, a list of materials precedes the clear, numbered directions. An unusually good craft book for the young.

National Wildlife Federation. *Wild and Crafty: Ranger Rick's NatureScope.* 1998. Hardcover: Chelsea House. Paperback: McGraw-Hill. 96 pages. Ages 5–14. NONFICTION.

Unlike most craft books, this guide includes useful patterns to trace or photocopy. All the craft projects relate to animals, from an Animated Alligator made of a shoebox to the American Black Bear Puppet. The carefully designed projects, which use easily obtained materials, indicate a recommended grade level of K–2, 3–5, or 6–8. Each craft has a sidebar with "Fun Facts" and ideas for learning more about the animal. A wonderfully versatile craft book for animal fans.

Bull, Jane. *Change Your Room.* 1999. Hardcover: DK. 95 pages. Ages 7 and up. NONFICTION.

"Paint it! Frame it! Stack it! Store it!" advises the vibrant cover of this decorating book for children. The ninety-five pages offer eye-catching ways to redecorate with minimal cost and lots of color, including suggestions for painting old chairs, making simple pillows and screens, creating storage space, and other projects. Most have step-by-step directions and give five versions of each idea using different colors and patterns. The pictures look like a skilled adult did the crafts, but the projects are accessible to children, possibly with adult guidance. Also fun for browsing.

Solga, Kim. *Make Clothes Fun!* 1993. Hardcover: Grolier. 48 pages. Ages 8–13. NONFICTION.

Decorated shoelaces, jazzed-up jackets, and T-shirts with great painted designs are three of the ten attractive projects in this crafts book. Glossy photographs of the activities make the directions easy to follow. Within each project, several variations suggest ideas to inspire readers. For example, the suggestions for stenciled T-shirts show stencils of a sun, word, soccer ball, snowflakes, and some beach items. The materials are inexpensive and the results will please children.

Smolinski, Jill. *The First-Timer's Guide to Origami.* Illustrated by Neal Yamamoto. 2000. Paperback: Lowell House. 80 pages. Ages 8 and up. Of interest to younger children. NONFICTION.

Learning origami from a book requires an ability to go from a two-dimensional page to a three-dimensional object, which can be challenging. This book does a good job of making that process possible thanks to clearly written directions and detailed step-by-step illustrated demonstrations. It opens with terminology, common folds, and three basic folded forms that are used as starting points later in the book. Readers can make thirty objects ranging from a simple paper airplane to a complicated "hot-air balloon." A welcome guide, more accessible than most origami books.

Valenta, Barbara. *Pop-O-Mania: How to Create Your Own Pop-ups.* 1997. Hardcover: Dial. 12 pages. Ages 8 and up. Of interest to younger children. NONFICTION.

Learn how to make fabulous pop-ups from a short book that has several pop-ups on every page. For example, the first large double-page spread includes a dinosaur on a sliding tab, a spiral pop-up, a flap to lift, a pop-up with a step, and a pop-up envelope with further directions in it. The combination of directions with 3–D models makes the process possible to understand even for children without strong spatial skills. More good ideas follow, guaranteeing hours of fun making cards, tags, invitations, books, and more.

Swain, Gwenyth. *Bookworks: Making Books by Hand.* 1995. Hardcover and paperback: Carolrhoda. 64 pages. Ages 9–13. NONFICTION.

Written in conjunction with the Minnesota Center for Book Arts, this thorough activity book grows out of extensive experience with children. The bright photographs show children learning to make paper and to craft a variety of attractive books. Step-by-step directions show how to make accordion books, pop-ups, marbled paper, and more. The history of paper and printing opens and closes this fine volume. Young writers will especially like making books to hold stories they've written.

Birdseye, Tom. *A Kids' Guide to Building Forts.* Illustrated by Bill Klein. 1993. Paperback: Roberts Rinehart. 62 pages. Ages 9–13. Of interest to younger children. NONFICTION.

This wonderful guide gives detailed directions for sixteen different outdoor, snow, and indoor forts. They range from simple structures that do not require much work or equipment to more complicated ones that involve thatching walls and lashing together many poles. Four of the five indoor forts are especially easy to construct. With black-and-white drawings that are both decorative and useful, this is written in a friendly, casual way. Highly recommended and sure to satisfy.

Solga, Kim. *Make Sculptures!* **1993. Hardcover: Grolier. 48 pages. Ages 9–13. Of interest to younger children. NONFICTION.**

This book offers lots of excellent sculpture ideas, although it doesn't always give specific directions. For example, it shows a wonderful fabric sculpture of a painted bug and describes how to make a pillow for the central body, but the reader must figure out how to add the button eyes, wire antennae, and pipe cleaner legs. Other attractive projects include time capsules, soft stone sculptures, giant food sculptures, clay pots, papier-mâché, and more. Geared toward children who are already conversant with crafts, this is inspirational and beautifully presented.

McGraw, Sheila. *Papier-Mâché for Kids.* **1991. Hardcover and paperback: Firefly. 72 pages. Ages 9–14. Of interest to younger children. NONFICTION.**

Helpful photographs show each step of these papier-mâché projects, making this an unusually usable crafts book. The book opens with a general guide to papier-mâché, then gives detailed instructions for eight appealing projects such as masks, bangles, cats, and monsters. The final section on "Finishing" describes painting, decoupage, and add-ons using clay and other materials. Although the reading level is not easy, younger children will also enjoy doing these projects with the help of adults or older children.

CRAFTS

Falick, Melanie. *Kids Knitting.* **Illustrated by Kristin Nicholas. Photographs by Chris Hartlove. 1998. Hardcover: Artisan. 128 pages. Ages 11 and up. Of interest to younger children. NONFICTION.**

This well-designed craft book offers basic instructions for knitting as well as fifteen projects that will get kids started. The striking color photographs of girls and boys knitting make it look like fun, and the projects from scarves to finger puppets to a sweater have appealing colors and jazzy designs. Each project includes detailed step-by-step directions. Also excellent for adults to use with younger children or for anyone who wants to learn to knit.

Dance and Theater

Walsh, Ellen Stoll. *Hop Jump.* 1993. Hardcover and paperback: Harcourt. 32 pages. Ages 3–7. PICTURE BOOK.

Playful collage illustrations abound with energy in this book about a frog who is an artist and dancer. Betsy is a blue frog, surrounded by green frogs who always go "hop jump, hop jump." To Betsy, "It's always the same." She prefers to try different moves, imitating floating leaves, twisting and turning gracefully. Her new movement proves irresistible and soon the green frogs switch to dancing. An outstanding picture-story book with a simple text about dance.

Hampshire, Susan. *Rosie's Ballet Slippers.* Illustrated by Maria Teresa Meloni. 1996. Hardcover and paperback: Harper. 32 pages. Ages 3–8. PICTURE BOOK.

Rosie loves her new pink ballet slippers and her first ballet lesson. Luminous watercolors show her meeting the teacher and other children, then starting on ballet exercises. The illustrations introduce the first two foot positions and the five basic arm positions, and teach a few basic ballet terms. The students, mostly girls but a few boys, look like modern children, as does Rosie on the final page as she dances with her Barbie doll. A positive picture of a first encounter with ballet lessons.

Hoffman, Mary. *Amazing Grace.* Illustrated by Caroline Binch. 1991. Hardcover: Dial. 32 pages. Ages 3–8. PICTURE BOOK.

Grace loves to dress up and act out different roles like Anansi the Spider, Joan of Arc, and Aladdin. Exuberant pictures show her in different costumes, with simple props, sometimes acting alone, sometimes with other children. When she learns that her class play is *Peter Pan*, Grace plans to try out for the lead role, but her classmates discourage her because she is black and female. Supported by her mother and grandmother, Grace practices and gets the part. The last pictures show her as a happy, successful Peter Pan.

Jones, Bill T., and Susan Kuklin. *Dance*. Photographs by Susan Kuklin. 1998. Hardcover: Hyperion. 32 pages. Ages 3–8. NONFICTION.

This tribute to dance is as elegant as a graceful modern dance. It features photographs of dancer Bill T. Jones demonstrating modern dance, his body set against a completely white background. The spare, lyrical text reflects his love of dance. "When I am dancing, I can fly high and soar through the air," are the words that accompany three photographs of him doing spectacular jumps. A joyful celebration in a beautifully designed book.

Lee, Jeanne M. *Silent Lotus*. 1991. Hardcover and paperback: Farrar, Straus & Giroux. 32 pages. Ages 3–8. PICTURE BOOK.

Large, lovely watercolors based on Asian art enhance the story of Silent Lotus, a girl growing up in rural Cambodia. Although unable to hear or talk, Silent Lotus loves to move gracefully, imitating the egrets and herons near her home. Her parents take her to a temple in a city, where she sees a troupe of women dancing and dances like them. To her great happiness, she finds a place dancing in the palace, a joyful ending to an elegant book.

Hayes, Ann. *Onstage & Backstage at the Night Owl Theater.* **Illustrated by Karmen Thompson. 1997. Hardcover: Harcourt. 36 pages. Ages 5–9. PICTURE BOOK.**

Readers will learn a lot about the theater while enjoying a story about animals who put on a production of *Cinderella.* With a bear as director and a kangaroo as stage manager, the action starts four weeks before showtime. Auditions, a read-through, publicity, props, costumes, scenery, and rehearsals all appear in the cartoonlike pictures and the action-packed text. A glossary of theater words provides a useful final touch in this thoughtful book that takes readers backstage.

Giff, Patricia Reilly. *Dance with Rosie.* **Illustrated by Julie Durrell. 1996. Hardcover: Viking. Paperback: Puffin. 80 pages. Ages 7–10. FICTION.**

The first in the "Ballet Slippers" series, this short chapter book introduces Rosie O'Meara. Rosie's grandmother, now dead, was a ballerina, and Rosie hopes to be one, too. But she waits too long to register for class, so she must peek in the studio window of the dance studio and follow the ballet steps in the alley. Discovered, she gets into the class, but is crestfallen to find she isn't immediately a star. Filled with ballet references, including a glossary at the back, this book will delight young dancers and other Patricia Giff fans.

Streatfeild, Noel. *Ballet Shoes.* **1937. Paperback: Random House. 281 pages. Ages 9–12. FICTION.**

This timeless story follows the fortunes of three adopted sisters—Pauline, Petrova, and Posy. When their uncle is late returning from a long journey, the girls need to earn money to help pay expenses. They enroll in a dancing school where Pauline shows talent in acting and Posy proves to be an outstanding dancer. Petrova would rather be fixing cars than dancing, but she takes her responsibility seriously. Filled with dance and performances, this book will pull readers into the hopes and dreams of three likable characters. Also see *Dancing Shoes*.

Avi. *Romeo and Juliet—Together (and Alive!) at Last.* 1987. Hardcover: Orchard. Paperback: Avon. 128 pages. Ages 9–13. FICTION.

In this funny novel, the middle school characters from Avi's *S.O.R. Losers* are back, this time putting on a production of Shakespeare's romantic play. Ed organizes the play in order to help his friend Saltz connect with a girl he has a crush on. With two weeks to rehearse and get everything else ready, the final product has a few problems but also some great results. From casting to costumes, it's all completely run by students who don't know what they are doing but learn fast. Very enjoyable.

Grau, Andrée. *Dance.* 1998. Hardcover: Knopf. 64 pages. Ages 9–14. Of interest to younger children. NONFICTION.

This entry in the "Eyewitness" series gives a broad view of dance, drawing from many cultures and going beyond the usual topic of ballet to jazz, folk, tango, flamenco, and more. Each double-page spread focuses on one subject, with a lead paragraph and large and small photographs with informative captions. Topics include "Themes and Messages," "Dance and Worship," and "Famous Dancers." Children will enjoy browsing through the well-designed book and stopping to learn more on the many aspects of dance.

Cooper, Susan. *King of Shadows.* 1999. Hardcover: McElderry. 186 pages. Ages 10–13. FICTION.

What actor wouldn't love to act in the first performance of *A Midsummer's Night Dream*, playing Puck to an Oberon acted by Shakespeare himself? Such is the fate of Nat Field, who travels back in time to 1599 London and finds himself at the original Globe Theatre. Befriended by Shakespeare and other actors among the Chamberlain's Men, and thrilled to be in the performance of a lifetime, Nat still worries about getting stuck in the past forever. A fine novel that conveys the magic of theater and tells a strong story.

Bolton, Reg. *Showtime! Over 75 Ways to Put on a Show.* 1998. Hardcover: DK. 48 pages. Ages 10–13. Of interest to younger children. NONFICTION.

In this oversized book, each double-page spread uses vivid photographs to illustrate a type of show that children could put on, from marionettes to mime to magic. Each topic includes several suggestions but not many step-by-step instructions. For "Shadow Theater," one section shows hand shadows to make; another shows a shadow box puppet theater, while a series of photos illustrate a shadow play with kids behind a backlit bedsheet. More useful for ideas than details, this will entertain and inspire young performers.

Varriale, Jim. *Kids Dance: The Students of Ballet Tech.* 1999. Hardcover: Dutton. 32 pages. Ages 10–14. Of interest to younger children. NONFICTION.

Located in New York City, Ballet Tech is the first high school for ballet. This photo-essay explains how third graders are recruited for free ballet lessons, how some keep taking them, and how even fewer end up at Ballet Tech for high school. Lots of photographs and quotations from ballet students convey the spirit of the ballet training, which is difficult but often rewarding. A short, enthusiastic book about ballet and an unusual school.

Castle, Kate. *My Ballet Book.* **1998. Hardcover: DK. 64 pages. Ages 10–14. Of interest to younger children. NONFICTION.**

Even readers who have no intention of pursuing ballet may enjoy this detailed introduction to the topic. Each double-page spread discusses one aspect, such as ballet clothing and shoes, life at a ballet school, joining a company, dressing and making up for a performance, ballet stars of past and present, and much more. The pages have large and small photographs, with one main paragraph of text and many detailed captions. Delightful for browsing or for future ballet stars to immerse themselves in.

Freedman, Russell. *Martha Graham: A Dancer's Life.* **1998. Hardcover: Clarion. 176 pages. Ages 11–14. BIOGRAPHY.**

Elegant black-and-white photographs add an extraordinary dimension to this biography of one of the world's great modern dancers. After describing her childhood and training, the narrative details how Graham formed her own troupe, began to choreograph, and evolved her own personal dance style. This well-written biography sets her career in the context of dance history and discusses her personal life, noting her strengths and weaknesses. Even readers without a strong interest in dance may be entranced by the power of Graham's personality and dreams, so palpable in the photographs.

Staples, Suzanne Fisher. *Shiva's Fire.* **2000. Hardcover: Farrar, Straus & Giroux. 276 pages. Ages 12–14. FICTION.**

Parveti, a girl with mystical powers, has always loved dance. Her strangeness makes her an outcast in her small village in India, until a guru hears of her extraordinary grace. He invites her to his dance *gurukulam*, where she grows into one of the best dancers in the country. The story moves leisurely, with exquisite descriptions of the countryside, food, clothing, and especially dance. The fine writing brings the reader palpably to another place and into the life of a dedicated Indian dancer.

Music and Musicians

Mahy, Margaret. *Boom, Baby, Boom, Boom!* **Illustrated by Patricia MacCarthy. 1997. Hardcover: Viking. 32 pages. Ages 2–7. PICTURE BOOK.**

Mama settles her baby in a high chair with lots of good food for lunch, then turns her back to play her drums, declaring, "Beating those drums makes me feel at ease with the world." What Mama doesn't know is that several animals have heard about lunch and start coming in the door to eat behind her back. The baby obliges them by dropping bits of her food on the floor. The mother ends her drumming with a sigh of happiness and turns just after a cow races out. Rounded, colorful pictures suit the happy spirit of this bouncing book.

Hurd, Thacher. *Mama Don't Allow.* **1984. Hardcover and paperback: Harper. 40 pages. Ages 3–8. PICTURE BOOK.**

When the possum Miles gets a saxophone for his birthday, his parents want him to practice outside. Walking through town making a racket, he finds three other musicians and they head to the swamp to practice. To their surprise, the "sharp-toothed, long-tailed, yellow-eyed alligators" like their music and invite them to play at the Alligator Ball on a riverboat, which turns out to be unexpectedly dangerous. Vivid colors, funny remarks in cartoon balloons, and a suspenseful plot make this a winner. It includes music and lyrics for the song "Mama Don't Allow."

Moss, Lloyd. *Zin! Zin! Zin! A Violin*. Illustrated by Marjorie Priceman. 1995. Hardcover: Simon & Schuster. Paperback: Aladdin. 32 pages. Ages 3–8. PICTURE BOOK.

In this joyful introduction to ten orchestra instruments, a witty rhyme bounces along from instrument to instrument as orchestra members assemble and tune up. The rhyme culminates in a performance before an enthusiastic audience, who demand an encore before everyone leaves for the night. Whimsical illustrations show musicians who resemble their instruments in amusing ways. Children will also enjoy the dog, mouse, and two cats that appear in many pictures but aren't mentioned in the text. A delightful Caldecott Honor Book.

Pinkney, Andrea Davis. *Duke Ellington: The Piano Prince and His Orchestra*. Illustrated by Brian Pinkney. 1998. Hardcover: Hyperion. 32 pages. Ages 4–9. PICTURE BOOK BIOGRAPHY.

Lively scratchboard artwork full of swirling colors conveys the memorable music of Duke Ellington in this Caldecott Honor Book. Starting with his childhood, it follows Ellington's musical career as he forms a band and plays at the famous Cotton Club. The colloquial language echoes the times, with phrases like "cuttin' the rug" and "soul-sweet music." A toe-tapping book with superb pictures, this introduces an important American musician in a way that will appeal to children.

Koscielniak, Bruce. *The Story of the Incredible Orchestra: An Introduction to Musical Instruments and the Symphony Orchestra*. 2000. Hardcover: Houghton. 40 pages. Ages 5–10. PICTURE BOOK NONFICTION.

This fully illustrated book describes the history of the orchestra and introduces many instruments. Watercolor-and-ink pictures show musicians through time playing different instruments drawn in detail. The Baroque, Classical, and Romantic periods each have several pages devoted to them. The text is clear and straightforward, while the pictures are energetic and informative. Overflowing with information, this is an attractive way to learn a lot about classical music.

Hopkinson, Deborah. *A Band of Angels: A Story Inspired by the Jubilee Singers*. Illustrated by Raúl Colón. 1999. Hardcover: Atheneum. 32 pages. Ages 6–10. PICTURE BOOK.

Extraordinary textured illustrations in browns and golds set the mood for this fictional story based on the real Jubilee Singers. The time is after the Civil War, and the main character, Ella, seeks an education at Fisk School, later to be Fisk University, a school for former slaves. When the school runs low on money, Ella and other musical students travel around the country to raise money by giving concerts. The story focuses on the chorus's switch from popular songs to spirituals. The dedication of the students and their exciting success come across powerfully in this inspiring tale of courage.

Venezia, Mike. *The Beatles*. 1997. Hardcover and paperback: Children's Press. 32 pages. Ages 6–10. NONFICTION.

Children familiar with the songs of the Beatles will enjoy learning more about this highly influential group. Venezia presents an enthusiastic introduction while also entertaining readers with occasional cartoons about the performers' lives. Photographs show the Beatles as children and teenagers as well as in their musical group. The large print and attractive design are characteristic of all the books in this excellent series, "Getting to Know the World's Greatest Composers," which mostly features classical musicians.

Krull, Kathleen, collector and arranger. *Gonna Sing My Head Off! American Folk Songs for Children.* **Illustrated by Allen Garns. 1992. Paperback: Knopf. 160 pages. Ages 7 and up. NONFICTION.**

This is an exceptional collection of well-loved American folk songs, arranged for piano and guitar. The sixty-two songs range from sad to serious to silly, from "Red River Valley" to "We Shall Overcome" to "Beans in My Ears." A paragraph discusses the origin of each song, most of which have no known composer. Notes identify which region of the country, if any, the songs come from. Illustrations add decoration, emotion, and a sense of place. A treasure house of music that singing families will enjoy.

Namioka, Lensey. *Yang the Youngest and His Terrible Ear.* **Illustrated by Kees de Kiefte. 1992. Hardcover: Little, Brown. Paperback: Dell. 134 pages. Ages 8–11. FICTION.**

Yingtao, whose family has recently moved from China to Seattle, is supposed to practice violin each day, even though he is terrible compared to his three siblings. The children are preparing a recital to showcase their father's music teaching skills, in hopes of bringing him more students. Yingtao fears his bad performance will defeat the purpose. When he realizes his new friend Matthew has a talent for violin, the two cook up a scheme to make the recital a success. Meanwhile, Yingtao discovers his talent for baseball. A thoughtful, entertaining story about music, sports and life in a new country. One in a series.

Curtis, Christopher Paul. *Bud, Not Buddy.* **1999. Hardcover: Delacorte. 245 pages. Ages 9–13. FICTION.**

This Newbery Award winner draws readers in with its engaging main character, lively dialogue, and vivid descriptions.

Ten-year-old Bud Caldwell, who has left his harsh foster home to seek the father he has never met, has reason to believe his only living parent is the jazz bandleader Herb Calloway. Herb's kindhearted band members take Bud in even when the cantankerous Calloway ignores him. Glimpses of life for African Americans during the Depression add a somber note, balanced by the upbeat attitude of the musicians. A wonderful book with a hopeful ending.

MacLachlan, Patricia. *The Facts and Fictions of Minna Pratt.* **1988. Hardcover and paperback: Harper. 144 pages. Ages 9–13. FICTION.**

Eleven-year-old Minna Pratt plays the cello and longs for order in her chaotic family. When she meets fellow musician Lucas, she is drawn to his ordered household. She and Lucas are part of a quartet practicing Mozart for a contest, which makes Minna wish more than ever for a vibrato, a certain richness musicians get in playing their instrument. Minna ponders life and music, and the quotation above her mother's writing desk: "Fact and fiction are different truths." An outstanding novel.

O'Connor, Barbara. *Beethoven in Paradise.* **1997. Hardcover and paperback: Farrar, Straus & Giroux. 160 pages. Ages 9–13. FICTION.**

What if you loved music and wanted to play an instrument more than anything else in the world, but your father hated the idea? That is Martin's situation. His father wishes that his adolescent son would excel at baseball, which Martin dislikes, and he considers Martin a "sissy" for loving music. Martin has friends but he has to face up to his father alone. A powerfully realistic portrait of a thoughtful boy and the father who doesn't appreciate him, this novel includes a lot of wonderful writing about music.

Geras, Adèle, reteller. *The Random House Book of Opera Stories*. 1997. Hardcover: Random House. 136 pages. Ages 9–14. FICTION.

This attractive, useful guide to operas retells Mozart's *The Magic Flute*, Verdi's *Aida*, Janácek's *The Cunning Little Vixen*, Puccini's *Turandot*, Rossini's *Cinderella*, Humperdinck's *Hansel and Gretel*, and Prokofiev's *The Love for Three Oranges*. A different, talented artist illustrates each well-told story, giving it a distinct flavor. Excellent for building up excitement before an opera and making the performance easier to understand.

Krull, Kathleen. *Lives of the Musicians: Good Times, Bad Times (And What the Neighbors Thought)*. Illustrated by Kathryn Hewitt. 1993. Hardcover: Harcourt. 96 pages. Ages 9–14. COLLECTIVE BIOGRAPHY.

The stories about twenty famous musicians in this witty volume offer information about their professional accomplishments plus intriguing personal details. For example, Johann Sebastian Bach had twenty children including five boys named Johann and two girls named Johanna, four of whom became respected composers. Influential European and American composers and performers are included, each pictured in a caricature. Specific pieces of music are mentioned, providing ways to learn more about the subjects. An ingenious way to introduce notable musicians.

Collier, James Lincoln. *Jazz: An American Saga*. 1997. Hardcover: Henry Holt. 104 pages. Ages 12–14. NONFICTION.

This well-written book introduces jazz as an art form, its history, and its most influential musicians. Anecdotes and frequent black-and-white photographs add texture to the fascinating story, which begins with a short overview of its place in the world today. The book explores jazz's African roots and its emergence in New Orleans, then describes major changes and the various styles that emerged over the years. A discography recommends music of performers discussed in the book. An elegant introduction to an American form of music.

Poetry

Kennedy, X. J., and Dorothy Kennedy, selectors. *Talking Like the Rain: A First Book of Poems*. Illustrated by Jane Dyer. 1992. Hardcover: Little, Brown. 96 pages. Ages 3–9. POETRY COLLECTION.

This exceptional array of more than one hundred poems lends itself to reading aloud, but is also accessible to strong younger readers for reading alone. Short, familiar words and short sentences characterize most of the poems, which are gracefully illustrated in watercolors on large, open pages. Readers will recognize older poets including Robert Frost, Robert Louis Stevenson, and Christina Rossetti, as well as newer ones like Jack Prelutsky and Karla Kuskin. A pleasure to look at, with poems to read and reread.

George, Kristine O'Connell. *Little Dog Poems*. Illustrated by June Otani. 1999. Hardcover: Clarion. 40 pages. Ages 3 and up. POETRY COLLECTION.

This exceptionally wonderful small collection of verse describes the world of Little Dog, a well-loved pet, from morning until night. Poems of three to eight lines capture life from the dog's point of view and from his young owner's: the vacuum as an enemy, the other dog hiding in the mirror, the girl coming home to a joyful dog. Uncluttered watercolors gently complement the poems without overwhelming them. Anyone who has loved a dog will appreciate this perceptive and entertaining tribute to Little Dog.

Lee, Dennis. Edited by Jack Prelutsky. *Dinosaur Dinner (With a Slice of Alligator Pie): Favorite Poems by Dennis Lee.* **Illustrated by Debbie Tilley. 1997. Hardcover: Knopf. Paperback: Dragonfly. 32 pages. Ages 5–11. POETRY COLLECTION.**

"Alligator pie, alligator pie / If I don't get some I think I'm gonna die"—so begins one of the title poems of this funny volume. Canadian poet Dennis Lee is a master at creating catchy verse that children love. Zany color illustrations complement the zany poems, most of which are short and bouncy. Food and friends, crazy creatures and animated animals provide the subjects. An irresistible collection for reading aloud and having a good time.

Stevenson, James. *Cornflakes.* **2000. Hardcover: Greenwillow. 48 pages. Ages 7–12. POETRY COLLECTION.**

Cartoonist and picture-book creator James Stevenson uses economy of language and line to craft this small poetry book of unusual charm. Most of the short poems take a fresh look at familiar objects like lawn chairs and guitars. The poems have watercolor-and-ink illustrations, some very simple, others cluttered in an attractive way, all united by a friendly feel. Also see his other poetry books, *Sweet Corn*, *Popcorn*, and *Candy Corn*.

Esbensen, Barbara Juster. *Echoes for the Eye: Poems to Celebrate Patterns in Nature.* **Illustrated by Helen K. Davie. 1996. Hardcover: Harper. 32 pages. Ages 8–12. POETRY COLLECTION.**

Esbensen, one of the finest poets for children, draws inspiration from nature for this slim collection. Her brief, evocative poems are about spirals such as shells, branches such as veins, polygons such as beehives, meanders such as snakes, and circles, which abound in nature. Each topic results in several poems, illustrated in soft watercolors that suit the mood. Readers may well look at the world around them differently after encountering these poems.

Kennedy, X. J., and Dorothy M. Kennedy. *Knock at a Star: A Child's Introduction to Poetry.* Illustrated by Karen Lee Baker. 1999 Revised Edition. Hardcover and paperback: Little, Brown. 180 pages. Ages 8–12. POETRY COLLECTION.

This is both an outstanding introduction to poetry and a fine anthology of more than 180 poems. Each chapter briefly explains one aspect of poetry, such as imagery or meter, or specific formats such as haiku, limericks, and more. A dozen or so poems illustrate each concept. The final sections offer ideas to children about writing poems and tips for adults on how to encourage children to enjoy poetry. A book to own, learn from, and enjoy.

McCord, David. *Every Time I Climb a Tree.* Illustrated by Marc Simont. 1967. Hardcover and paperback: Little, Brown. 48 pages. Ages 8–12. POETRY COLLECTION.

McCord was one of the great poets to write for children, as this slim collection demonstrates. His poems combine love of language and sounds with humor on topics that appeal to kids. Award-winning artist Marc Simont complements the poetry with watercolors that enhance but don't overwhelm the words. Most of the twenty-five poems are short and perfect for reading aloud. A wonderful combination of word and picture, rhythm and sometimes rhyme. Highly recommended.

Schwartz, Alvin. *And the Green Grass Grew All Around: Folk Poetry from Everyone*. Illustrated by Sue Truesdell. 1992. Paperback: Harper. 210 pages. Ages 8–14. POETRY COLLECTION.

This is a terrific collection of children's folklore that bounces off the page with verse children will love. For example, one rhyme starts, "Mary had a little lamb, a little pork, a little ham." The chapters include traditional rhyming songs and song parodies, jump-rope rhymes, superstitions, riddles, wishes, and far more. Although some adults may not like the "Taunts" and "Teases," children may recognize a piece of their own experience. Funny black-and-white drawings add to the collection's irresistible appeal.

Worth, Valerie. *All the Small Poems and Fourteen More*. Illustrated by Natalie Babbitt. 1994. Hardcover and paperback: Farrar, Straus & Giroux. 194 pages. Ages 8–14. POETRY COLLECTION.

In this lovely book, each page contains a short, deceptively simple poem, accompanied by a small, exquisite black-and-white illustration. The subjects come from everyday life: a safety pin, turtle, cat bath, lawn mower, and more. The poems, which number more than one hundred, play with language and ideas, relying on concrete images delivered in well-chosen words. Beautifully arranged in a small volume, the poems will inspire the reader to look at ordinary objects in a fresh way.

Silverstein, Shel. *Falling Up*. 1996. Hardcover: Harper. 172 pages. Ages 8 and up. Of interest to younger children. POETRY COLLECTION.

Most of the poems in this collection are short and funny. Many draw on a subject of great interest to kids such as treasure, ghosts, and food, with broad humor touching on themes like nose picking or throwing up. Black line drawings provide many of the laughs or add funny twists to the poems. Great for reading aloud, the rhythmic verses will satisfy fans of his earlier collections *Where the Sidewalk Ends* and *A Light in the Attic*.

Prelutsky, Jack. *A Pizza the Size of the Sun.* Illustrated by James Stevenson. 1996. Hardcover: Greenwillow. 160 pages. Ages 9–13. Of interest to younger children. POETRY COLLECTION.

Popular children's poet Jack Prelutsky showers his readers with humor in this popular collection. His catchy poems play with words, rhyme, rhythm, and format, often on high appeal subjects like monsters and bugs. Poems of three or four stanzas alternate with short ones, with something for everyone. Stevenson's pen-and-watercolor illustrations suit the mood of the poems, mostly funny but occasionally more reflective. One of many fine collections by Prelutsky.

Frost, Robert. *You Come Too: Favorite Poems for Young Readers.* Illustrated by Thomas W. Nason. 1959. Hardcover and paperback: Henry Holt. 96 pages. Ages 9–14. POETRY COLLECTION.

This classic poetry collection for children provides an excellent introduction to America's best-loved poet. The selection of fifty-one poems includes many well-known ones such as "Birches," "Mending Wall," "The Road Not Taken," and "Stopping by Woods on a Snowy Evening." A few longer poems, including "Death of a Hired Man" and "Two Tramps at Mud-Time," are interspersed with the short ones. The poems read-aloud well and lend themselves to memorizing. With a small number of lovely woodcuts, this is an exceptionally fine poetry book.

Janeczko, Paul B., selector. *The Place My Words Are Looking For: What Poets Say About and Through Their Work.* **1990. Hardcover: Bradbury. 150 pages. Ages 10–14. POETRY COLLECTION.**

This original volume combines short essays by poets with a sampling of their poetry. The sixty-plus poems, most of them short, span an array of subjects and feelings. Some are funny, some serious, some haunting. Photographs show the thirty-nine poets who comment on how and why they write poetry. They present different viewpoints, of interest to aspiring poets and to those who love reading poems. A thoughtful, inspiring approach to poetry.

Carlson, Lori M., editor. *Cool Salsa: Bilingual Poems on Growing Up Latino in the United States.* **1994. Hardcover: Henry Holt. Paperback: Fawcett. 123 pages. Ages 11–14. POETRY COLLECTION.**

More than three dozen poems by different writers convey feelings about growing up bilingual in the United States. Most are given in English and Spanish, although a few combine the two languages. A glossary at the back translates Spanish words. Divided into categories such as "School Days," "Hard Times," and "Time to Party," the poems span a wide range of emotions. Some reflect a life of hardship, while others rejoice in a Latino heritage. A fine collection.

Nye, Naomi Shihab, selector. *This Same Sky: A Collection of Poems from Around the World.* 1992. Hardcover: Four Winds. Paperback: Aladdin. 224 pages. Ages 12–14. POETRY COLLECTION.

This rich collection brings together poems, many in translation, from sixty-eight countries. Readers will be struck by the commonality of feelings and themes expressed. Nye groups the poems by general categories such as "Words and Silences," "Dreams and Dreamers," "Families," "Losses," and so on. Most of the poems are short and laced with effective images. Notes at the back give dates and some biographical information on each poet. A wonderful way to travel the world in words.

Folklore and Fantasy

Dragons, Wizards, and Other Magic

Whitcher, Susan. *The Key to the Cupboard.* Illustrated by Andrew Glass. 1997. Hardcover: Farrar, Straus & Giroux. 32 pages. Ages 3–7. PICTURE BOOK.
What child wouldn't like a key to a secret cupboard that leads up to a room with a friendly witch? The young narrator and her witch concoct a magic brew together. Energetic illustrations fill the large pages as the girl and the witch take off on a broomstick in a sky filled with magical creatures. An encounter with a scruffy wizard proves dangerous until the liquid from their brew saves the day, "Drip! *Drop!* POP!" A wild adventure full of magic and mayhem.

Gibbons, Gail. *Behold the Dragons!* 1999. Hardcover: Morrow. 32 pages. Ages 3–8. PICTURE BOOK NONFICTION.

Using a picture-story-book format, Gibbons supplies a lot of colorful information about dragons in history and throughout the world. She describes five groups defined by "dracontologists," including serpent dragons and sky dragons. The mundane watercolor-and-pen illustrations add more details, as does a one-page appendix about related topics such as the komodo dragon, which is really a large lizard. Read this one in conjunction with a story about dragons.

Mitchell, Adrian. *Nobody Rides the Unicorn.* Illustrated by Stephen Lambert. 2000. Hardcover: Scholastic. 32 pages. Ages 3–8. PICTURE BOOK.

A king who fears poisoning seeks to kill a unicorn for its horn in order to make magic utensils that will guarantee his safety. He tricks Zoe, a good-natured beggar girl, into helping him capture the gentle creature. But he underestimates the courage of the girl, who risks her life and banishment from her home to save the unicorn. The large, haunting illustrations, full of strong shadows and strange details, create the perfect setting for a unicorn tale.

Nolen, Jerdine. *Raising Dragons.* Illustrated by Elise Primavera. 1998. Hardcover: Harcourt. 32 pages. Ages 3–8. PICTURE BOOK.

A farm girl finds a dragon's egg and tends the dragon when it hatches. She names him Hank, feeds him and reads to him, and some nights goes on grand flights on his back. He grows enormous and increasingly lovable, but when he starts drawing attention from outsiders, the girl knows it's time for a change. She comes up with the perfect solution for her dragon. A magical, original story with illustrations that suit it perfectly.

Van Allsburg, Chris. *The Widow's Broom.* **1992. Hardcover: Houghton. 32 pages. Ages 5–9. PICTURE BOOK.**

In this wonderfully strange story, Widow Shaw helps a fallen witch and ends up with her old broom. The magical broom proves to be a big help, sweeping by itself, chopping wood, and even playing the piano. But the widow's self-righteous neighbor sees the broom working and insists she get rid of it. With the help of the broom, the widow outsmarts him and sends him packing. Outstanding brown-and-white pencil illustrations enhance the spooky mood of this tale. Not to be missed.

Gannett, Ruth Stiles. *My Father's Dragon.* **Illustrated by Ruth Chrisman Gannett. 1948. Hardcover: Random House. Paperback: Knopf. 86 pages. Ages 6–9. FICTION.**

In this magical adventure, a boy named Elmer Elevator journeys to the Wild Island, where he has close escapes from a lion, rhino, and tiger, among others. Luckily, he has packed everything he needs to distract the animals. In the end, Elmer rescues the captive flying dragon he came for. Despite a harsh scene where Elmer's mother whips him, this Newbery Honor Book endures thanks to an imaginative plot and charming pictures. Followed by *Elmer and the Dragon* and *The Dragons of Blueland.*

Hunt, Jonathan. *Bestiary: An Illuminated Alphabet of Medieval Beasts.* **1999. Hardcover: Simon & Schuster. 40 pages. Ages 6–10. PICTURE BOOK NONFICTION.**

From amphisbaena, a two-headed reptile, to ziphius, a vicious water-owl, this large book introduces twenty-six strange creatures. A paragraph describes the characteristics of each beast, while a large, ornate picture shows it in action. Readers learn about creatures encountered in fantasies and myths, many of them obscure and fascinating. The author's note discusses the history of books called bestiaries, while a bibliography suggests further reading. A companion book is *Illuminations*.

Yolen, Jane. *Merlin and the Dragons*. Illustrated by Li Ming. 1995. Paperback: Puffin. 40 pages. Ages 6–10. PICTURE BOOK.

This well-told tale gives one version of Merlin's childhood and coming of age in which he is born of a royal mother but grows up without a father. Early on he can foretell the future and see spirits, making him an outcast as a child. A visiting king threatens his life until the boy saves himself by detecting two dragons beneath the earth, one red and one white, that fight each other in the air. Unusually large, dramatic pictures reveal that it is an older Merlin telling this story about his past to young King Arthur.

San Souci, Robert D. *Sukey and the Mermaid*. Illustrated by Brian Pinkney. 1992. Hardcover: Four Winds Press. Paperback: Aladdin. 32 pages. Ages 6–10. PICTURE BOOK.

Delicately colored scratchboard illustrations set this folktale on the South Carolina shore, where a girl named Sukey lives with her mother and harsh stepfather. When she can get away from her chores, Sukey goes to the beach where she one day meets "a beautiful, brown-skinned, black-eyed mermaid." The encounter improves Sukey's life, takes her on a strange adventure, and finally leads her to happiness. An unusual, haunting mermaid tale from the African-American tradition.

Coville, Bruce. *Jeremy Thatcher, Dragon Hatcher.* **Illustrated by Gary A. Lippincott. 1991. Hardcover: Harcourt. Paperback: Minstrel. 148 pages. Ages 8–13. FICTION.**

When Jeremy buys a dragon's egg at a mysterious magic shop, it's a dream come true, but a dream with many complications. He conscientiously follows the directions about hatching the egg and caring for the fantastic little creature that only one other person can see. But the dragon gets huge fast, and meanwhile, Jeremy has a few problems of his own at school to deal with. A popular dragon tale about a likable boy and the magic that enters his life.

Ibbotson, Eva. *The Secret of Platform 13.* **Illustrated by Sue Porter. 1994. Hardcover: Dutton. Paperback: Puffin. 224 pages. Ages 9–13. FICTION.**

Ghosts, wizards, ogres, harpies, and many more magical creatures appear in this original British fantasy in which the baby prince of a magical island is kidnapped in London. Nine years later, four magical islanders go to rescue him. To their dismay, they greatly dislike the boy they believe to be the prince and he has no interest in being rescued. Sympathetic characters, lots of magic, and a few Roald Dahl touches of nastiness make for an exciting read.

Jones, Diana Wynne. *Witch Week.* **1982. Hardcover: Greenwillow. Paperback: Morrow. 248 pages. Ages 9–13. FICTION.**

Larwood House seems like a modern school, but in this fictional England witches exist. Since witches come into their powers around adolescence, several students are starting to realize what they can do: make themselves invisible, make wishes come true, and fly on broomsticks. Their new powers are exhilarating but dangerous because witches are burned. When an inquisitor comes to the school, five young witches run away, with only a strange spell to bring them to safety. A clever fantasy, with moments of absurd humor. Highly recommended.

Rowling, J. K. *Harry Potter and the Sorcerer's Stone.* Illustrated by Mary GrandPre. 1998. Hardcover and paperback: Scholastic. 312 pages. Ages 9–13. FICTION.

Harry Potter, who has been living with gruesome relatives, enrolls in a wizard academy where he learns about his heritage and finds out how important he really is. Harry makes close new friends, excels at the magical sport of Quidditch, and proves his heroism to save the school. While seemingly set in modern times, the fantasy and its sequels suffer from frequent stereotyped images of females, who rarely perform key actions and often need rescuing. Nevertheless, the imaginative magical details and humor have an uncanny ability to capture children's interest and keep them reading. A stunningly popular fantasy.

Hill, Douglas. *Witches and Magic-Makers.* Photographs by Alex Wilson. 1997. Hardcover: Knopf. 64 pages. Ages 9 and up. NONFICTION.

This "Eyewitness" book uses photographs, long captions, and limited text to discuss different topics on each double-page spread. The first part of the book focuses on the traditional European view of witchcraft and wizardry, with photographs of cauldrons, broomsticks, herbs, and amulets. The pages on witch hunts are grim, showing some instruments of torture, after which the scope widens to look at magical practices around the world. Good photographs and well-chosen details will capture the interest of those who want to know more about the history of magic.

Wrede, Patricia C. *Dealing with Dragons*. 1990. Hardcover: Harcourt. Paperback: Scholastic. 212 pages. Ages 10–13. FICTION.

Cimorene, a strong-minded princess, finds castle life so boring that she runs away and gets a job as the cook and librarian for a dragon named Kazul. When the King of the Dragons dies, and Kazul is laid low from poisoning, Cimorene and some of her magical friends outwit the evil wizards who caused the trouble. Full of funny twists on fairy tales, this action-packed adventure has an appealing cast of dragons, witches, smart princesses, and ruthless wizards. The first of four "Enchanted Forest Chronicles."

Tolkien, J.R.R. *The Hobbit, or There and Back Again*. 1966. Hardcover: Houghton. Paperback: Ballantine, Houghton. 290 pages. Ages 11–14. FICTION.

Hobbits are smaller than humans, inclined to be stout, and like a cozy life. Bilbo Baggins, a hobbit, has led a respectable life until the wizard Gandalf persuades him to go on an adventure disguised as a burglar. Bilbo and thirteen dwarves set off to recover treasure stolen by a dragon long ago. On the journey, they encounter trolls, goblins, and elves, and engage in a dreadful battle in this engaging magical tale. Followed by the *Lord of the Rings* trilogy, one of the greatest fantasy series ever written.

Vande Velde, Vivian. *Never Trust a Dead Man*. 1999. Hardcover: Harcourt. 192 pages. Ages 11–14. FICTION.

Because his fellow villagers believe that Selwyn has killed his romantic rival Farold, they shut him in a cave with Farold's body. Luckily, a witch comes along and agrees to help—for a price. In exchange for years of Selwyn's service, she temporarily awakens Farold from the dead and provides Selwyn with a disguise. Selwyn and Farold, who is resurrected in a bat's body, return to the village to figure out who committed the murder. Full of funny plot twists, with a gratifying ending, this fantasy is a winner.

Jenkins, Martin. *Informania: Vampires.* **1998. Hardcover and paperback: Candlewick. 92 pages. Ages 11–14. NONFICTION.**

"Everything you ever wanted to know about vampires— but were too afraid to ask!" proclaims this book's cover, under the picture of a red-eyed, fanged vampire. The enjoyable text recaps Bram Stoker's book *Dracula* in comic-strip format, then goes on to explore various aspects of blood-sucking creatures in nature, history, and the movies. It traces the origin of the belief in vampires and how the belief has manifested itself through the years. A jaunty design with lots of humorous pictures and asides livens up the dark topic.

Jones, Diana Wynne. *Dark Lord of Derkholm.* **1998. Hardcover: Greenwillow. 352 pages. Ages 11–14. FICTION.**

Derk has no interest in playing the part of an evil wizard to entertain visiting tourists, but that is a requirement in his world. He and other creatures including his griffin children serve as entertainment for tourists from Earth. As they pit themselves against a huge commercial enterprise, Derk and his magical family enter a grand battle against evil. Fast-moving with plenty of danger and humor, this outstanding fantasy is by one of the finest writers of the genre. Followed by *Year of the Griffin.*

Le Guin, Ursula K. A *Wizard of Earthsea*. Illustrated by Ruth Robbins. 1968. Hardcover: Atheneum. Paperback: Bantam. 197 pages. Ages 11–14. FICTION.

Ged, a poor boy talented in magic, goes to the island of Roke to be trained as a wizard. Proud and impatient, he experiments with powers beyond his control and calls up a dark spirit from the dead. Although he survives the encounter, he must give up his dreams of glory and leave Roke. In his wanderings, he fights dragons and other enemies, but ultimately has to face the darkness again. Le Guin has created a richly detailed world with its own history, languages, and magic. First in an outstanding series.

Folktales from Around the World

Sierra, Judy. *Tasty Baby Belly Buttons.* **Illustrated by Meilo So. 1999. Hardcover: Knopf. 40 pages. Ages 3–7. PICTURE BOOK.**

The title of this retold Japanese folktale will draw children in, and the mixture of humor and courage will keep them listening. When terrible monsters steal a village's babies in order to eat their "tasty baby belly buttons," a girl born from a watermelon, who has no belly button herself, sets out to save the children. With three helpful companions, a sword, and some millet dumplings, she succeeds. Lovely watercolors that evoke Japanese artwork match the amusing tale.

McDermott, Gerald. *Anansi the Spider: A Tale from the Ashanti.* **1972. Hardcover and paperback: Henry Holt. 48 pages. Ages 3–8. PICTURE BOOK.**

In this short tale about Anansi the spider and his six sons, Anansi falls into trouble a long way from home. Luckily, each of his sons has a special talent that helps rescue Anansi when he is swallowed by a huge fish. One son can build roads, another can throw stones perfectly, and so on. They put their talents into effect until Anansi is safe. A creative design and inventive graphics make the illustrations in this Caldecott Honor Book a standout. The rhythmic text reads aloud well, and the story delights young children.

Sierra, Judy, selector. *Nursery Tales Around the World.* Illustrated by Stefano Vitale. 1996. Hardcover: Clarion. 114 pages. Ages 3–8. FOLKLORE COLLECTION.

This excellent folktale collection divides its tales into themes, then gives three examples of each. The theme "Runaway Cookies" includes the well-known story about the gingerbread man, a Swedish story about a runaway pancake, and a Russian one about a baked bun. Thanks to their rhythm and repetition, the stories lend themselves to reading aloud, especially to younger children. The oil paintings on wooden panels have a folk art flavor that draws from traditions of different countries. This outstanding book may well become a family treasure.

Taback, Simms. *Joseph Had a Little Overcoat.* 1999. Hardcover: Viking. 32 pages. Ages 3–8. PICTURE BOOK.

In this simple Yiddish tale, Joseph uses his worn coat to make a jacket, the jacket to make a vest, the vest to make a scarf, and so on. Each brightly colored double-page spread has a garment-shaped hole that children can peek through to see the next garment. The clever collage illustrations, which echo primitive folk paintings, brim over with funny details to delight children and adults. A Caldecott Medal winner.

San Souci, Robert D., reteller. *A Weave of Words: An Armenian Folktale.* Illustrated by Raúl Colón. 1998. Hardcover: Orchard. 32 pages. Ages 4–9. PICTURE BOOK.

Prince Vachagan, a warm-hearted, handsome man used to getting his own way, is shocked when he wants to marry a weaver's daughter and she refuses. She won't marry a man who can't read, as she can, and who knows no craft. The prince learns to read and weave, and they marry. But when the prince goes to investigate trouble in the kingdom, a three-headed demon

FOLKLORE AND FANTASY

enslaves him. Thanks to his new knowledge and his brave wife, he is saved. A beautifully illustrated story of love and loyalty.

Gregorowski, Christopher. *Fly, Eagle, Fly: An African Tale.* Illustrated by Niki Daly. 2000. Hardcover: McElderry. 32 pages. Ages 5–9. PICTURE BOOK.

When a farmer finds a baby eagle and raises it with his chickens, the eagle learns to act like an earthbound bird. After the eagle is grown, a visiting friend vows to teach the bird its true nature. One morning the farmer and his friend climb a mountain where the blazing sunrise calls to the eagle and it soars away. In the words of Archbishop Desmond Tutu's foreword, "We are made for the sublime, the transcendent." Daly's luminous illustrations add spirit and some humor to the inspiring tale.

McCully, Emily Arnold. *Beautiful Warrior: The Legend of the Nun's Kung Fu.* 1998. Hardcover: Scholastic. 40 pages. Ages 5–10. PICTURE BOOK.

Jingyong was a Chinese girl educated as a boy who excelled at the martial art of kung fu. When grown she became a nun called Wu Mei, or Beautiful Warrior. In this story, Wu Mei saves a girl named Mingyi from bandits and the girl apprentices herself to Wu Mei to learn kung fu. After a challenging year, Mingyi fights to save herself from an unwanted marriage and vows to devote her life to kung fu. Superb watercolors show lots of martial arts drama.

Yolen, Jane, editor. *Favorite Folktales from Around the World.* **1986. Hardcover: Pantheon. 498 pages. Ages 5 and up. FOLKLORE COLLECTION.**

For the child who loves folklore, this extensive collection of tales from around the world is a gold mine. Yolen has done a masterful job of assembling and editing tales that retain the sound of oral tradition. Because they use traditional phrasing and uncluttered language, they are just right for reading aloud. Thirteen sections divide the tales into logical groupings such as numskull and noodle tales, ghost stories, trickster stories, tales of heroes, tales about the devil, and more. Under each title, the country or culture of origin is listed, with sources at the back of the book.

Phelps, Ethel Johnston. *Tatterhood and Other Tales.* **Illustrated by Pamela Baldwin Ford. 1978. Paperback: Feminist Press. 166 pages. Ages 6–13. FOLKLORE COLLECTION.**

This fine collection features twenty-five tales about females who have adventures and who do the rescuing rather than be rescued as in so many traditional stories. Some of the heroines are old, others young. Some of the stories are funny, while others are romantic. Each tale has a note describing its country of origin and its source. Drawn from many countries, the stories retain the cadence of traditional storytelling. Occasional black-and-white illustrations accompany the stories. Also see the companion volume *The Maid of the North*, which has tales about independent girls and women, too.

Hamilton, Virginia. *The People Could Fly: American Black Folktales.* Illustrated by Leo and Diane Dillon. 1985. Hardcover and paperback: Knopf. 178 pages. Ages 7–12. FOLKLORE COLLECTION.

This outstanding folktale collection assembles twenty-four tales from American black folklore, accompanied by graceful black-and-white illustrations. Notes after each story and an extensive bibliography add to its high quality. Seven animal tales tell of small animals tricking bigger ones, while in several other tales, the slave character John the Conqueror outwits slave owners. The magical, scary, funny, and moving stories read aloud beautifully. A tribute to African-American oral tradition.

Folktales from Europe

Marshall, James. *Goldilocks and the Three Bears.* 1988. Hardcover: Dial. Paperback: Puffin. 32 pages. Ages 3–8. PICTURE BOOK.

James Marshall, one of the funniest illustrators ever, turned his talents to illustrating several Grimms' tales. In this irreverent version of Goldilocks, which generally follows the standard plot, Goldilocks takes a shortcut clearly marked "Very risky!" and "Not a good idea." At a delightful small Victorian house, she tries the porridge, the chairs, and finally the beds, where she is discovered and quickly makes her escape. The little house is packed with humorous details that children will enjoy looking at as they laugh at the story. A Caldecott Honor Book. Also see Marshall's versions of Red Riding Hood, Hansel and Gretel, and the Three Little Pigs.

Perrault, Charles. Translated by Malcolm Arthur. *Puss in Boots.* Illustrated by Fred Marcellino. 1990. Hardcover and paperback: Farrar, Straus & Giroux. 32 pages. Ages 3–9. PICTURE BOOK.

When the miller's youngest son is left with only a cat after his father dies, the cat asks for a pair of boots and a sack, and sets out to make his master rich. He manages beautifully by tricking the king into believing the miller's son owns abundant land. Then the cat fools a wealthy ogre. The youngest son ends up with riches and he marries the king's daughter. Beautifully rendered artwork, full of detail and humor, and a striking design made this a Caldecott Honor Book.

Hyman, Trina Schart, reteller. *Little Red Riding Hood.* **1983. Hardcover and paperback: Holiday House. 32 pages. Ages 4–9. PICTURE BOOK.**

Delightful illustrations create a fairy-tale world in this Caldecott Honor Book that retells a well-known Grimms' story. Following the familiar plot, Red Riding Hood walks through the woods, picks flowers at the wolf's suggestion, mistakes the wolf for her grandmother, and ends up in his stomach. A local huntsman saves the day. A conversational tone characterizes the retelling. Charming borders surround the text, and cunning details fill the pictures. Certain to please young fairy-tale fans.

Kimmel, Eric A., reteller. *Seven at One Blow: A Tale from the Brothers Grimm.* **Illustrated by Megan Lloyd. 1998. Hardcover: Holiday House. 32 pages. Ages 4–9. PICTURE BOOK.**

After a tailor kills seven flies in one swipe, he embroiders his belt with the slogan "Seven at One Blow." Everyone he encounters as he makes his way in the world assumes the seven were men or giants. By good luck, he then tricks giants, ogres, a wild boar, and a unicorn and wins his fortune. His persistent cheerfulness in the face of challenges makes him a real hero. A good retelling with wonderful pen-and-watercolor illustrations.

Lesser, Rika, reteller. *Hansel and Gretel.* **Illustrated by Paul O. Zelinsky. 1999 Reissue. Hardcover: Dutton. Paperback: Paper Star. 40 pages. Ages 4–9. PICTURE BOOK.**

Rich oil paintings create a dark forest where Hansel and Gretel are abandoned in this fine retelling of a Grimms' tale. In this version, the mother rather than a stepmother insists on leaving the children. Hansel saves them once but the second time they end up at the candied home of a cruel witch. Gretel saves them this time by pushing the witch into the oven. The candy house yields up jewels, sending the children home to their father rich and happy in this beautifully illustrated tale.

Andersen, Hans Christian. Adapted and illustrated by Jerry Pinkney. *The Ugly Duckling.* **1999. Hardcover: Morrow. 40 pages. Ages 5–9. PICTURE BOOK.**

Luminous watercolors depict the familiar story of a swan born into a duck family. He feels ugly as a duck but later finds he is a beautiful swan. Award-winning illustrator Pinkney achieves remarkably transparent effects in the many large pictures where swans and ducks dive and swim. The winter scene reflects the swan's desolation, while the light-filled spring ones radiate with joy. The retelling follows the original story line, but the illustrations set it in nineteenth-century rural America. An unusually beautiful version of an old favorite, this is a Caldecott Honor Book.

Andersen, Hans Christian. Retold by Andrew Matthews. *Stories from Hans Christian Andersen.* **Illustrated by Alan Snow. 1993. Hardcover: Orchard. 96 pages. Ages 6 and up. FOLKLORE COLLECTION.**

"The Princess and the Pea," "The Ugly Duckling," and "The Emperor's New Clothes" are among the stories in this collection that every child should know because of their place in our culture. Matthews has retold these and eleven other Andersen tales in an accessible fashion, striking a tone between casual and formal. The humorous artwork, which includes at least one small illustration on most pages, softens some of the more tragic tales like "The Little Match Girl" and "The Steadfast Tin Soldier." Fans of the Disney movie may be surprised to hear the differences in the original "The Little

Mermaid." Altogether, a good introduction to an important storyteller.

Bader, Barbara. *Aesop & Company with Scenes from His Legendary Life.* **Illustrated by Arthur Geisert. 1990. Hardcover and paperback: Houghton. 64 pages. Ages 8–11. Of interest to younger children. FOLKLORE COLLECTION.**

This elegant book tells nineteen fables of Aesop in simple, lyrical language. The stories have become such a part of Western culture that even children who have not heard them before may recognize the morals such as "Easier said than done" from the tale about belling the cat. The collection includes famous tales like "The Tortoise and the Hare," "The Fox and the Grapes," "The Shepherd Boy Who Cried 'Wolf,' " and lesser-known ones. An informative introduction discusses fables in history, and the final pages recount legends about Aesop. A charming collection of stories every child should know.

Lunge-Larsen, Lise. *The Troll with No Heart in His Body and Other Tales of Trolls, from Norway.* **Illustrated by Betsy Bowen. 1999. Hardcover: Houghton. 96 pages. Ages 9–13. Of interest to younger children. FOLKLORE COLLECTION.**

This is a beautifully made book for a family to treasure and hand down over the years. Loving attention to detail characterizes the design and especially the elegant woodcuts that accompany the nine stories. Because the writer retelling the stories grew up in Norway, the tales reflect what she heard as a child and flow with the rhythms of traditional storytelling. The trolls can be nasty at times, so these tales may not be best for bedtime reading, but they are excellent for sharing at other times.

Philip, Neil, reteller. *Fairy Tales of the Brothers Grimm.* Illustrated by Isabelle Brent. 1997. Hardcover: Viking. 144 pages. Ages 9–13. Of interest to younger children. FOLKLORE COLLECTION.

"The Frog Prince," "Snow White," "Rumpelstiltskin," "Rapunzel," and sixteen other Grimms' tales are gracefully retold in an attractive volume. In these traditional stories, kindness often pays while arrogance and laziness are punished. Princesses tend to be beautiful and passive, although a few stories have girls who shape their own fates. The stories retain the rhythm and simplicity of the oral tradition, making them good for reading aloud. Gold-tinged paintings help create a fairy-tale world.

Fractured Folktales

Brett, Jan. *Gingerbread Baby.* **1999. Hardcover: Putnam. 32 pages. Ages 3–8. PICTURE BOOK.**

In this original variation on the "Gingerbread Man," Matti and his mother are baking a gingerbread boy. When Matti opens the oven too early, a gingerbread baby pops out. The cookie escapes through the door into a wintry Scandinavian landscape where it is chased by Matti's parents, then a cat, a dog, and more. Meanwhile, Matti himself is concocting a gingerbread house that finally lures the cookie back. Ornate illustrations with elaborate borders will please Brett's many fans.

Ketteman, Helen. *Bubba the Cowboy Prince: A Fractured Texas Tale.* **Illustrated by James Warhola. 1997. Hardcover: Scholastic. 32 pages. Ages 3–8. PICTURE BOOK.**

Although Bubba's wicked stepdaddy and two stepbrothers make him do all the work on their Texas ranch, he never complains because he loves ranching. But when the rich rancher Miz Lurleen announces she is throwing a ball to "find herself a feller," Bubba wishes he could go. Sure enough, he shows up in fancy cowboy duds thanks to his fairy godcow. Children will recognize the Cinderella story and laugh at the funny pictures that suit this zany tale.

Sturges, Philemon. *The Little Red Hen (Makes a Pizza).* **Illustrated by Amy Walrod. 1999. Hardcover: Dutton. 32 pages. Ages 3–8. PICTURE BOOK.**

Jaunty cut-paper illustrations provide humorous details in this retelling of a well-known tale. The little red hen plans to make a pizza rather than a loaf of bread, but she can get no help from her neighbors—a duck in a swimming cap, a frolicking dog, and a saxophone-playing cat. So the hen herself makes several shopping trips, always coming back with lots of extras. She makes the pizza, which her friends help eat and then, happily, they do the cleaning up. Great fun.

Lowell, Susan. *The Bootmaker and the Elves*. Illustrated by Tom Curry. 1997. Hardcover and paperback: Orchard. 32 pages. Ages 4–8. PICTURE BOOK.

"Whoopee-ki-yi-yay!" It's a Western retelling of the tale about elves who help a poor shoemaker. In this sassy new version set in the Wild West, the elves make dazzling cowboy boots at night, which magically fit the next day's customers and so save the bootmaker from poverty. Droll illustrations exaggerate the Westerners who come in to buy, like the "rootin' tootin' cowboy from the back of the beyond." Wonderfully playful language matched by the exuberant pictures makes this fractured fairy tale a treat.

Scieszka, Jon, and Lane Smith. *The Stinky Cheese Man & Other Fairly Stupid Tales*. 1992. Hardcover: Viking. 32 pages. Ages 5–10. PICTURE BOOK.

This hilarious collection turns well-known tales on their heads. Even before the title page—labeled "Title Page" in huge letters—the little red hen begins her story. Then comes the tale of Chicken Licken in which the Table of Contents falls instead of the sky, followed by "The Princess and the Bowling Bowl" and "Little Red Riding Running Shorts," among others. Imaginative collages and playful book design made this a Caldecott Honor Book. Sure to have children howling with laughter.

Stanley, Diane. *Rumpelstiltskin's Daughter.* 1997. Hardcover: Morrow. 32 pages. Ages 5–10. PICTURE BOOK.

In this clever fractured fairy tale, Rumpelstiltskin proves to be a conscientious, friendly, family-oriented man who wins the heart of the miller's daughter in some very funny dialogue. The two of them escape from the king and live happily together. But there's more. They have a daughter who attracts the greedy king's interest as her mother did. This time, though, Rumpelstiltskin's daughter gets the best of the king while she also helps the impoverished people of the kingdom. Outstanding.

Scieszka, Jon. *The True Story of the Three Little Pigs.* Illustrated by Lane Smith. 1989. Hardcover: Viking. Paperback: Puffin. 32 pages. Ages 6–10. PICTURE BOOK.

In this fractured fairy tale, the reader learns the story of the three little pigs from the viewpoint of the wolf, who claims he was just sneezing and the houses fell in. He had simply gone to the first pig's house to borrow a cup of sugar to bake his granny a birthday cake. Wonderfully funny pictures, which repay close study, include newspaper coverage of the story. A clever, very popular book, not to be missed.

O'Neal, Shaquille. *Shaq and the Beanstalk.* Illustrated by Shane W. Evans. 1999. Hardcover: Scholastic. 80 pages. Ages 8–12. Of interest to younger children. FICTION.

"I was lucky," writes basketball star Shaquille O'Neal in his note to readers. "I grew up in a loving home where my parents read to me a lot." Now he has taken some of his favorite stories and put himself into them as a child: "Shaq and the Beanstalk," "Little Red Riding Shaq," and three more. The funny retellings have a modern tone with constant allusions to basketball. The jaunty pen-and-watercolor pictures incorporate photos of Shaq, matching the narrative's spirit of fun.

Datlow, Ellen, and Terri Windling, editors. *A Wolf at the Door and Other Retold Fairy Tales.* **2000. Hardcover: Simon & Schuster. 166 pages. Ages 10–13. FICTION.**

In this entertaining collection, thirteen fine writers take favorite fairy tales and turn them into new stories or poems. Readers will recognize most of the underlying tales such as "Cinderella," "Snow White," and "The Twelve Dancing Princesses." Many of the updated versions inject elements of modern life into the tales. Ali Baba meets forty aliens instead of thieves in one, and a Sony Playstation shop lures Hansel and Gretel in another. Some add darkness to the original tales, while others add humor. Great fun.

Brooke, William J. *Teller of Tales.* **1994. Hardcover and paperback: Harper. 170 pages. Ages 10–14. FICTION.**

Teller is an old man who hears voices that compel him to write. First he writes newspapers and, with the help of a young girl who is a pickpocket, sells them. But they offend the Emperor, who demands that Teller write stories instead. All the stories somehow incorporate Teller and the girl. Is he Rumpelstiltskin? Is she Goldilocks? Readers will have to decide for themselves. Clever and sometimes funny, these stories will change how the reader looks at "The Emperor's New Clothes," "Red Riding Hood," and other well-known fairy tales.

Ghosts, Aliens,
and UFOs

Marshall, Edward. *Space Case*. Illustrated by James Marshall. 1980. Hardcover and paperback: Dial. 40 pages. Ages 3–7. PICTURE BOOK.

"It came from outer space" is how this funny book about a robotlike alien begins. The small creature arrives on Halloween and finds the natives on the planet very interesting indeed. It starts trick-or-treating with some children and follows one, Buddy, home. The creature studies a dictionary and starts to talk, then goes to school with Buddy and volunteers to be his science project. Disappointed that school is every day and Halloween only once a year, it decides to leave, at least until Christmas. Cartoonlike pictures perfectly suit the story.

Sierra, Judy. *The House That Drac Built*. Illustrated by Will Hillenbrand. 1995. Hardcover and paperback: Harcourt. 32 pages. Ages 4–8. PICTURE BOOK.

Sounding like "The House That Jack Built," this version incorporates Halloween creatures into the verses, each increasingly larger: a bat, cat, werewolf, manticore, and so on. Large, wide pictures in grays and browns portray ugly but not terrifying creatures who themselves are finally caught by surprise when other, shorter creatures knock at their door on Halloween night. Keep in mind that some children like Halloween books all year round. Great for reading aloud.

Del Negro, Janice. *Lucy Dove.* **Illustrated by Leonid Gore. 1998. Hardcover: DK Ink. 32 pages. Ages 5–9. PICTURE BOOK.**

This tale's creepy setting, clawed monster, and haunting pictures will satisfy children who crave scary books. "When wishes were horses and beggars could ride," it begins, a rich, superstitious laird offered gold to anyone who would sew him trousers by moonlight in an old graveyard. Old Lucy Dove, who has more courage than money, resolves to win the gold. In the moonlit graveyard, she encounters a fearsome monster and defeats it with her wit. Illustrated with deliciously ghostly paintings.

Schwartz, Alvin. *Ghosts! Ghostly Tales from Folklore.* **Illustrated by Victoria Chess. 1991. Hardcover and paperback: Harper. 64 pages. Ages 5–9. EASY READER.**

This "I Can Read" book is perfect for beginning readers who like ghost stories. In simple language, the tales tell about a haunted house, a ghost cat, a nasty ghost girl, and more. The final chapter offers advice on scaring away ghosts. While not terribly scary, the collection is a good starting point for a lifetime of suspenseful reading. The color illustrations, which show suitably strange characters with a haunted air, also add a note of humor.

Herbst, Judith. *The Mystery of UFOs.* **Illustrated by Greg Clarke. 1997. Hardcover: Atheneum. Paperback: Aladdin. 40 pages. Ages 6–10. PICTURE BOOK NONFICTION.**

This short illustrated book provides a lot of information about UFOs. The author, who is open to the idea that some UFOs are genuine, reviews the major "sightings" in the United States, starting with the incident that introduced the term *flying saucer.* The account discusses reported appearances around Roswell, New Mexico, and the government's reactions to them. Maps add information, but most of the other illustrations have a lighthearted spirit. The book offers an upbeat introduction to a high-interest topic.

Etra, Jonathan, and Stephanie Spinner. *Aliens for Breakfast.* **Illustrated by Steve Björkman. 1988. Hardcover and paperback: Random House. 64 pages. Ages 7–10. FICTION.**

The last thing Richard expects to emerge from his breakfast cereal is an alien, a tiny creature named Aric who desperately needs Richard's help. He claims that an evil Drane plans to take over Earth and they only have a few days to stop it. The Drane turns out to be the new kid who has charmed everyone else in Richard's class. Short chapters, large print, a quick-moving plot, and some funny dialogue make this a good choice for younger readers.

Gauthier, Gail. *My Life Among the Aliens.* **1996. Hardcover: Putnam. Paperback: Paper Star. 112 pages. Ages 8–12. FICTION.**

By the end of this jaunty short novel, it seems entirely plausible that aliens visit Will and his brother, Robby, on a regular basis. The aliens differ in appearance and temperament, but each one is curious about Earth and particularly drawn to the healthy food Will's mother cooks, which Will himself could live without. The dialogue and characters are remarkably realistic, with lots of humor and warmth. Readers will only wish the inconvenience of alien visitors would happen to them.

Yolen, Jane, and Heidi Elisabet Yolen Stemple. *The* **Mary** **Celeste:** *An Unsolved Mystery from History.* **Illustrated by Roger Roth. 1999. Hardcover: Simon & Schuster. 32 pages. Ages 8–12. NONFICTION.**

In 1872, the *Mary Celeste* was found adrift at sea one month after leaving New York. Mysteriously, the ship showed no signs of mutiny, sickness, or pirate attack. This short, intriguing book lays out the mystery in detail, ultimately offering six possible explanations. Fully illustrated pages relay the story in narrative form, with additional information and nautical definitions on what look like "stickies" and pages from a notebook. Readers must draw their own conclusions about the strange occurrence based on all the clues.

Simon, Seymour. *Strange Mysteries from Around the World.* **1997 Revised Edition. Hardcover and paperback: Morrow. 64 pages. Ages 8–14. NONFICTION.**

A ghost ship, a strange crystal skull, and big bangs are among the mysteries Simon explores in this intriguing book. The diverse topics share one trait: No one can completely explain them. How do humans walk on burning coals without blistering their feet? Why does it sometimes rain frogs and fish? Experts have recorded such events but cannot pinpoint how they happen. Curious readers will enjoy these strange occurrences and the questions they raise.

DeFelice, Cynthia. *The Ghost of Fossil Glen.* **1998. Hardcover: Farrar, Straus & Giroux. Paperback: Camelot. 168 pages. Ages 9–12. FICTION.**

This supernatural thriller opens with sixth-grader Allie clinging to a cliff face, where she has been looking for fossils and climbed too high. A calm voice encourages her to save herself, but when she does she discovers that there's no one around. Could it have been the voice of a sixth-grade girl who died before Allie moved to town? Was she murdered? Allie endangers her own life as she tries to find out the truth and bring the murderer to justice. A fast-paced combination of murder mystery and ghost story.

Mackel, Kathy. *Can of Worms*. 1999. Hardcover: Avon. Paperback: Camelot. 144 pages. Ages 9–13. FICTION.

Mike Pillsbury's strange memories of aliens convince him that he is from another planet. Only his younger neighbors believe his stories until, humiliated in school one day, he summons help from outer space—and it arrives! In fact, alien after alien arrives in answer to his radio signal. Some are helpful, others dangerous. Mike's life quickly improves, so he doesn't want to leave the planet, but he may not have any choice. An action-packed, often funny, science fiction novel.

Blackwood, Gary L. *Alien Astronauts*. 1999. Hardcover: Benchmark. 64 pages. Ages 9–14. NONFICTION.

This intriguing book divides its information into two parts: "The Long, Strange History of Alien Encounters" and "Everything You Always Wanted to Know About UFOs." The author presents his overview in a straightforward style, accepting some UFO sightings and encounters, and rejecting others. Heavily illustrated with photographs, the book offers tips on what to do if you see a UFO and where to watch for them. It also includes a glossary and references to books, museums, organizations, and more. Fun even for those who don't believe.

Schwartz, Alvin, collector. *Scary Stories to Tell in the Dark.* **Illustrated by Stephen Gammell. 1981. Hardcover and paperback: Harper. 112 pages. Ages 9–14. FOLKLORE COLLECTION.**

Children who can't get enough of scary stories love this collection from American folklore. One chapter retells urban legends, stories of more recent origin, such as "The Hook," often told at camp or slumber parties. In the final chapter, humorous stories provide a chance to laugh at scary things. Most of the tales focus on death, danger, cemeteries, ghosts, and other magical creatures, illustrated with creepy black-and-white drawings. Also see *More Scary Stories to Tell in the Dark* and *Scary Stories 3.*

Krull, Kathleen. *They Saw the Future: Oracles, Psychics, Scientists, Great Thinkers, and Pretty Good Guessers.* **Illustrated by Kyrsten Brooker. 1999. Hardcover: Atheneum. 108 pages. Ages 10–13. COLLECTIVE BIOGRAPHY.**

The twelve people in this entertaining book either predicted the future or made scientific guesses about it. The list starts with the Oracle at Delphi, women in ancient Greece who gave answers in riddles. Other entries include Mayans who believed in astrology; Nostradamus, a doctor in the middle ages who made predictions that came true; and Jeanne Dixon, who advised world leaders. More scientific in their future-gazing were Leonardo da Vinci and Jules Verne. The chapters—about eight or nine pages each—enlighten as well as amuse.

Boot, Andy. *ESP: Are You a Mind Reader?* **1998. Hardcover: Element. 128 pages. Ages 10–14. NONFICTION.**

The British author of this chatty book believes in extrasensory perception, although he does include some notes of caution. After basic information about ESP, the book looks at several different ways it manifests itself, including mind-reading; dowsing to find water or minerals; and seeing the future in dreams. Simple experiments allow readers to test their ESP potential. The remainder of the book offers stories and anecdotes about ESP. Also in the "Elements of the Extraordinary" series are *Handwriting* and *Prophecies*.

Hoobler, Dorothy and Thomas Hoobler. *The Ghost in the Tokaido Inn.* 1999. Hardcover: Philomel. 214 pages. Ages 10–14. FICTION.

Fourteen-year-old Seikei wishes more than anything to be a samurai, but he was born into the wrong class. Traveling with his merchant father, Seikei encounters the good and bad sides of samurai when a jewel is stolen from a brutal samurai and another is called in as judge. The judge takes Seikei under his wing and the two of them try to solve the mystery. Steeped in samurai tradition, this mystery, set in eighteenth-century Japan, will keep readers in suspense from beginning to end.

Mahy, Margaret, editor. *Don't Read This! and Other Tales of the Unnatural.* 1998. Hardcover: Front Street. 180 pages. Ages 11–14. FICTION.

Do people in different countries find the same things scary? This collection of eleven stories written by outstanding authors from around the world may answer that question. Supernatural creatures and episodes fill the book. A Japanese mirror sucks in a girl and casts her nasty mirror double out into the world. An ivory door in a story from the Netherlands teaches a prince an important lesson, too late. Ghosts, spirits, a mysterious and invisible tennis player—spooky elements make this a satisfyingly haunting book.

Mythology

Craft, Charlotte. *King Midas and the Golden Touch.* Illustrated by K. Y. Craft. 1999. Hardcover: Morrow. 32 pages. Ages 5–11. PICTURE BOOK.

Ornate, framed illustrations glow with gold in this retelling of a well-known story. The king lives in a sumptuous palace with his young, loving daughter, but when he is offered a reward for a good deed, he foolishly asks that all he touches turn to gold. He quickly realizes his mistake and must make a journey to a river's source to lose the curse. Everyone should become familiar with this story, presented here in romantic pictures.

Yolen, Jane. *Wings.* Illustrated by Dennis Nolan. 1991. Hardcover and paperback: Harcourt. 32 pages. Ages 6–11. PICTURE BOOK.

Lyrical language tells the dramatic Greek story of the inventor Daedalus and his son Icarus. It describes Daedalus's life and travels, but focuses mostly on his attempt to fly and his son's fatal flight too close to the sun. Romantic paintings show the gods' faces in the clouds, hovering over Daedalus and deciding his fate. With far more text than most short books, this extended mythological tale is full of action and tragedy.

Fisher, Leonard Everett. *The Gods and Goddesses of Ancient Egypt.* 1997. Hardcover and paperback: Holiday House. 32 pages. Ages 7–12. NONFICTION.

This short book provides a wonderful introduction to Egyptian mythology. Each colorful double-page spread describes one of thirteen gods or goddesses with a few paragraphs about their parentage, powers, and history. Pictures with an Egyptian flavor show the deities and symbols related to them. The endpapers carry a map of the region; an endnote includes a family tree, pronunciation guide, and bibliography. An excellent starting place for the rich subject of Egyptian myths.

Hutton, Warwick, reteller. *Odysseus and the Cyclops.* **1995. Hardcover: McElderry. 32 pages. Ages 8–13. PICTURE BOOK.**

This gruesome tale will surprise children who think horror stories are a recent invention. Blown off-course on their way home from the Trojan War, Odysseus and his companions land on a green island replete with fruit trees and grazing sheep. To their dismay, they encounter a one-eyed giant, a Cyclops named Polyphemus. He eats several of the men before the wily Odysseus tricks him and extracts revenge. Impressionistic pen-and-watercolor illustrations tone down the violence while they help tell the suspenseful story.

Hamilton, Virginia. *In the Beginning: Creation Stories from Around the World.* **Illustrated by Barry Moser. 1988. Hardcover and paperback: Harcourt. 162 pages. Ages 8–14. FOLKLORE COLLECTION.**

In this splendid book, creation myths from cultures around the world are retold in beautifully honed language. Well-known stories from the Bible and Greek mythology stand side-by-side with less familiar myths from Australian aborigines, Native Americans, and African and Asian cultures. Dramatic full-page oil paintings enhance the tales as does the unusually elegant book design. Excellent for reading aloud, these myths also lend themselves to discussions. This Newbery Honor Book is highly recommended.

Lattimore, Deborah Nourse. *Medusa.* **2000. Hardcover: Harper. 32 pages. Ages 9–12. Of interest to younger children. PICTURE BOOK.**

Readers may not realize that Medusa began life unusually beautiful, but lost her beauty when she bragged that it outshone Athena's. The goddess Athena cursed her, turning Medusa's hair to snakes and declaring that anyone who saw her would turn to stone. Then Athena arranged to have the young hero Perseus find Medusa and cut off her head. Large, elaborate illustrations filled with movement convey the interwoven stories of Perseus and the ill-fated Medusa in this classic story.

Low, Alice. *The Simon & Schuster Book of Greek Gods and Heroes.* **Illustrated by Arvis Stewart. 1985. Hardcover: Simon & Schuster. 184 pages. Ages 9–13. FOLKLORE COLLECTION.**

This lyrical collection of the most famous stories from Greek mythology uses relatively large print and straightforward language to make the tales accessible to upper elementary school students. The large book opens with the origin of the Greek gods and the story of Zeus defeating his father, Cronos. It goes on to describe the gods and goddesses of Mount Olympus and their adventures. The book's second half relates exciting stories of heroes such as Perseus and Jason. Stylized watercolors illustrate the gripping time-tested myths.

Osborne, Mary Pope, reteller. *Favorite Norse Myths.* **Illustrated by Troy Howell. 1996. Hardcover: Scholastic. 96 pages. Ages 9–14. FOLKLORE COLLECTION.**

The adventures of Norse gods, giants, and monsters fill the pages of this fine collection. It starts with the creation of the nine worlds, then moves on to Odin's quests for wisdom, poetry, and the ability to read runes. The gods repeatedly fight giants and other monsters until the death of Balder and the final battle. Dramatic paintings convey key scenes, and charming drawings based on Viking art open each chapter. Also see Osborne's other mythology collections.

Riordan, James. *The Twelve Labors of Hercules.* **Illustrated by Christina Balit. 1997. Hardcover: Millbrook. 64 pages. Ages 9–14. PICTURE BOOK.**

Fans of mythology or superheroes will find plenty of action in this retelling of Hercules's labors. From slaying the Nemean lion to fetching the hound Cerberus from Hades, each task pits Hercules, the son of a god and a mortal woman, against fearsome monsters and powerful enemies. His strength and cunning triumph after each struggle. Ornate, colorful pictures expand the action and setting of these powerful adventures.

Sutcliff, Rosemary. *The Wanderings of Odysseus: The Story of the Odyssey.* **Illustrated by Alan Lee. 1996. Hardcover: Delacorte. 120 pages. Ages 12–14. FOLKLORE.**

Graceful yet powerful language retells the adventures of Odysseus on his long journey back home from Troy, during which he encounters monsters, brutal storms, beautiful sorceresses, and the vagaries of the gods. Meanwhile, his faithful wife and son deal with greedy suitors who want Odysseus's wife and estate. Even when the hero arrives in Ithaca, he must fight before he can reclaim his home. Large watercolors portray the journey, which is sometimes gory and sometimes beautiful. A masterful retelling of one of the world's most exciting epics.

History and Adventure

Archaeology and the Ancient World

Aliki. *Mummies Made in Egypt.* 1979. Hardcover and paperback: Harper. 32 pages. Ages 4–9. PICTURE BOOK NONFICTION.

This terrific "Reading Rainbow" book explores the different aspects of Egyptian mummies in a succinct narrative. It explains how the bodies were prepared, describes amulets and other objects buried with them, shows the coffins, and discusses the pyramids and funerals. Many of the detailed color illustrations are based on paintings and sculptures found in Egyptian tombs. One page shows the Egyptian gods and goddesses, while another discusses mummified animals. A fine introduction to a subject with high child appeal.

Brown, Don. *Rare Treasure: Mary Anning and Her Remarkable Discoveries.* **1999. Hardcover: Houghton. 32 pages. Ages 4–9. PICTURE BOOK BIOGRAPHY.**

Mary Anning, who lived from 1799 to 1847, grew up hunting fossils with her father on the beach and cliffs of England. When her father died, she carried on his work, selling her finds to support her mother and brother. Although Anning had little schooling, she taught herself geology and related sciences. Her discoveries were so impressive that she became internationally known among geologists. Evocative watercolors show Anning at work, mostly on the beach, in this fine short biography.

Duke, Kate. *Archaeologists Dig for Clues.* **1997. Hardcover and paperback: Harper. 32 pages. Ages 5–9. PICTURE BOOK NONFICTION.**

Two boys and a girl accompany an archaeologist to her local dig, where they learn about archaeology. At first, the children are disappointed—the dig is just a hole in the ground and they won't be excavating anything exotic. But as the day goes on, they get drawn into the digging process and especially the discovery of an Archaic awl, a needle without a hole used for sewing. Cheerful pictures plus diagrams and sidebars deliver plenty of interesting information. This is one of the high-quality "Let's-Read-and-Find-Out Science" series that introduces many topics.

Rumford, James. *Seeker of Knowledge: The Man Who Deciphered Egyptian Hieroglyphs.* **2000. Hardcover: Houghton. 32 pages. Ages 5–10. PICTURE BOOK BIOGRAPHY.**

This beautifully designed book recounts how Jean-Francois Champollion found the key to understanding ancient Egyptian hieroglyphic writing and so greatly expanded knowledge of the ancient world. Richly colored watercolors and a concise narrative convey his childhood and studies, and his exciting discovery in 1822. Woven into the text and the borders are hieroglyphs, which also appear in an appendix and on the endpapers. An inspiring story about the search for knowledge.

Guiberson, Brenda Z. *Mummy Mysteries: Tales from North America.* **1998. Hardcover: Henry Holt. 64 pages. Ages 7–10. NONFICTION.**

Although most people associate mummies with Egypt, this informational book for younger readers focuses on preserved bodies of animals and people found in North America. It begins with a successful search for Aleut mummies in the far north. Another intriguing chapter discusses well-preserved bodies from ships lost in the Arctic in 1845. The book is gruesome in spots, but full of satisfying information about mummies, supplemented by black-and-white drawings and photographs.

Reinhard, Johan. *Discovering the Inca Maiden: My Adventures on Ampato.* **1998. Hardcover: National Geographic. 48 pages. Ages 9–13. NONFICTION.**

Superb photographs show the mountainous setting in Peru where anthropologist and mountain climber Reinhard and his assistant discovered a remarkably well-preserved mummy and many striking artifacts from five hundred years ago. Reinhard tells his exciting story day by day as the two climb a mountain and make the discoveries. He describes the follow-up expedition and the results of scientific studies that use technological equipment to examine the findings. Although grim at times, this is a gripping true-life story.

Patent, Dorothy Hinshaw. *Lost City of Pompeii.* **2000. Hardcover: Benchmark. 64 pages. Ages 9–14. NONFICTION.**

The city of Pompeii, stopped in time by a volcanic explosion, offers a unique look at life in the past. This overview explains the disaster and how the city came to be so well-preserved, then looks at details of daily life that archaeologists have uncovered. Color photographs of Pompeii today, color reproductions of wall paintings, and speculative illustrations of life then provide a strong sense of the place. Sidebars delve into topics such as religion, food, gladiators, and more. A well-written book on a memorable topic.

Service, Pamela F. *The Reluctant God.* **1988. Hardcover: Atheneum. Paperback: Juniper. 212 pages. Ages 10–13. FICTION.**

Lorna loves Egypt, where her archaeologist father excavates ancient Egyptian sites. When she visits him at an ancient quarry, Lorna discovers the door to an unusual tomb. Initially, this engaging novel alternates between the modern world and ancient Egypt, where the main character is Ameni, twin brother to a future pharaoh. With the help of Egyptian gods, Ameni ends up in modern times. Together, he and Lorna try to retrieve a precious urn that has been sent to England. Archaeology and ancient Egypt are an integral part of this time-travel novel.

Perl, Lila. *Mummies, Tombs and Treasure: Secrets of Ancient Egypt.* **Illustrated by Erika Weihs. 1987. Hardcover and paperback: Clarion. 114 pages. Ages 10–14. NONFICTION.**

Smooth writing, fascinating facts, and a keen sense of what will interest young readers makes this an outstanding book. It starts with a brief history of early Egypt and Egyptian mummies. Using drawings and photographs, the book explains why Egyptians made mummies and provides detailed descriptions of the mummifying process. Pyramids, funerals, Egyptian mythology, mummified animals, tomb robbers, and archaeological digs fill out the book, which will captivate mummy fans.

Deem, James M. *Bodies from the Bog.* **1998. Hardcover: Houghton. 48 pages. Ages 10–14. Of interest to younger children. NONFICTION.**

While Egyptians carefully preserved dead bodies, nature itself has preserved a number of bodies in Western European waterlogged areas called bogs. The many excellent photographs in this book, which readers may find gruesome, show the remarkable state of some bog mummies. The six chapters discuss why the bodies last, how they are found, how they died, and how scientists study them. One chapter shows cauldrons, jewelry, and other artifacts also found in bogs. The cover will pull in readers and the subject matter will keep them entranced.

Dickinson, Peter. *A Bone from a Dry Sea.* **1993. Hardcover: Delacorte. Paperback: Laurel Leaf. 200 pages. Ages 11–14. FICTION.**

Vinny is visiting her father, who works on a paleontological dig in Africa. Chapters about her participation in the dig alternate with chapters about a young female hominid called

Li, who lived four million years ago in the same spot. A vivid picture emerges of the grueling work at an archaeological dig and the political and fund-raising aspects of such an enterprise. Equally as vivid is the speculative portrayal of life in the past. Thought-provoking and well-written.

Stanley, Diane. *A Time Apart*. 1999. Hardcover: Morrow. 264 pages. Ages 11–14. FICTION.

Thirteen-year-old Ginny, who barely knows her father, reluctantly leaves Texas to join him in England while her mother undergoes cancer treatment. Because her father is part of a university experiment about the Iron Age, Ginny ends up living in primitive conditions, grinding grain into flour, cooking in a stone oven, and living in one large structure with fifteen others, mostly adults. She slowly grows to appreciate her new accomplishments and the strong sense of community. An engrossing, informative novel.

Stefoff, Rebecca. *Finding the Lost Cities*. 1997. Hardcover and paperback: Oxford. 192 pages. Ages 13 and up. NONFICTION.

Imagine being the first person in centuries to see the walls of Troy or the ancient city of Ur. The twelve chapters in this fine book describe those historical episodes and more. Almost all of the "lost cities" were rediscovered during the 1800s and early 1900s. Photographs enhance the skillfully written text that combines exciting narratives with facts about history and archaeology. Perfect for those who want to read about real life counterparts of Indiana Jones.

Black History

Thomas, Joyce Carol. *I Have Heard of a Land.* Illustrated by Floyd Cooper. 1998. Hardcover and paperback: Harper. 32 pages. Ages 4–8. PICTURE BOOK.

"I have heard of a land / Where the earth is red with promises"—so begins this poetic tribute to black pioneers. The speaker, a black woman, has staked a claim in the Oklahoma territory, willing to put in the hard physical labor to earn her new land. Superb illustrations show her sod hut with a goat on the roof, surrounded by empty prairie. The lyrical text extends from her arrival until she has prospered enough to have a log house. The author's note discusses black settlers in the West. Outstanding.

Johnson, Dolores. *Now Let Me Fly: The Story of a Slave Family.* 1993. Hardcover: Macmillan. Paperback: Aladdin. 32 pages. Ages 5–9. PICTURE BOOK.

As the author's note states, this "is not a pleasant story, nor does it have a happy ending. Yet it is a story that must be told." It begins in Africa, where the narrator is sold into slavery as a child. On an American plantation, she and her husband have four children, then the husband and oldest boy are sold. One daughter escapes north and a son escapes to live with Seminole Indians in Florida. In the end, the narrator is still in slavery with her youngest daughter. Richly colored oil paintings add depth to the story and its powerful emotional effect.

Sanders, Scott Russell. *A Place Called Freedom.* **Illustrated by Thomas B. Allen. 1997. Hardcover: Atheneum. 32 pages. Ages 5–9. PICTURE BOOK.**

This simple, inspiring story tells about the narrator's family, who left Tennessee in 1832, no longer slaves. They headed north for Indiana, where Quakers helped them start farming. Thanks to hard work, they prospered and returned south to bring back other relatives. When southern blacks heard about the family's success, they came, too, and ultimately formed a town. They chose to call it Freedom and celebrated the new name by building a school. Soft, colored-pencil illustrations, with a feeling of long ago, match the beauty of the story.

Ringgold, Faith. *If a Bus Could Talk.* **1999. Hardcover: Simon & Schuster. 32 pages. Ages 5–10. PICTURE BOOK.**

When a black girl named Marcie gets on a bus one day, the bus starts to tell her the story of Rosa Parks and the Montgomery bus boycott. Striking paintings show Parks's childhood and her momentous choice not to give up her bus seat to a white passenger. The story conveys injustices of the time as well as the hardships of the boycott. In the end, Marcie meets Rosa Parks to wish her happy birthday. An accessible introduction for younger children to an important woman and her role in changing the world.

Lowery, Linda. *Aunt Clara Brown: Official Pioneer.* **Illustrated by Janice Lee Porter. 1999. Hardcover and paperback: Carolrhoda. 48 pages. Ages 6–9. BIOGRAPHY.**

This biography for younger readers describes the remarkable life of Clara Brown, a freed slave who went West in 1859. Searching for her daughter who had been sold when the girl was ten, Brown made her way to Colorado, where she set up a thriving laundry business, then shrewdly invested in real estate. She used her wealth to help other former slaves, and eventually found her grown daughter. Brown also fought successfully for the recognition and pension awarded other pioneers. The bold illustrations echo the story's main character.

Wright, Courtni C. *Wagon Train: A Family Goes West in 1865.* **Illustrated by Gershom Griffith. 1995. Hardcover: Holiday House. 32 pages. Ages 7–10. PICTURE BOOK.**

This picture-story book recounts a black family's trip from Virginia to California. Told from the perspective of a girl named Ginny, the story starts after the Civil War, when the family leaves the plantation where they were slaves. The book highlights episodes of the wagon train trip such as dealing with a rattlesnake bite, encountering friendly Arapaho Indians, suffering through the desert, and finally arriving in California. Large watercolors illustrate the varying terrain of their long journey.

Duncan, Alice Faye. *The National Civil Rights Museum Celebrates Everyday People.* **Photographs by J. Gerard Smith. 1995. Hardcover and paperback: Bridgewater. 64 pages. Ages 7–11. NONFICTION.**

Located in the Lorraine Motel in Memphis, where Martin Luther King, Jr., was shot, the National Civil Rights Museum focuses on the civil rights movement from 1954 through 1968. As the large color photographs show, the museum re-creates scenes such as lunch-counter protests, Rosa Parks's act of courage, and the freedom riders in the South, using life-size statues. The text reviews the history, while the photos show today's children interacting with the exhibits.

Bridges, Ruby. *Through My Eyes.* **1999. Hardcover: Scholastic. 64 pages. Ages 9–13. AUTOBIOGRAPHY.**

In 1960, first-grader Ruby Bridges integrated an all-white elementary school in New Orleans, walking through angry mobs each day to get there. When none of the white parents sent their children to join her, Ruby spent the days alone with her teacher. In this elegant book illustrated with glossy black-and-white photographs, Bridges looks back at her feelings and understanding at the time of this important event. A moving story of courage and faith.

McKissack, Patricia C., and Fredrick L. McKissack. *Black Hands, White Sails: The Story of African-American Whalers.* **1999. Hardcover: Scholastic. 152 pages. Ages 9–13. NON-FICTION.**

"During the 'golden age' of whaling (1800–60), African Americans comprised 25 percent of the whaling crews" that left the United States, explains the introduction to this engaging book. Free black men and escaped slaves served as crew, and some ended up as captains and ship owners. Meanwhile, a number of black whalers helped slaves escape from the South. This readable book, which weaves together information about whaling, abolitionism, and black social history, enriched by quotations from the time, reveals a fascinating slice of history.

Robinet, Harriette Gillem. *Washington City Is Burning.* **1996. Hardcover: Atheneum. 160 pages. Ages 9–13. FICTION.**

Twelve-year-old Virginia, a slave owned by James Madison, moves from his Virginia plantation to Washington to work in the White House. Authentic details of luxury in the White House contrast with the slave markets all over the capital city. Virginia quickly starts helping runaway slaves, and although she makes a mistake in judgment, she plays a crucial role in several escapes. Meanwhile, the War of 1812 brings British soldiers closer to the city until the White House itself is in danger. A turbulent time seen through the eyes of a perceptive girl.

Myers, Walter Dean. *One More River to Cross: An African American Photograph Album*. 1995. Hardcover and paperback: Harcourt. 176 pages. Ages 9–14. NONFICTION.

This host of visual images from the past offers an effective way to gain a sense of the history of African Americans. Myers has brought together an impressive array of black-and-white photographs from the days of slavery to the present, showing black Americans in every aspect of life and society. The well-designed pages show a broad spectrum of life—young, old, poor, wealthy, rural, urban, happy, sad—with a minimal, poetic text. An outstanding and moving book, not to be missed.

Curtis, Christopher Paul. *The Watsons Go to Birmingham— 1963*. 1995. Hardcover: Delacorte. Paperback: Dell. 210 pages. Ages 10–13. FICTION.

The mood of this fine novel changes when the Watsons, an African-American family, go from Michigan to Alabama near the story's end. Early on, a humorous tone prevails as ten-year-old Kenny describes his skirmishes with his irascible older brother, Byron, who is starting to worry their parents. Hoping that time with his grandmother will straighten Byron out, his parents load up their car and drive into the turbulent South of 1963 and the worst trouble the family has ever known. This Newbery Honor Book creates a memorable family and their struggles.

Schlissel, Lillian. *Black Frontiers: A History of African American Heroes in the Old West.* 1995. Hardcover: Simon & Schuster. Paperback: Aladdin. 80 pages. Ages 10–13. NONFICTION.

Many evocative black-and-white photographs illustrate this overview of how African Americans helped settle the West. It opens with a section on "Mountain Men, Trappers, and Guides," then moves to black homesteaders. Well-chosen details explain the successes and problems of the pioneers. The narrative then discusses cowboys, gunmen, and soldiers, and wraps up with important women and the role of Black Indians. A readable history that supplies missing pieces in the pioneer story.

McKissack, Patricia C., and Fredrick L. McKissack. *Rebels Against Slavery: American Slave Revolts.* 1996. Hardcover and paperback: Scholastic. 192 pages. Ages 10–14. NONFICTION.

Historians have often recorded the roles that whites played in ending slavery, overlooking the efforts made by free blacks and slaves. This welcome book focuses on slave revolts and black abolitionists. It describes the work of Haiti's leader Toussaint-Louverture, and blacks who led revolts in the United States such as Gabriel Prosser, Denmark Vesey, and Nat Turner. Other chapters discuss the ship *Amistad*, the underground railroad, John Brown, and black abolitionists in the North. Illustrated with occasional prints and photographs, this is a useful book about an important cause.

Taylor, Mildred D. *Roll of Thunder, Hear My Cry.* 1976. Hardcover: Dial. Paperback: Puffin. 276 pages. Ages 10–14. FICTION.

This gripping novel chronicles the life of the Logans, the only black family to own land in their Mississippi town.

A white plantation owner wants it, but for narrator nine-year-old Cassie and her family, the land gives them an independence they will fight to keep. While her parents and grandmother face this problem, hot-tempered Cassie and her brothers come up with their own ways of dealing with racial hate. Winner of the Newbery Medal, this long, complex book vividly re-creates the South during the Depression.

Hamilton, Virginia. *The House of Dies Drear*. 1968. Hardcover: Simon & Schuster. Paperback: Aladdin. 280 pages. Ages 11–14. FICTION.

When twelve-year-old Thomas and his family move into an Ohio house that was part of the Underground Railroad, he discovers a frightening tunnel under the house. Thomas and his father love history and take pride in their African-American heritage, but hostility in their new community and from the house's mysterious old caretaker start to bother them. The father and son persist in trying to unravel a series of strange events, leading to a wild, ghostly evening in the woods, the climax of this historical mystery. Followed by *The Mystery of Drear House*.

Cowboys, Cowgirls, and the Wild West

Demarest, Chris. *The Cowboy ABC.* 1999. Hardcover: DK Ink. 32 pages. Ages 3–8. PICTURE BOOK.

Watercolors with an old-fashioned flair show an object or word associated with cowboy life for each letter of the alphabet. "A is for Appaloosa, a trusty steed. B is for Buckaroo, who rides at top speed." The rhymes are easy and natural, and the pictures will be of great interest to cowboy fans, who get to see cowboys—a few of whom seem to be female—at their work.

Gardella, Tricia. *Casey's New Hat.* Illustrated by Margot Apple. 1997. Hardcover: Houghton. 32 pages. Ages 3–8. PICTURE BOOK.

Casey, a dedicated cowgirl, always wears cowboy boots, and her room is full of toy horses. When she needs a new cowboy hat, she and her cowboy father go to town to shop, but nothing suits her. It isn't until she goes to feed horses with her grandfather that she finds the perfect hat, Grandpa's crumpled, old, dusty cowboy hat. In the final picture, Casey and her grandfather perch on the back of his pickup truck, each happy in a cowboy hat. Appealing colored-pencil illustrations show an energetic girl who loves ranch life.

Antle, Nancy. *Sam's Wild West Show.* Illustrated by Simms Taback. 1995. Hardcover: Dial. Paperback: Puffin. 40 pages. Ages 4–8. EASY READER.

In this easy-to-read book, Sam's Wild West Show comes to a small western town. Funny, energetic pictures show cowgirls and cowboys balancing on horses, shooting flying cans, and wielding lassoes. Their skills become vital when a telegram announces that bandits are coming to town. The scared marshal and mayor turn the problem over to Sam and his talented performers, who lasso the bandits and recover stolen money. A lively western tale illustrated by a Caldecott-winning illustrator.

Brusca, María Cristina. *On the Pampas.* **1991. Paperback: Henry Holt. 32 pages. Ages 4–8. PICTURE BOOK.**

The narrator is thrilled to be spending the summer on her grandparents' ranch in Argentina. She and her cousin Susanita devote their time to horseback riding and learning from a gaucho how to use a lasso, which takes hours of practice. In honor of her new ranching skills, her grandmother gives the girl a gaucho belt decorated with silver coins. Set on a ranch on the pampas, or plains, this brightly illustrated story shows the joys and challenges of a ranching life.

Carlson, Laurie. *Boss of the Plains: The Hat That Won the West.* **Illustrated by Holly Meade. 1998. Hardcover and paperback: DK Ink. 32 pages. Ages 4–9. PICTURE BOOK BIOGRAPHY.**

Everyone knows what cowboy hats look like, but where did they first come from? This charming book answers that question by telling the story of John Stetson, a hat maker from New Jersey who went West to seek gold in 1859. He created the first Stetson for himself to keep off rain and sun, but eventually he supplied a great number of cowboys with his hats. Two double-page spreads show all the uses of the Stetson that make it such a special hat. Splendid mixed-media pictures expand the story.

Lowell, Susan. *Cindy Ellen: A Wild Western Cinderella.* Illustrated by Jane Manning. 2000. Hardcover: Harper. 40 pages. Ages 4–9. PICTURE BOOK.

"What you need first, gal, is some gravel in your gizzard. Grit! Guts!" her gun-toting fairy godmother tells Cindy Ellen, a crying cowgirl whose mean stepsisters have gone to the rodeo without her. In this sparkling western retelling of the old favorite, Cindy Ellen rides a bucking bronco, wins the trick roping event, and beats Joe Prince in the horse race. When she loses her diamond spur at the square dance, Joe finds her and they get hitched. Colorful exaggerated illustrations express the tall-tale tone of this fractured "Cinderella."

Pinkney, Andrea D. *Bill Pickett: Rodeo-Ridin' Cowboy.* Illustrated by Brian Pinkney. 1996. Hardcover and paperback: Harcourt. 32 pages. Ages 5–9. PICTURE BOOK BIOGRAPHY.

This picture-book biography tells the remarkable story of the African-American cowboy and rodeo star Bill Pickett. Growing up in Texas in the late 1800s, Pickett was fascinated with cowboys. After he came up with the idea of "bull-dogging" cattle by biting their upper lips to subdue them, his fame soared. His skill with cattle and his "bulldogging" earned him a place in the rodeo circuit and Wild West shows, with which he traveled around the world. A well-illustrated action-packed story.

Walter, Mildred Pitts. *Justin and the Best Biscuits in the World.* Illustrated by Catherine Stock. 1986. Hardcover: Lothrop. Paperback: Random House. 122 pages. Ages 8–10. FICTION.

Justin dislikes doing his chores around the house until he visits his grandfather's ranch. A fine housekeeper and cook, his cowboy grandfather shows Justin how to do chores right and to bake great biscuits. He also tells Justin stories about black pioneers and cowboys, and takes him to a rodeo. Back home, Justin shows off his new skills by making dinner for his mother and sisters. Large print and pencil sketches help make this fine story accessible to younger readers.

Glass, Andrew. *Bad Guys: True Stories of Legendary Gunslingers, Sidewinders, Fourflushers, Drygulchers, Bushwhackers, Freebooters, and Downright Bad Guys and Gals of the Wild West.* **1998. Hardcover: Doubleday. Paperback: Yearling. 48 pages. Ages 8–12. COLLECTIVE BIOGRAPHY.**

Andrew Glass, who loved reading about outlaws when he was young, suffuses this enjoyable book with his enthusiasm. He focuses on famous and less famous figures of the Wild West, describing each in a few pages. Vigorous, humorous illustrations add to every double-page spread. Wild Bill Hickok, Calamity Jane, and five more legendary westerners fight, shoot, and cheat their way through the book's pages—with no moral lessons attached.

Anderson, Joan. *Cowboys: Roundup on an American Ranch.* **Photographs by George Ancona. 1996. Hardcover: Scholastic. 46 pages. Ages 8–13. NONFICTION.**

In this photo-essay, thirteen-year-old Leedro and his younger brother Colter help round up eight hundred cattle on their family's ranch. The entire family and hired hands work together, riding out to find the cattle, chasing strays, branding them, and shipping some to market. The boys spend days in the saddle in the beautiful New Mexico mesas, captured in the many photographs. A vivid look at the hardships and pleasures of some cowboys today, from an adolescent's point of view.

Crum, Robert. *Let's Rodeo: Young Buckaroos and the World's Wildest Sport.* **1996. Hardcover: Simon & Schuster. 48 pages. Ages 8–13. Of interest to younger children. NONFICTION.**

Action-packed photographs show boys and girls of different ages participating in Oregon rodeos. The littlest ones ride sheep and tie ribbons on goats' tails, while the older ones rope cattle, barrel race, ride bareback, and try to stay on bucking broncos. Their courage and excitement is palpable, encouraged by the support of their families. The abundance of details will satisfy cowboy and rodeo fans. Younger children will enjoy hearing this read aloud and studying the pictures.

Alter, Judy. *Wild West Shows: Rough Riders and Sure Shots.* **1997. Hardcover and paperback: Watts. 64 pages. Ages 9–13. NONFICTION.**

Wild West shows changed our national image of the cowboy from a ruffian to a romantic hero. This short history focuses on Buffalo Bill's Wild West, the most influential of the shows, which featured sharpshooter Annie Oakley and the famous Sioux chief Sitting Bull. Buffalo Bill's troupe staged fights, often between Native Americans and cowboys, reenacted a Pony Express ride, and acted out a stagecoach robbery. Illustrated with posters and photographs, this recounts a vital part of cowboy history.

Freedman, Russell. *Cowboys of the Wild West.* **1985. Hardcover and paperback: Clarion. 104 pages. Ages 9–14. NONFICTION.**

Freedman has assembled striking black-and-white photographs from the second half of the nineteenth century that show cowboys at work and at rest. The well-written text dispels many mistaken beliefs about cowboys and their ways, yet leaves the reader with an admiration for the young men who drove herds thousands of miles over the open range. Full of details about cowboys, their horses, possessions, and work, these hundred pages will draw in cowboy fans and those who love history.

Myers, Walter Dean. *The Journal of Joshua Loper: A Black Cowboy*. 1999. Hardcover: Scholastic. 158 pages. Ages 10–13. FICTION.

Joshua Loper, a sixteen-year-old cowboy, goes on his first cattle drive from Texas to Kansas in 1871. Like many cowboys at the time, he is black and has to deal with the trail boss's racial bias. The hardships of riding all day on the Chisholm Trail, interrupted sleep, and poor weather challenge Joshua, who keeps a journal of his experiences and thoughts full of fascinating details. Deceptively packaged to look as if it is a historical document, this is nevertheless a good novel about cowboy life and black history.

Naylor, Phyllis Reynolds. *Walker's Crossing*. 1999. Hardcover: Atheneum. 232 pages. Ages 12–14. FICTION.

Seventh-grader Ryan isn't a full-fledged cowboy yet, but that's his ambition. He helps out any way he can on the Wyoming ranch where his father is the caretaker. Ryan grows more and more troubled by his older brother Gil's growing involvement in a local militia, and struggles to understand why Gil hates Jews, Mexicans, and anyone he considers "different," including people Ryan likes. Questions of tolerance split the small ranching community, and Ryan must decide what he believes is right. With many scenes about ranching, this novel also raises some important issues.

Explorers and Adventurers

Brown, Don. *Alice Ramsey's Grand Adventure*. 1997. Hardcover and paperback: Houghton. 32 pages. Ages 5–10. **PICTURE BOOK BIOGRAPHY.**

"On June 9, 1909, Alice Ramsey drove out of New York City and into a grand adventure." Ramsey became the first woman, and only the third person, to drive a car across the United States. Few roads and no good maps existed, and Ramsey had to take care of her car herself. The text conveys the excitement as well as the constant obstacles, while the charming watercolors provide a sense of the vastness of the country and its varying terrain in a less populated age. Highly recommended.

Armstrong, Jennifer. *Spirit of Endurance: The True Story of the Shackleton Expedition to the Antarctic*. Illustrated by William Maughan. 2000. Hardcover: Crown. 32 pages. Ages 6–10. **PICTURE BOOK NONFICTION.**

This unusually oversized book tells the thrilling story of Shackleton's dangerous expedition to the Antarctic. The narrative follows the journey that started in England in August 1914 and ended with the sensational final rescue in August 1916. Black-and-white photographs from the expedition and large, dramatic paintings convey the bleak conditions and life-threatening dangers the men experienced. The well-written text highlights the main points of an exciting story that will capture the imagination of young adventurers.

Burleigh, Robert. *Black Whiteness: Admiral Byrd Alone in the Antarctic*. Illustrated by Walter Lyon Krudop. 1998. Hardcover: Atheneum. 40 pages. Ages 6–10. PICTURE BOOK BIOGRAPHY.

This gripping story, told in lyrical language, tells how Admiral Byrd stayed alone in the Antarctic during the winter of 1934. Living in a tiny, snow-covered shack, he took weather measurements every day and kept a diary. Even inside the shack, temperatures sank to well below zero. Told in the present tense, with excerpts from Byrd's own writing, the story has such an immediacy, especially when he loses strength and hope, that the reader will rejoice when help arrives. A remarkable tale, well-told.

Maestro, Betsy, and Giulio Maestro. *The Discovery of the Americas*. 1991. Hardcover: Lothrop. Paperback: Mulberry. 48 pages. Ages 7–10. NONFICTION.

This fine book offers a balanced history of the peoples and explorers who came to the Americas before and after Columbus. The concise text begins with the last Ice Age, discusses the civilizations in America that followed it, and then describes European explorers including Eriksson, Columbus, Cabot, and Magellan. The authors note that explorers often mistreated native people, bringing hardship, disease, and death. Sweeping illustrations show the Americas, while maps and appendixes add information.

Steger, Will, and Jon Bowermaster. *Over the Top of the World: Explorer Will Steger's Trek Across the Arctic*. Photographs by Gordon Wiltsie. 1997. Hardcover: Scholastic. 64 pages. Ages 8–13. NONFICTION.

In March 1994, four men, two women, and thirty-three dogs set off across the Arctic Ocean with the goal of crossing it in under five months. This suspenseful account of their journey conveys the dangers and hardships they faced daily, and describes the terrain, weather, animals, and ecosystem of the Arctic. Lots of color photographs add details and atmosphere. A compelling story, well-told, and sure to satisfy young armchair adventurers.

Cummings, Pat, and Linda Cummings, editors. *Talking with Adventurers.* **1998. Hardcover: National Geographic. 96 pages. Ages 9–14. COLLECTIVE BIOGRAPHY.**

Jane Goodall, expert on chimpanzees, and Robert Ballard, who discovered the *Titanic*, are two of the twelve adventurers interviewed in this captivating book. The others include a rain forest scientist, underwater photographer, archaeologists, anthropologists, and wildlife filmmakers, all of whom travel to far-off, often dangerous, locations. Clear color photographs show them at work, while well-crafted interviews recount their challenges and discoveries. Interesting and inspiring.

Jenkins, Steve. *The Top of the World: Climbing Mount Everest.* **1999. Hardcover: Houghton. 32 pages. Ages 9–14. Of interest to younger children. PICTURE BOOK NONFICTION.**

Extraordinary cut-paper illustrations combined with a high-interest subject make this a winner. It introduces mountain climbing and specifically how people climb Mount Everest. A double-page spread lays out the equipment that serious mountain climbers use, just one of the many thoughtful details. The book addresses the geology of mountains as well as the reasons people engage in the dangerous pursuit of mountain climbing. An outstanding nonfiction book with a wide age range.

Karwoski, Gail Langer. *Seaman: The Dog Who Explored the West with Lewis & Clark.* Illustrated by James Watling. 1999. Hardcover: Peachtree. 184 pages. Ages 10–13. FICTION.

The journals of Lewis and Clark mention Lewis's dog Seaman nearly thirty times. Using the Newfoundland dog as a focus, this historical novel describes the famous journey from beginning to end. On the dangerous, difficult trip, Seaman helped hunt and fish, and probably saved lives when he chased away buffalo at night. He warned the corps when he sensed outsiders approaching and once was almost stolen. This historical novel provides an entertaining way to learn about an important event in American history.

Myers, Edward. *Climb or Die.* 1994. Hardcover and paperback: Hyperion. 180 pages. Ages 10–13. FICTION.

Danielle, who is fourteen, and thirteen-year-old Jake have to save their parents, who are trapped on a mountain road after a car accident. The two set off through the snow, relying on Jake's scientific skills and Danielle's wilderness training. Jake rigs up tools, while Danielle gives him a quick course in mountaineering. Faced with a perilous climb and repeated setbacks, they must pool their strengths and cooperate to survive. A suspenseful story with many physical challenges.

Paulsen, Gary. *Hatchet.* 1987. Hardcover and paperback: Simon & Schuster. 142 pages. Ages 11–14. FICTION.

When the small plane's pilot suffers a fatal heart attack over Canada, Brian manages a crash landing and survives. But now he is stranded alone in the wilderness with a hatchet as his only tool. How he struggles for months, encountering snakes, porcupines, wolves, and other hazards makes a mesmerizing story. The taut writing and a gripping plot have made this a great favorite especially among boys. Sequels to this Newbery Honor Book are *The River*, *Brian's Winter*, and *Brian's Return*.

Armstrong, Jennifer. *Shipwreck at the Bottom of the World: The Extraordinary True Story of Shackleton and the Endurance.* **1999. Hardcover: Crown. Paperback: Random House. 128 pages. Ages 12–14. NONFICTION.**

Even a reader who knows the ending will get caught up in this nearly unbelievable true story about twenty-eight men stranded in the Antarctic in winter. On Shackleton's 1914 voyage to the bottom of the world, everything went wrong and chances of survival were painfully slim. The courage and ingenuity of the crew and the remarkable leadership of Shackleton come across in this detailed account, illustrated with a crew member's stunning black-and-white photographs. Anyone who loves adventure will love this book.

Aronson, Marc. *Sir Walter Ralegh and the Quest for El Dorado.* **2000. Hardcover: Clarion. 222 pages. Ages 12–14. BIOGRAPHY.**

Sir Walter Ralegh (more commonly spelled "Raleigh"), who lived in the time of Elizabeth the First, repeatedly embraced adventure and danger. A sailor and soldier, he fought for England against Spain and staged sea raids against rich merchant ships. He sailed to the New World hoping to find gold in the mythical El Dorado, and sponsored the famous Lost Colony on Roanoke Island. Ralegh wrote poetry and best-selling books about his travels. This well-written biography vividly conveys his larger-than-life qualities and sets him in a broad historical context.

Knights and Castles

Gibbons, Gail. *Knights in Shining Armor*. 1995. Hardcover and paperback: Little, Brown. 32 pages. Ages 3–8. PICTURE BOOK NONFICTION.

Lots of information comes across in the text and pictures of this short book about the history of knights, the stages from page to squire to knighthood, and their skills. Labeled pictures explain the parts of a castle and the parts of a suit of armor. The final pages touch briefly on famous knights of Arthur's Round Table and a few dragons. Although the pictures are a bit stiff, the book answers the kind of questions children have about knights and their battles.

San Souci, Robert. *Young Arthur*. Illustrated by Jamichael Henterly. 1997. Hardcover: Doubleday. Paperback: Yearling. 32 pages. Ages 6–10. PICTURE BOOK.

This romantic story begins with King Arthur's childhood. After his mother died, the infant Arthur was taken by Merlin to Sir Ector, who raised Arthur with his own son, Kay. One day Arthur, who was serving as Kay's apprentice, forgot to bring the right sword to a great tournament. Rather than go home, he pulled a sword out of a stone, not realizing the act revealed his royalty. The story goes on to describe how he got the sword Excalibur and won his first battle. Dramatic pictures paint a heroic England.

Gravett, Christopher. *The Knight's Handbook: How to Become a Champion in Shining Armor.* **1997. Hardcover: Cobblehill. 32 pages. Ages 6–11. NONFICTION.**

This small book examines the daily lives and activities of knights and gives instructions for seven well-designed crafts such as making a castle and a helmet. The first brief chapter addresses armor and weapons, and includes a well-labeled photograph of armor. Other chapters explain heraldry, parts of a castle, tournaments, the Crusades, and more. The text is profusely illustrated with color pictures from tapestries and other medieval art. The small print may challenge some readers, but those fascinated by knights will not want to miss this book.

Skurzynski, Gloria. *The Minstrel in the Tower.* **Illustrated by Julek Heller. 1988. Paperback: Random House. 64 pages. Ages 7–10. FICTION.**

Eleven-year-old Roger and his younger sister, Alice, must find their uncle, a nobleman they have never met. The children's father never returned from the Crusades and now their mother seems to be dying. During the three-day journey, Roger sings for their meals while Alice climbs trees to scout the land ahead. When ruffians capture them, the children must quickly devise an escape. Their courage leads to a happy ending. Occasional black-and-white pictures depict the adventure's medieval setting.

Osborne, Will, and Mary Pope Osborne. *Knights and Castles: Magic Tree House Research Guide #2.* **Illustrated by Sal Murdocca. 2000. Hardcover and paperback: Random House. 120 pages. Ages 7–11. NONFICTION.**

This companion to the "Magic Tree House" books describes knights and castles, with occasional asides from Annie and Jack, characters from the series. It introduces the Middle Ages, then presents three chapters on castles and castle life. Other chapters discuss knights, armor, weapons, and battles. Black-and-white illustrations, diagrams, sidebars, and photographs add to the information. Fans of the "Magic Tree House" series will especially enjoy this companion to *The Knight at Dawn*.

Talbott, Hudson. *Lancelot*. 1999. Hardcover: Morrow. 40 pages. Ages 7–11. PICTURE BOOK.

In this version of his story, Lancelot excels as the strongest fighter in King Arthur's court and defeats all other knights in a tournament. Arthur loves Lancelot, although the other knights do not all respect him. But the worst befalls the hero when he realizes that he loves Queen Guinevere. To punish himself and escape from her presence, he retreats to the woods and lives by himself as a wild man until Arthur himself seeks out his old friend. Lancelot's adventures unfold in sweeping romantic illustrations.

Platt, Richard. *Castle Diary: The Journal of Tobias Burgess, Page*. Illustrated by Chris Riddell. 1999. Hardcover: Candlewick. 64 pages. Ages 8–12. Of interest to younger children. NONFICTION.

Presented in diary form, this oversized book describes life in an English castle in 1285. Eleven-year-old Toby has gone to live with his wealthy uncle, a baron, where he learns the duties of a page, hoping to become a squire and then a knight. The diary entries cover aspects of castle days from food to harvesting to jousting. Information-filled illustrations add more details and humor. Highly recommended.

Hodges, Margaret, adaptor. *Saint George and the Dragon.* **Illustrated by Trina Schart Hyman. 1984. Hardcover and paperback: Little, Brown. 32 pages. Ages 8–13. PICTURE BOOK.**

Superb illustrations, which won the Caldecott Medal, create an awesome dragon and the courageous knight who defeats him. In the romantic tale, adapted from Edmund Spenser's *Faerie Queene*, the Red Cross Knight follows a lovely woman to her country where a dragon is ravaging the land. Described in striking detail, the extended fight ends with the knight triumphing over his dreaded opponent. A lyrical retelling combined with wonderfully rich pictures.

Kimmel, Eric A. *Sword of the Samurai: Adventure Stories from Japan.* **1999. Hardcover: Harcourt. 64 pages. Ages 8–13. FICTION.**

Those who wanted to be samurai, like those who aspired to be knights, spent long, hard years training in the martial arts before they went into service for a lord. These eleven stories tell of brave and some not so brave samurai, and of a female warrior. Several rely on supernatural elements, such as a dragon and a talking head. Martial arts are woven in some way into most of the stories, which read aloud well.

Morris, Gerald. *The Squire's Tale.* **1998. Hardcover: Houghton. Paperback: Laurel Leaf. 212 pages. Ages 9–13. FICTION.**

Raised by a hermit, Terence has never seen a knight before Sir Gawain rides into the woods. The far-seeing hermit explains that it is Terence's future to serve Sir Gawain, so the boy goes off on adventures with the famous knight of the Round Table. The two travelers, who become friends, encounter wizards, sorceresses, fairies, magic lakes, and magic castles on their quests. The novel successfully adds a young character and amusing dialogue to well-known Arthurian tales.

Paterson, Katherine. *Parzival: The Quest of the Grail Knight*. 1998. Hardcover: Lodestar. Paperback: Puffin. 144 pages. Ages 9–13. FICTION.

This elegant, pocket-sized book retells the tale of Parzival, who grew up ignorant of the world but became an important knight in King Arthur's court. Although known for his chivalry and honor, he makes a crucial mistake when he fails to aid a dying king who turns out to be dedicated to the Holy Grail. The failure sends Parzival on a long, adventure-filled quest that finally leads him back to the wounded king. A lyrical story of heroism.

Pierce, Tamora. *First Test*. 1999. Hardcover and paperback: Random House. 224 pages. Ages 9–13. FICTION.

Keladry knows that by law girls can study to be knights at the King of Tortall's court, but no girl has for years. When Kel applies, they put her on probation for a year just because she is female. Plagued by bullies, Kel draws on her martial arts background to fight for fair treatment. Eventually she makes friends, and sometimes excels in the warfare training. Will they let her return for the second year? An engaging first book in the "Protector of the Small" series by a popular fantasy author. Followed by *Page*.

Byam, Michele. *Arms and Armor*. 1988. Hardcover: Knopf. 64 pages. Ages 9–13. Of interest to younger children. NONFICTION.

Each double-page spread of this history of arms and armor intersperses short paragraphs of information with clear photographs that have extensive captions. It moves chronologically from Bronze Age and Celtic tools such as flint arrowheads and bronze helmets, through medieval crossbows, longbows, and knights' armor, and ends with a look at weapons of the westward expansion. Although the print in the captions is small, the book will captivate those who love knights and arms.

Watkins, Richard. *Gladiator.* **1997. Hardcover and paperback: Houghton. 96 pages. Ages 10 and up. NONFICTION.**
    Be prepared for a lot of violence when you open this book in which each description of gladiators in ancient Rome seems bloodier than the last. Written with enthusiasm, the beautifully designed volume describes gladiators in detail, the schools where they trained, the arenas where they fought, and the crowds who watched them battle to the death. Black-and-white drawings provide more information and a sense of time and place. An eye-opening book about a violent society.

Cadnum, Michael. *The Book of the Lion.* **2000. Hardcover: Viking. 220 pages. Ages 13 and up. FICTION.**
    Edmund considers himself lucky when he escapes death, threatened because his master is a counterfeiter. Instead, moody Sir Nigel takes the bright teenager on as a squire to accompany him to the Crusades, via London, France, and Italy. Edmund is lucky to share his adventures with a friendly fellow squire, but their idealism suffers from the brutality of their companions and of the war in the Holy Land. A gritty picture of medieval knighthood and the violence of the Crusaders.

Kings and Queens

Wood, Audrey. *King Bidgood's in the Bathtub.* **Illustrated by Don Wood. 1985. Hardcover: Harcourt. 32 pages. Ages 2–7. PICTURE BOOK.**

King Bidgood plans to spend the day in his bathtub. When a courtier suggests he get out to fish, the bathtub becomes wreathed with water plants and filled with fish. Another who says it's time to lunch finds the tub bedecked with an astonishing array of food. Superb illustrations create magical effects, with the bathtub transformed into delightfully detailed scenes. Children will want to listen to this Caldecott Honor Book again and again.

Shields, Carol Diggory. *I Am Really a Princess.* **Illustrated by Paul Meisel. 1993. Hardcover: Dutton. Paperback: Puffin. 32 pages. Ages 3–8. PICTURE BOOK.**

What child wouldn't like to be a prince or princess, with everything they want, no chores, and nothing unpleasant—like eating lima beans? The girl in this comical book imagines such a life in glorious detail, with new royal parents who are aghast to hear how her real parents treat her. " 'What?' the queen will frown. 'They won't let you have a pony? But every princess needs a pony.' " A highly appealing story well matched by lively pictures.

Paterson, Katherine. *The Wide-Awake Princess.* **Illustrated by Vladimir Vagin. 2000. Hardcover: Clarion. 48 pages. Ages 4–9. FICTION.**

Princess Miranda's fairy godmother gives her the gift of being awake in all her waking hours, so the girl spends her childhood paying attention to everything. But when her parents die, the powerful noblemen don't want a twelve-year-old queen. Instead, Miranda mingles with the poor people of her country, and finds them discouraged and heavily taxed. Her friendship with them leads to a splendid, unexpected ending to this original fairy tale. The many illustrations add color and touches of humor.

Wolkstein, Diane, reteller. *The Glass Mountain.* **Illustrated by Louisa Bauer. 1999. Hardcover: Morrow. 32 pages. Ages 4–9. PICTURE BOOK.**

A king, hoping to find the best husband for his daughter, announces that she will be married to the man who climbs a nearby glass mountain. All those who try fail, and many die trying, until a whistling young man named Jared attracts the princess by his good nature. She climbs with him, and herself falls into unexpected, dangerous adventures. With unusually charming, old-fashioned pictures, this story will delight fairy-tale fans.

Loehr, Mallory. *The Princess Book.* **Illustrated by Jan Palmer. 1996. Hardcover: Random House. 48 pages. Ages 5–10. NONFICTION.**

Each chapter in this short activity book centers around a princess from folklore or fiction, some specific, like Cinderella, others general, like fairy princesses. A paragraph describes the princess, followed by ideas for crafts, costumes, parties, and simple recipes. For example, the Twelve Dancing Princesses chapter gives directions for princess hats, a "magic potion" punch, a simple dance, and more. Many of the projects require adult help. Perfect for readers who dream of being princesses.

Shepard, Aaron, reteller. *The Sea King's Daughter: A Russian Legend.* **Illustrated by Gennady Spirin. 1997. Hardcover: Atheneum. 40 pages. Ages 5–10. PICTURE BOOK.**

Expansive, ornate illustrations create the magical world of this Russian tale in which a young musician journeys beneath the sea. Sadko's love for the river causes the King of the Sea to invite him to his court to play music. At the bottom of the ocean, the king's daughters, all dressed in gorgeous gowns, admire the musician. The king tells Sadko that he may choose one daughter in marriage, but only at a high price. Romantic enough to please any fairy-tale fan.

Fritz, Jean. *Can't You Make Them Behave, King George?* **Illustrated by Tomie de Paola. 1977. Hardcover: Coward McCann. 48 pages. Ages 7–10. BIOGRAPHY.**

With an attractive combination of facts and humor, this biography introduces King George III, the British monarch during the American Revolution. Amusing illustrations capitalize on the details and anecdotes in the narrative, and convey the king's uncertainties about ruling. Children interested in the American Revolution will especially enjoy this view of the man who ruled the other side. This slim book is one in a series of popular biographies about famous historical figures.

Fleischman, Sid. *The Whipping Boy.* **Illustrated by Peter Sis. 1986. Hardcover: Greenwillow. Paperback: Troll. 90 pages. Ages 8–11. FICTION.**

Prince Brat constantly gets into trouble around the palace, but never pays for it. The whipping boy Jemmy gets punished instead. Jemmy decides to run away, never expecting that the prince will go with him. During their adventures with a pair of ruffians, a dancing bear, and other colorful characters, Prince

Brat starts to grow up and Jemmy sees that being royalty has its drawbacks. Winner of the Newbery Medal.

Climo, Shirley, reteller. *A Pride of Princesses: Princess Tales from Around the World.* **Illustrated by Angelo Tillery. 1996. Paperback: Harper. 112 pages. Ages 8–12. FOLK-LORE COLLECTION.**

For the child ready to expand beyond Grimms' tales, here are seven tales about princesses from China, Arabia, Russia, Africa, Germany, Central America, and Greece. In some, the princess relies on her own strength and powers, while in others she has a more passive role. Each tale has an introduction to set it in context, with source notes at the back. This is a good way to explore tales of different countries, united by the ever-popular theme of princesses.

Fisher, Leonard Everett. *Prince Henry the Navigator.* **1990. Hardcover: Macmillan. 32 pages. Ages 8–12. PICTURE BOOK BIOGRAPHY.**

This picture-book biography, with its dramatic black-and-white paintings, introduces the far-seeing Portuguese prince Henry. In 1415, he established the first school of navigation where ship captains, mapmakers, astronomers, and geographers improved navigation tools and built better ships. He backed expeditions for forty years, influencing major explorers but also perpetuating the slave trade. An interesting introduction to a man who used his power and money to further knowledge.

Levine, Gail. *Ella Enchanted.* **1997. Hardcover and paperback: Harper. 240 pages. Ages 9–13. FICTION.**

This Newbery Honor Book weaves an enchanting story about a princess named Ella who is under a curse: She must obey anyone who tells her to do something. In a series of entertaining episodes and adventures, she grows up enough to break the power of the curse and save her romance with a worthy prince. Alert readers will enjoy the allusions to the Cinderella story, which is transformed here into a rich, lively tale with a likable heroine.

Stanley, Fay. *The Last Princess: The Story of Princess Ka'iulani of Hawai'i*. Illustrated by Diane Stanley. 1991. Hardcover: Four Winds. 40 pages. Ages 9–14. PICTURE BOOK BIOGRAPHY.

Beautiful paintings full of precise details depict the life of the young woman who would have become the queen of Hawaii had the United States not annexed the islands in 1898. It shows her upbringing in the islands, her schooling in Europe, and her attempts to save her country. This well-written biography, with large illustrations on every page, tells a gripping story of courage and loss that will touch readers' hearts.

Lasky, Kathryn. *Elizabeth I: Red Rose of the House of Tudor*. 1999. Hardcover: Scholastic. 240 pages. Ages 10–13. FICTION.

This entry in the "Royal Diaries" series focuses on Elizabeth I from ages eleven through thirteen. The diary is fictional, which may confuse readers because the distinction between fact and fiction is not clear. The entries incorporate large historical facts and interesting details of daily life including the girl's studies and her tangled family relationships. Elizabeth, who longs for attention from her father King Henry VIII, is intelligent and politically alert in a way that foreshadows her successful reign.

Alexander, Lloyd. *The Remarkable Journey of Prince Jen.* **1991. Hardcover: Dutton. Paperback: Yearling. 273 pages. Ages 10–14. FICTION.**

Good-natured Prince Jen, the son of a fictional Chinese emperor, would like to know how the ruler in a nearby kingdom has such a prosperous, happy country. So he embarks on a quest with his faithful servant. A mysterious old man gives the prince six seemingly pointless gifts, including a bowl and a kite, that each play a key role in his quest. Prince Jen meets a wonderful cast of characters in this rich, colorful story full of plot twists, humor, and love of language.

Myers, Walter Dean. *At Her Majesty's Request: An African Princess in Victorian England.* **1999. Hardcover: Scholastic. 144 pages. Ages 10–14. BIOGRAPHY.**

In 1848, when a West African village was overrun by neighboring warriors, one of the villagers kidnapped was a young princess. She was saved from death by a British naval officer, who took her to England where she met Queen Victoria. Photographs, drawings, and letters bring alive her fate as she returns to Africa under Victoria's patronage, then back to England. A remarkable, moving story of a princess torn between two worlds.

More History

Van Leeuwen, Jean. *Going West*. Illustrated by Thomas B. Allen. 1992. Hardcover and paperback: Dial. 32 pages. Ages 4–8. PICTURE BOOK.

Told from a child's point of view, with details of interest to children, this simple story about a family of pioneers describes their journey across harsh lands and rivers. The family settles on the prairie, a lonely environment that, by the end of the book, feels like home to the young narrator. Smudged drawings on a brown background give a sense of life long ago. An effective, lyrical introduction to America's pioneer days.

Corey, Shana. *You Forgot Your Skirt, Amelia Bloomer!* Illustrated by Chesley McLaren. 2000. Hardcover: Scholastic. 32 pages. Ages 4–9. PICTURE BOOK BIOGRAPHY.

Dashing, richly colored illustrations set the tone for this story about Amelia Bloomer, who campaigned for women's voting rights in the mid-1800s. One day she had a visit from a friend who was wearing baggy pantaloons under a short skirt. In a time when women's clothing weighed as much as forty pounds, Bloomer wrote enthusiastically about the new clothing in the women's newspaper she edited. This charming account of how she changed women's fashions relies heavily on the pictures, with minimal but snappy text. Great fun.

HISTORY AND ADVENTURE

Lasky, Kathryn. *Marven of the Great North Woods.* Illustrated by Kevin Hawkes. 1997. Hardcover: Harcourt. 48 pages. Ages 5–8. PICTURE BOOK.

In this heartwarming story based on a true episode, ten-year-old Marven is sent by his loving family from Duluth to a lumber camp to avoid the deadly 1918 flu epidemic. Large, evocative paintings show his fear as he takes the train north, then skis five miles to the camp. But he finds that the men at the camp welcome him warmly, especially the enormous Jean Louis who becomes his friend. Fields of snow, snow-covered trees, and larger-than-life woodsmen fill the pages of this vivid tale from the past.

Hest, Amy. *When Jessie Came Across the Sea.* Illustrated by P. J. Lynch. 1997. Hardcover: Candlewick. 40 pages. Ages 5–9. PICTURE BOOK.

In this story about a thirteen-year-old Jewish immigrant, three generations of women earn their living. Jessie's grandmother in the old country sews lace, saves her money, and teaches her orphaned granddaughter to sew. When Jessie goes to the United States, she works for her rabbi's sister in her dress shop. Jessie goes to school but also saves money to bring her grandmother to New York. The large pictures vary between dramatic close-ups of faces and expansive vistas of the village, ocean, and New York City.

Hearne, Betsy. *Seven Brave Women.* Illustrated by Bethanne Andersen. 1997. Hardcover: Greenwillow. 32 pages. Ages 7–11. PICTURE BOOK.

To show that history is more than men fighting in wars, this slim, illustrated book looks at seven women from the time of the Revolutionary War until the present. "My great-great-great-grandmother did great things," opens the first brief chapter in which the brave woman crosses mountains and ocean to come to this country. Down through the generations, each woman makes her own contribution in farming, home-making, raising children, teaching, painting, and more. Large, flowing paintings show the women in action. A welcome approach to history, which puts women solidly in the picture.

Hesse, Karen. *Letters from Rifka.* **1992. Hardcover: Henry Holt. Paperback: Puffin. 148 pages. Ages 9–13. FICTION.**

Rifka's Jewish family flees Russia to seek a new home in the United States. But after a hard journey to Warsaw, they find that twelve-year-old Rifka cannot board the ship because she has ringworm. The rest continue their trip and she stays behind until she is cured. After lonely months, Rifka finally endures a harsh voyage to Ellis Island where she needs all her strength and intelligence if she is to be reunited with her family. Told in the form of letters, this outstanding novel engages readers with its suspenseful plot and well-drawn characters.

Van Leeuwen, Jean. *Bound for Oregon.* **Illustrated by James Watling. 1994. Hardcover: Dial. Paperback: Puffin. 164 pages. Ages 9–13. FICTION.**

Based on a true story, this memorable novel set in 1852 recounts the journey of nine-year-old Mary Ellen Todd and her family from their home in Arkansas to the rich farmland of Oregon. They must leave the girl's beloved grandmother behind as well as the school Mary Ellen loves. The six-month-long trip in a covered wagon includes illness, an Indian attack, mountains, deserts, and much more. Vivid descriptions bring the trail to life and convey Mary Ellen's fear and excitement along the way. A moving story replete with historical detail.

Warren, Andrea. *Orphan Train Rider: One Boy's True Story.* **1996. Hardcover and paperback: Houghton. 80 pages. Ages 9–13. NONFICTION.**

From 1859 to 1929, orphan trains carried 200,000 children from the East Coast to new families in the Midwest. This compelling true story about a boy and his two brothers describes the journey and the agony of being sent to separate homes. Although the ending is relatively happy, readers will sympathize with the plights of the orphans. Told with well-chosen details, apt quotations, and black-and-white photographs, this fine book combines a personal story with information about the orphan trains.

Warren, Andrea. *Pioneer Girl: Growing Up on the Prairie.* **1998. Hardcover: Morrow. Paperback: Harper. 96 pages. Ages 9–13. NONFICTION.**

History comes alive in this account of one girl's life on the frontier. As a young child, Grace McCance Snyder moved to Nebraska where she lived in a house made from sod, herded cattle, harvested, and reveled in her outdoor life. Based on interviews and Grace's memoir, the book brims with lively incidents and absorbing details. Black-and-white photographs, some of Grace herself, add information and atmosphere. Readers will be sorry to reach the end of this wonderful journey to the past.

Blackwood, Gary. *The Shakespeare Stealer.* **1998. Hardcover: Dutton. Paperback: Puffin. 216 pages. Ages 10–13. FICTION.**

Widge, an orphan, is apprenticed to Dr. Bright, who teaches him a unique form of shorthand. Bright then sells Widge to a curt stranger, who takes the boy to London where he attends a performance of *Hamlet* in order to copy the play's dialogue. By a strange twist, Widge starts acting with Shakespeare's company and then realizes the consequences of stealing a play. Meanwhile, for the first time in his life, Widge has friends and experiences kindness. An engaging novel full of vivid details about Shakespeare's time. Followed by *Shakespeare's Scribe*.

DeFelice, Cynthia. *The Apprenticeship of Lucas Whitaker*. 1996. Hardcover: Farrar, Straus & Giroux. Paperback: Camelot. 152 pages. Ages 10–13. FICTION.

Lucas Whitaker is on his own at age twelve after tuberculosis has killed his family. A kind, intelligent doctor in a small Connecticut town asks Lucas to be his apprentice and teaches him a lot. But the boy broods on the thought that he could have saved his mother through a gruesome ritual that involves digging up bodies and taking out the hearts in order to save the dying. Despite the doctor's skepticism, Lucas needs to learn for himself if this grim cure works. Based on historical research, this novel offers a powerful picture of the past and the limited role of medicine then.

Miller, Brandon Marie. *Dressed for the Occasion: What Americans Wore 1620–1970*. 1999. Hardcover: Lerner. 88 pages. Ages 10–14. NONFICTION.

This engaging history looks at the fashions of the wealthy and the workers, and what it signified. For many years, women were not supposed to show their legs and went so far as to wear enormous hoops under their skirts to hide their shape altogether. Wars dictated fashion by limiting available materials, while prosperous times and social classes displayed their wealth through clothing in different ways. Black-and-white photographs—although not enough of them—illustrate some of the trends.

Calabro, Marian. *The Perilous Journey of the Donner Party.* **1999. Hardcover: Clarion. 192 pages. Ages 11–14. NONFICTION.**

The Donner party's grim journey is associated with cannibalism, but there is much more to the story. The trip from Illinois to California described in compelling prose paints a picture of life in a wagon train and the difficulties of travel. The party made a bad decision that stranded them in the Sierras in snowy November, thus leading to starvation conditions. Letters give the viewpoint of a thirteen-year-old girl who lived through the disaster. A gripping account of a gruesome historical episode.

Colman, Penny. *Girls: A History of Growing Up Female in America.* **2000. Hardcover: Scholastic. 192 pages. Ages 11–14. NONFICTION.**

This substantial book gives a fine overview of U.S. history with special emphasis on the roles girls played from before the Colonial era to 1999. Colman frequently quotes from girls' diaries and letters, and the memoirs of women looking back on their childhoods. Photographs and other illustrations feature girls over the years, showing what they wore and some of their activities and jobs. Highly recommended for those who love history or who like historical fiction series like the "Dear America" or "American Girl" books.

Cushman, Karen. *Catherine, Called Birdy.* **1994. Hardcover: Clarion. Paperback: Harper. 212 pages. Ages 12–14. FICTION.**

This outstanding historical novel records the daily life of Catherine, a young girl who was known as Birdy. She keeps a diary of her humorous view of the world, complaining often but also having a good time. She chafes at the ladylike behavior expected of a nobleman's daughter and worries about her father's plan to sell her off in marriage to the highest bidder. Many entries open with a wry comment about the saint whose feast day it is, and express the narrator's bawdy sense of humor. Readers will sympathize with her constraints and rejoice at the hopeful ending of this Newbery Honor Book.

Jennings, Peter, and Todd Brewster. Adapted by Jennifer Armstrong. *The Century for Young People*. 1999. Hardcover: Doubleday. 240 pages. Ages 12–14. NONFICTION.
Well-chosen photographs and interviews, and a concise text sum up the twentieth century remarkably well. Adapted from an even longer book, this large volume progresses through the years highlighting important historical events but also reflecting on social changes. The many excerpts from interviews merge gracefully into the narrative and present a wonderful, balanced variety of voices. The photographs make the historical eras more immediate. Much of the book focuses on war and other tragedies, but it ends on a note of hope for the next century.

Native Americans
Past and Present

Ata, Te. Adapted by Lynn Moroney. *Baby Rattlesnake*. Illustrated by Veg Reisberg. 1989. Hardcover and paperback: Children's Book Press. 32 pages. Ages 3–8. PICTURE BOOK.

Told for many years by Chickasaw storyteller Te Ata, this tale shows "what happens when you get something before you're ready for it." Baby Rattlesnake wants a rattle and cries all the time because he doesn't have one. When he keeps all the Rattlesnake People awake at night, they decide to let him have a rattle to teach him a lesson. He cannot resist using it to scare others, which proves to be a big mistake. The rhythmic text and wonderfully patterned pictures create a terrific book.

McDonald, Megan. *Tundra Mouse: A Storyknife Tale*. Illustrated by S. D. Schindler. 1997. Hardcover: Orchard. 32 pages. Ages 3–9. PICTURE BOOK.

"Yup'ik girls in southwestern Alaska still practice the art of storyknifing, a unique tradition of drawing pictures with the tip of a knife in mud or snow while telling a story," explains the author's note. In a charming, original tale, a tundra mouse ends up by mistake in the house where a Yup'ik woman and her two granddaughters are celebrating Christmas. The story is told by one of the girls, accompanied by colored-pencil illustrations and traditional storyknife drawings. A jaunty mouse tale that incorporates an unusual, authentic storytelling practice.

Smith, Cynthia Leitich. *Jingle Dancer.* **Illustrated by Cornelius Van Wright and Ying-Hwa Hu. 2000. Hardcover: Morrow. 32 pages. Ages 4–9. PICTURE BOOK.**

Jenna, a personable girl from the Muscogee, or Creek, Nation, wants to be a jingle dancer like her grandmother, but she needs to get the jingles for her costume. Warm, large watercolors, which set the story in a prosperous suburb, show Jenna going to favorite relatives and friends to ask each for a row of jingles. Details about traditional food, dance, and ceremonies combine seamlessly with the modern setting in this well-told, well-illustrated story. An author's note adds useful information.

Swamp, Chief Jake. *Giving Thanks: A Native American Good Morning Message.* **Illustrated by Erwin Printup, Jr. 1995. Hardcover and paperback: Lee & Low. 24 pages. Ages 5–9. PICTURE BOOK.**

"To be a human being is an honor, and we offer thanksgiving for all the gifts of life"—so begins this traditional Iroquois message still spoken at ceremonial gatherings. Stylized acrylic paintings on every page use bold colors to illustrate earth, water, sky, animals, and other gifts to human beings. The evocative words make this a fine bedtime book to close a day with thanks. An author's note at the beginning sets the tone, while the final page gives the words in the Mohawk language.

Bunting, Eve. *Cheyenne Again.* **Illustrated by Irving Toddy. 1995. Hardcover: Clarion. 32 pages. Ages 6–10. PICTURE BOOK.**

The narrator of this book must leave his family to attend a boarding school as so many Native American children were forced to do during the last two centuries. At school, the officials cut off his braids and take away his old clothes, saying, "No more Cheyenne. You have lost nothing of value. You will be like us." His loneliness and homesickness are palpable, and only his dreams and a kind teacher keep him going. A sad but important story told in simple terms.

Turtle, Eagle Walking. *Full Moon Stories: Thirteen Native American Legends.* **1997. Hardcover: Hyperion. 48 pages. Ages 6–11. FOLKLORE COLLECTION.**

This unusually graceful book brings together thirteen folktales, one for each full moon in a year. The author heard the stories from his grandfather while growing up on the Northern Arapahoe Indian Reservation in Wyoming. Most of the lyrical short tales concern magical animals, and weave in traditions and history as well as details from the writer's life as a child. The mixed media illustrations beautifully combine folk art and modern art techniques.

Wood, Ted, with Wanbli Numpa Afraid of Hawk. A *Boy Becomes a Man at Wounded Knee.* **1992. Paperback: Walker. 48 pages. Ages 8–10. NONFICTION.**

In 1890, American soldiers killed 360 unarmed Lakota Sioux at Wounded Knee Creek. The men, women, and children had just made a harsh journey in temperatures below zero trying to reach protection. In recent years, modern Lakota have duplicated the journey by horse to "heal the Lakota nation and bring the suffering of the massacre to an end." This photo-essay follows eight-year-old Wanbli Numpa Afraid of Hawk on the snowy December trip. Told in the first person, the narrative records the six days of hard riding and the final solemn ceremony.

Bruchac, Joseph. *Eagle Song.* **Illustrated by Dan Andreasen. 1997. Hardcover: Dial. Paperback: Puffin. 80 pages. Ages 8–12. FICTION.**

Fourth-grader Danny Bigtree longs to be back on the Mohawk reservation where he grew up and not in Brooklyn. After two months, he still has no friends at school, where kids call him "Chief." He misses his dad, who is often away working as an ironworker. But when his father tells him a story from Iroquois history and then visits Danny's classroom, things slowly start changing for the boy. Readers will sympathize with Danny's problems and cheer at the hopeful ending of this fine, short novel.

Erdrich, Louise. *The Birchbark House.* **1999. Hardcover: Hyperion. 244 pages. Ages 8–12. FICTION.**

Seven-year-old Omakayas lives with her family on an island in Lake Superior, in the year 1847. This novel, full of descriptions of the traditional Ojibwa life, follows Omakayas through a year of learning and heartbreak. The family builds their summer birchbark house, plants and harvests corn, gathers wild rice, and moves to town for a tragic winter. A slow-paced but satisfying long novel.

Roessel, Monty. *Kinaaldá: A Navajo Girl Grows Up.* **1993. Hardcover: Lerner. Paperback: First Avenue. 48 pages. Ages 9–12. NONFICTION.**

Thirteen-year-old Celinda McKelvey lives near the Navajo Reservation in New Mexico, where she celebrates her coming of age with the Kinaaldá ceremony. This photo-essay depicts the two-day event and discusses its place in the Navajo tradition. The ceremony includes singing, running, sitting up all night, and cooking a large corn cake. Family and friends gather during the days to share in prayers and help with the ceremony.

Color photographs show a modern girl entering enthusiastically into an ancient tradition in a starkly beautiful setting.

Hoyt-Goldsmith, Diane. *Buffalo Days*. Photographs by Lawrence Migdale. 1997. Hardcover: Holiday House. 32 pages. Ages 9–13. NONFICTION.

Ten-year-old Clarence Three Irons, Jr., better known as "Indian," lives in Montana and is a member of the Crow tribe. In this attractive photo-essay, the reader meets the boy and his family, learns about the role of the buffalo and its recent comeback in Crow life, and attends the colorful Crow Fair, a huge meeting of the Crow tribe. Sharp, color photographs give a sense of the people and place.

Sterling, Shirley. *My Name Is Seepeetza*. 1992. Hardcover: Douglas & McIntyre. Paperback: Groundwood. 126 pages. Ages 9–13. FICTION.

Through the yearlong journal of twelve-year-old Seepeetza, readers get a vivid picture of life in an Indian boarding school in the late 1950s. To balance the bleak time at school, Seepeetza also writes lovingly of her vacations at home in British Columbia. At school, the routine is strict and the work hard. Luckily, Seepeetza has sisters and cousins around her to provide some enjoyment and relief. Written faithfully from a child's point of view, the story provides a wealth of details and incidents that create a memorable picture of a time, place, and painfully unfair treatment. Highly recommended.

Freedman, Russell. *Indian Chiefs*. 1987. Hardcover and paperback: Holiday House. 152 pages. Ages 9–14. COLLECTIVE BIOGRAPHY.

Great leaders emerged in the nineteenth century as Native Americans found their way of life threatened and often devastated by whites. This outstanding collective biography describes six such leaders: Red Cloud, Satanta, Quanah Parker, Washakie, Joseph of the Nez Percé, and Sitting Bull. These men took different approaches to dealing with settlers, soldiers, and a government that repeatedly broke its promises. Some were renowned warriors, others remarkable orators and statesmen. Black-and-white photographs and paintings enrich these true stories of courage.

Bruchac, Joseph. *Sacajawea: The Story of Bird Woman and the Lewis and Clark Expedition.* 2000. Hardcover: Harcourt. 200 pages. Ages 10–14. FICTION.

This fine historical novel alternates between the voices of Sacajawea, the young Shoshone woman who helped guide the Lewis and Clark expedition, and William Clark, one of the expedition leaders. The journey from North Dakota to the Pacific Ocean and back, full of hardships and close calls, keeps the plot moving quickly. Clark's entries especially reveal Sacajawea's intelligence and strength, which are set in historical context. Folktales and excerpts from expedition journals open each chapter, and a map shows the route. An exciting book about a perilous trip.

Pirates and
Buried Treasure

Fox, Mem. *Tough Boris*. Illustrated by Kathryn Brown. 1994. Hardcover and paperback: Harcourt. 32 pages. AGES 3–7. PICTURE BOOK.

The dashing pirate Boris has traits typical of pirates, described in minimal words such as "He was tough. All pirates are tough." In the end, readers learn that even pirates cry. The large pictures reveal a story not in the text, in which Boris and his crew dig up a buried chest by following a treasure map. Little do they know they are being watched by a boy who sneaks onto their ship. Caught, the boy saves himself by playing a violin for the scary pirates.

McPhail, David. *Edward and the Pirates*. 1997. Hardcover: Little Brown. 32 pages. Ages 3–7. PICTURE BOOK.

Edward loves to read adventure stories, which come so alive for him that it's as if he's taking part in the action, riding to war with Joan of Arc or in Sherwood Forest with Robin Hood. When a pirate story comes to life, and the pirates want his library book, Edward refuses. His parents—or are they Joan of Arc and Robin Hood?—come to the rescue. The shadowy pictures lend an air of mystery to Edward's escapades. An engaging tribute to the joys of reading.

Gibbons, Gail. *Sunken Treasure.* **1988. Hardcover and paperback: Harper. 32 pages. Ages 3–9. PICTURE BOOK NONFICTION.**

This short book describes the true story of the search for the *Atocha*, a Spanish galleon that sank near Florida in 1622. In the 1960s, treasure hunters began to look for the sunken ship and its treasure of gold, jewels, and silver. Pictures on every page and a brief text describe the search as well as instruments used in searching and excavating, some restoration processes, and what happened to the treasure. The final pages highlight four other famous treasure hunts.

McCully, Emily Arnold. *The Pirate Queen.* **1995. Hardcover: Putnam. Paperback: Paper Star. 32 pages. Ages 5–9. PICTURE BOOK.**

Grania O'Malley was an Irish pirate who ruled part of the waters off the coast of Ireland, taking money and goods from passing ships. She commanded her own fleet of ships and pirates, and owned five castles. Action-filled paintings show her as a girl leaping into a pirate battle, as a young woman running her ship, and finally as an older woman confronting Queen Elizabeth I. Based on fact and legend, the story is filled with high spirits, fighting, and lawlessness.

MacGill-Callahan, Sheila. *To Capture the Wind.* **Illustrated by Gregory Manchess. 1997. Hardcover: Dial. 32 pages. Ages 5–10. PICTURE BOOK.**

The heroine Oonagh has a successful farm and is happily engaged to the weaver Conal. But when pirates kidnap Conal, Oonagh summons her impressive wit and strength to save him. Pretending to seek the pirate captain's son in marriage, she agrees to solve four riddles. She solves them, but in the end must cross swords with the pirates. A Celtic tale with lyrical language and dramatic paintings.

Donnelly, Judy. *True-Life Treasure Hunts*. Illustrated by Thomas La Padula. 1993. Hardcover and paperback: Random House. 48 pages. Ages 7–11. NONFICTION.

Four chapters discuss the high-interest topic of treasure hunts, using large print and vocabulary accessible to younger readers. The book opens with descriptions of pirates including Blackbeard, then describes a successful dive for pirate treasure near Jamaica. Another chapter concerns a well in Mexico sacred to the Mayans, that had gold, jewelry, and skeletons at the bottom. The book wraps up with a review of different types of treasure found in a variety of places.

Scieszka, Jon. *The Not-So-Jolly Roger*. Illustrated by Lane Smith. 1991. Hardcover: Viking. Paperback: Puffin. 58 pages. Ages 8–12. FICTION.

In the second of the "Time Warp Trio" series, a magical book sends Joe, Fred, and Sam back in time to a desert island to look for buried treasure. But the famous pirate Blackbeard takes them prisoner, and they get pulled into a battle against another ship. By good luck, the three boys help save the pirates and ask for buried treasure as a reward. Back on the desert island, they start digging for treasure—or are they digging their own graves? Snappy dialogue, outrageous pictures, and high-speed plots make this a very popular series.

Gregory, Kristiana. *The Stowaway: A Tale of California Pirates*. 1995. Hardcover and paperback: Scholastic. 126 pages. Ages 9–13. FICTION.

When eleven-year-old Carlito boards a pirate ship in 1818, he is seeking revenge. The pirates have destroyed Carlito's town of Monterey, California, and killed his father. Carlito is caught and pressed into service as a cabin boy for the vicious captain, Hippolyte de Bouchard. Will he accomplish his goal and escape? Or will the pirate's ship take him too far from home ever to return? A stirring historical novel based on facts about nineteenth-century pirates.

Deem, James M. *How to Hunt Buried Treasure*. Illustrated by True Kelley. 1992. Hardcover: Houghton. 192 pages. Ages 9–13. Of interest to younger children. NONFICTION.

This impressive book goes far beyond the usual stories about sunken ships and treasure maps, to treasure hunting ideas children can actually try. It expands the idea of treasure to include historical artifacts like arrowheads and old buttons, emphasizing the pleasure of learning about the past rather than getting rich. It gives advice on library research, how to locate good spots for finding old things, and more. Full of anecdotes, techniques, and useful tips, with entertaining illustrations, this is a gem among treasure books.

Garwood, Val. *The World of the Pirate*. Illustrated by Richard Berridge. 1997. Hardcover: Peter Bedrick. 48 pages. Ages 9–13. Of interest to younger children. NONFICTION.

Corsairs, buccaneers, the Spanish Main—words associated with pirates are explained throughout this solid overview. Each double-page spread covers one of twenty topics including weapons, navigation, treasure, and clothing. The utilitarian pictures are occasionally gruesome, such as one of a leg being amputated. Overall, though, the reader gets the impression of lives largely similar to those of other sailors. The book, which is better than most informational books on pirates, neither romanticizes nor vilifies them beyond historical fact.

Schwartz, Alvin, collector. *Gold and Silver, Silver and Gold: Tales of Hidden Treasure.* **Illustrated by David Christiana. 1988. Hardcover and paperback: Farrar, Straus & Giroux. 128 pages. Ages 9–14. NONFICTION.**

Who hasn't dreamed of finding buried treasure? This enjoyable collection brings together dozens of stories—factual and folklore—about different kinds of hidden treasure. They range from old to recent, from pirates who leave maps of their buried gold, to children who dig up coins in a vacant lot. Many of the stories have an element of tragedy as people risk, and sometimes lose, their lives hoping for great wealth. Black-and-white drawings complement the tales of adventure and greed.

Hobbs, Will. *Ghost Canoe.* **1997. Hardcover: Morrow. Paperback: Avon. 160 pages. Ages 10–13. FICTION.**

Buried Spanish gold is at the heart of this mystery set in the Northwest in 1874. Fourteen-year-old Nathan, son of the local lighthouse-keeper, finds himself embroiled in a dangerous hunt for buried treasure. First, a ship's captain is murdered. Then, a box of gold dollars is stolen. Finally, Nathan puts the pieces together but ends up in danger. The exciting novel also describes whale hunting and salmon fishing, which Nathan does with the Makah Indians. Full of suspense and action.

Morpurgo, Michael. *The Ghost of Grania O'Malley.* **1996. Hardcover: Viking. 184 pages. Ages 10–13. FICTION.**

Ten-year-old Jessie has always wanted to climb Big Hill, but her cerebral palsy has made it too difficult. Finally she succeeds and at the top she encounters the ghost of the Irish pirate queen Grania O'Malley. Miners are planning to bulldoze the beautiful, ecologically important Big Hill, a concern that unites Jessie, her mother, her American cousin, and the pirate's ghost in a battle against the miners and others on the Irish island. An engaging story that combines ecology and ghosts.

Stevenson, Robert Louis. *Treasure Island.* **Illustrated by N. C. Wyeth. 1911. Hardcover: Scribners. Paperback: Scholastic. 270 pages. Ages 10–14. FICTION.**

In this classic, young Jim Hawkins obtains a treasure map from a mysterious stranger and shows it to the local doctor and squire. The men plan an expedition to Treasure Island and take Jim along as cabin boy, never suspecting that the crew, led by the one-legged Long John Silver, plans to mutiny. The adventure unfolds in a series of dangerous episodes on the ship, then on the island. Although the dialogue is not always easy to follow, readers who get caught up in the suspense will find this novel thrilling to the end.

Wars

Garland, Sherry. *Voices of the Alamo.* Illustrated by Ronald Himler. 2000. Hardcover: Scholastic. 40 pages. Ages 5–9. PICTURE BOOK NONFICTION.

Voices of real people at different times through history convey the story of the Alamo. The book opens with a Payaya woman in 1500, moves to a Spanish conquistador, Franciscan priest, Spanish soldier at the Alamo, and on through the siege of the Alamo. Soft-edged watercolors give a feeling of long ago. Both men and women speak briefly and a modern child closes the book with a visit to the Alamo. An imaginative, effective approach to the history of one place and its many dimensions.

Kirkpatrick, Katherine. *Redcoats and Petticoats.* Illustrated by Ronald Himler. 1999. Hardcover: Holiday House. 32 pages. Ages 5–9. PICTURE BOOK.

During the Revolutionary War, ordinary people on Long Island risked their lives spying on the British. This story draws from a real-life episode in which Nancy Strong—mother of eight and wife of a captured soldier—hung out petticoats to signal the location of British soldiers for patriots hoping to cross the water to Connecticut. In this fictionalized account her son also uses a rowboat to spy on the British. Large watercolors add drama, and an afterword separates fact from fiction.

Lee, Milly. *Nim and the War Effort.* **Illustrated by Yangsook Choi. 1997. Hardcover: Farrar, Straus & Giroux. 40 pages. Ages 5–9. PICTURE BOOK.**

During World War II, young Nim vows to win her school's contest to collect the most newspapers, but her grandfather insists that time-consuming Chinese classes come first. Nevertheless, Nim's success is matched by only one other student, a boy named Garland. When it appears that Garland has cheated, Nim concocts an ingenious plan for winning. Large, elegant paintings depict a Chinese-American family in San Francisco while the story conveys the patriotism of Asian-Americans during the war and the biases they encountered.

Griffin, Judith Berry. *Phoebe the Spy.* **Illustrated by Margot Tomes. 1977. Hardcover and paperback: Scholastic. 48 pages. Ages 7–9. FICTION.**

In this tale, based on a true story from the Revolutionary War, Phoebe Fraunces, an African-American girl whose father runs a New York City tavern, becomes a servant to George Washington, then commander of the American army. She serves as a spy, eavesdropping and putting together clues, in order to prevent an unidentified enemy from harming Washington. At the last minute, her spying proves vital for saving the future president. A simple but exciting short novel, well-illustrated.

Lowry, Lois. *Number the Stars.* **1989. Hardcover: Houghton. Paperback: Dell. 137 pages. Ages 9–12. FICTION.**

Set in Denmark during World War II, this moving story of friendship focuses on two girls, Annemarie and her friend Ellen, who is Jewish. When Nazi occupation endangers Ellen and her family, Annemarie's family helps their brave friends escape. Near the Danish coast, Annemarie's courage is tested in a life-threatening encounter with Nazis. The extraordinary courage of the Danish people, both Jewish and Christian, comes forcefully to life in this Newbery Award winner that is based on a true story.

Sandler, Martin W. *Civil War: A Library of Congress Book.* **1996. Hardcover: Harper. 96 pages. Ages 9–13. NONFICTION.**

In this well-designed overview of the Civil War, each page features photographs and illustrations from the Library of Congress. The text outlines the war in a comprehensible way. With a balanced view, it discusses the causes, casualties, camp life, major battles and turning points, roles of women and blacks, and more. Plentiful sidebars quote from letters, songs, speeches, and other writings, enriching the powerful overall picture of those tragic years.

Booth, Martin. *War Dog.* **1997. Hardcover: McElderry. 144 pages. Ages 9–14. FICTION.**

In this compelling novel, a dog named Jet serves as a British military dog during World War II. Raised by a poacher, Jet is not only obedient, she can sense hidden humans at a distance, a skill that saves soldiers' lives. She and her handler spend months along enemy lines in France, and later she works with another handler to find civilians injured in bombings and explosions. An unusual historical novel, great for dog fans and war buffs.

Dolan, Edward F. *America in World War I.* **1996. Hardcover: Millbrook. 96 pages. Ages 9–14. NONFICTION.**

This straightforward history looks at World War I before the United States entered in 1917, then focuses on how America helped the Allied forces win. Black-and-white photographs convey the bleak conditions of trench warfare and show major historical figures; two maps pinpoint the areas of U.S. fighting. It combines information on specific battles with an overview of the Allied offensives. Sidebars discuss the U.S. homefront, the role of women, and Wilson's Fourteen Points for Peace. A fine book for learning about "the war to end all wars."

O'Grady, Captain Scott, with Michael French. *Basher Five-Two: The True Story of F-16 Fighter Pilot Captain Scott O'Grady.* 1997. Hardcover: Doubleday. Paperback: Yearling. 134 pages. Ages 9–14. NONFICTION.

What is it like to be shot down behind enemy lines, not knowing if you will be rescued or die? In 1995, while he was flying an F-16 over Bosnia, the author's plane was shot and destroyed. Only his training and an ejector seat kept him alive. This exciting story takes the reader along on his dangerous journey to survive, occasionally backtracking to explain how O'Grady became a fighter pilot. A suspenseful true account, this is hard to put down.

Reit, Seymour. *Behind Rebel Lines: The Incredible Story of Emma Edmonds, Civil War Spy.* 1988. Paperback: Harcourt. 114 pages. Ages 10–13. BIOGRAPHY.

During the Civil War, Emma Edmonds disguised herself as a man and served two years in the Union Army, one of many women who passed as male soldiers. A skillful spy, she completed eleven missions behind Confederate lines to collect information on troop size and plans, disguised as a handsome Confederate sympathizer and a matronly Irish peddler, among others. Her army career ended when she was hospitalized and her secret discovered. A fascinating biography that makes a good read-aloud.

Bachrach, Susan D. *Tell Them We Remember: The Story of the Holocaust.* 1994. Hardcover and paperback: Little, Brown. 109 pages. Ages 10–14. NONFICTION.

Written in conjunction with the U.S. Holocaust Memorial Museum, this book bears witnesses to the children and teenagers, more than a million total, who died in the Holocaust. An opening page shows twenty "identity" photographs of young people, and throughout the text, the photos reappear with more information about their fates. Other photos show the Nazis' rise to power, the ghettos, and the death camps. The text discusses Nazi Germany and the Final Solution, resistance fighters and others who risked their lives. An extraordinarily moving account told in clear prose with powerful photographs.

Myers, Walter Dean. *Fallen Angels.* 1988. Hardcover and paperback: Scholastic. 309 pages. Ages 12–14. FICTION.

In 1967, Richie Perry graduates from high school and enlists in the army, knowing he can't afford college and hoping his income will help his younger brother. He ends up in Vietnam, fighting a war he doesn't fully understand. His buddy Peewee, a quick-witted fellow black soldier, helps Richie survive, literally and figuratively. But every day brings possible death, a bewildering reality that changes the men in Richie's platoon. A remarkable novel about war, its intense friendships, and its pain. Not to be missed.

Paulsen, Gary. *Soldier's Heart: A Novel of the Civil War.* 1998. Hardcover: Delacorte. Paperback: Laurel Leaf. 128 pages. Ages 12–14. FICTION.

"Being the Story of the Enlistment and Due Service of the Boy Charley Goddard in the First Minnesota Volunteers" is the subtitle of this wrenching novel based on a real person.

Fifteen-year-old Charley lies about his age to join the Union Army, certain that the war will be short. His first fight—the Battle of Bull Run—stuns him with its brutality. He fights in many places, but the book focuses on the first two battles at Bull Run, life in camp, and the Battle of Gettysburg. Although short, the novel embeds Charley's terrible experiences in the reader's mind, not to be forgotten soon. Highly recommended.

Games, Puzzles, Hobbies, and Holidays

Brain Teasers and Riddles

Falwell, Cathryn. *Word Wizard*. 1998. Hardcover: Clarion. 32 pages. Ages 3–8. PICTURE BOOK.

Playing with her cereal letters one morning, Anna discovers the pleasures of anagrams, using the same letters to form different words. She starts with "dawn" and turns it into "wand," then goes on an adventure based on the anagrams, magically transforming the world around her as she rearranges letters. A note at the end gives more suggestions for playing with words. Cheerful, appealing collage artwork celebrates the magic of words.

Hall, Katy, and Lisa Eisenberg. *Chickie Riddles.* **Illustrated by Thor Wickstrom. 1997. Hardcover: Dial. Paperback: Puffin. 48 pages. Ages 4–8. EASY READER.**

"Why did the turkey cross the road? To show he wasn't chicken." This easy-to-read book of chicken jokes succeeds far better than most joke collections, hitting a level that kids can understand and enjoy. The goofy pictures make even the less obvious jokes funny. Kids will find a number of jokes they'll want to try out on their friends. Look for the many other collections by Hall and Eisenberg, including *Batty Riddles, Bunny Riddles,* and *Spacey Riddles.*

Christensen, Bonnie. *Rebus Riot.* **1997. Hardcover: Dial. 32 pages. Ages 5–9. PICTURE BOOK.**

Rebuses are pictures that take the place of words, such as an orange for the words "aren't you" or a head of lettuce for "let us." In this jaunty book, each double-page spread has a rhyme that uses pictures for some of the words. The charming scratchboard illustrations hint at the meanings, and a guide on the page explains each clue. Chosen for the child appeal, the subjects of the rhymes vary from monsters to valentines, cats to elephants. A lot of fun.

Schwartz, Alvin. *Busy Buzzing Bumblebees and Other Tongue Twisters.* **Illustrated by Paul Meisel. 1992. Hardcover and paperback: Harper. 64 pages. Ages 5–10. EASY READER.**

"Six sharp smart sharks!" Say it three times as quickly as you can, suggest the directions in this collection of tongue twisters for beginning readers. In this "I Can Read" book, Schwartz has compiled forty-six tongue-tangling phrases, some fairly easy to say, others quite challenging. While the collection includes "She sells seashells," most of the tongue twisters will be new to the reader and will provide hours of fun for those who respond to the challenge of this crowd pleaser.

Shannon, George. *Tomorrow's Alphabet*. **Illustrated by Donald Crews. 1996. Hardcover: Greenwillow. Paperback: Mulberry. 32 pages. Ages 6–10. PICTURE BOOK.**

This clever approach to the alphabet requires children to think about connections between the present and the future. The letters follow this format: "D is for puppy, tomorrow's dog," and "O is for acorn, tomorrow's oak." Children who already know the alphabet will solve the puzzle each letter presents, and then can come up with their own ideas for each letter. Large clean pictures illustrate both objects connected with each letter such as the acorn and the oak.

Agee, Jon. *Sit on a Potato Pan, Otis!: More Palindromes*. **1999. Hardcover: Farrar, Straus & Giroux. 80 pages. Ages 7–11. PICTURE BOOK NONFICTION.**

Readers will marvel at the inventiveness of these wacky palindromes, demonstrated by the title. The comical pictures add to the humor and help elucidate the phrases. For example, in one picture a man has stepped into a cage with a bear and asks, "Won't I be bit now?" While some of the palindromes work better than others, on the whole this book and other palindrome collections by Agee will delight word lovers.

Steig, William. *CDB!* **2000 Revised Edition. Hardcover: Simon & Schuster. 48 pages. Ages 8 and up. PICTURE BOOK.**

Renowned picture-story-book creator and cartoonist William Steig plays with the alphabet in this book of visual brain teasers. A sentence or two comprised only of letters and numerals accompanies each humorous picture. "CDB?" translates as "See the bee?" The scraggly drawings by Steig supply clues that help solve the puzzles. Although some of the puzzles are difficult, many children enjoy spending the time it takes to crack them. The revised edition gives answers in the back. Also try the similar *CDC*.

Sklansky, Amy E. *Zoom Zingers*. 1999. Paperback: Little, Brown. 64 pages. Ages 9–13. NONFICTION.

Brain teasers, word games, number games, and jokes fill this glossy book. Based on the public television show "ZOOM," it starts with physical challenges, such as juggling, balancing coins, and hanging spoons from one's nose. Most of the book, though, offers challenges for the mind: rebuses, card tricks, number or geometry puzzles, and more. The bright format features photographs of children and many sidebars with jokes and quotations. An appealing package of pastimes.

Shannon, George. *Stories to Solve: Folktales from Around the World*. Illustrated by Peter Sís. 1985. Hardcover: Greenwillow. Paperback: Harper. 56 pages. Ages 9–14. FOLKLORE COLLECTION.

Few children can resist these fourteen "mini-mysteries," short stories that give the reader a puzzle to solve, with the solution on the following page. In one tale, a father promises to leave his farm to the son who takes one coin and buys something that will fill a whole room. The first two buy straw and feathers, but the third buys two small things that fill the room completely. Many children love stretching their minds on such puzzles. Also enjoy *More Stories to Solve*, *Still More Stories to Solve*, and *True Lies*.

Cooking

Goss, Gary. *Blue Moon Soup: A Family Cookbook.* Illustrated by Jane Dyer. 1999. Hardcover: Little, Brown. 60 pages. All ages. NONFICTION.

This attractive cookbook gives recipes for two dozen soups suitable for winter, spring, summer, and fall, plus a few dishes that go well with soup. The recipes are to be made by a family, although a child ten or older could use them with adult supervision while using a knife. Each page features sprightly watercolors, sometimes small and sometimes a full page. An appetizing, specialized cookbook that will make cooking together a pleasure.

Kennedy, Jimmy. *The Teddy Bears' Picnic.* Illustrated by Alexandra Day. 1983. Hardcover: Green Tiger Press. Paperback: Aladdin. 40 pages. Ages 3–7. PICTURE BOOK.

"If you go down to the woods today / You're sure of a big surprise," begins this popular children's song, illustrated in soft watercolors with bears in many costumes. The bears are having a picnic with lots of food and games, joined by a human family in bear costume. Perfect for reading in conjunction with a picnic or even a birthday party to which teddy bears are invited. Also fun to read in conjunction with one of the many recordings of the song.

Katzen, Mollie, and Ann Henderson. *Pretend Soup and Other Real Recipes.* Illustrated by Mollie Katzen. 1994. Hardcover: Tricycle Press. 95 pages. Ages 3–9. NONFICTION.

The author of the *Moosewood Cookbook* joins forces with a preschool teacher to produce a wonderful cookbook for children. Nineteen recipes vary from quesadillas to blueberry pancakes, noodle pudding to chocolate-banana shakes. Each has advice "To the Grown-ups," cooking hints, a list of tools, directions, and a double-page spread that illustrates each step. Most require adult supervision, unless the child is old enough to use a knife and stove. Beautifully illustrated, this stands out among cookbooks for the younger set.

Douglass, Barbara. *The Chocolate Chip Cookie Contest*. Illustrated by Eric Jon Nones. 1985. Hardcover: Lothrop. 32 pages. Ages 4–8. PICTURE BOOK.

Hoping to win tickets to the circus, Cory and his friend Kevin decide to enter a cookie contest to be judged that afternoon. They go looking for help, first to Cory's baby-sitter, who lends them a recipe, then to his grandmother, who gives them raisins to add. So it goes, with relatives and neighbors giving advice and special ingredients. Finally, a neighbor, who happens to be a clown, supervises them as he makes himself up and dons his costume. The result is a happy surprise. The book includes the recipe.

Rattigan, Jama Kim. *Dumpling Soup*. Illustrated by Lillian Hsu-Flanders. 1993. Hardcover and paperback: Little, Brown. 32 pages. Ages 4–8. PICTURE BOOK.

Seven-year-old Marisa helps her relatives make dumplings to celebrate the New Year. The dumplings she makes turn out lumpy but are declared delicious by her large family, which includes adults and children of Korean, Japanese, Chinese, Hawaiian, and Caucasian descent. Delightful watercolors show the congenial family in a Hawaiian setting. Although it includes no recipes, this delightful book has a lot in it about food.

Dooley, Norah. *Everybody Cooks Rice.* **Illustrated by Peter J. Thornton. 1991. Hardcover: Carolrhoda. Paperback: First Avenue. 32 pages. Ages 4–10. PICTURE BOOK.**

Early one evening, Carrie goes from house to house in her friendly urban neighborhood where everybody is cooking or eating a rice dish. A warm feeling prevails as she is welcomed by neighbors, many of whom come from other countries. Cheerful pictures add to the ambiance, and nine rice recipes are included, to be cooked by an adult, perhaps with a child assistant. Also see *Everybody Bakes Bread* by the same team.

van Dam, Johannes. *Play with Your Pumpkins.* **Illustrated by Joost Elffers and Saxton Freymann. 1998. Hardcover: Stewart, Tabori and Chang. 79 pages. Ages 6 and up. NON-FICTION.**

In this creative book, photographs show pumpkins carved in remarkable facial expressions with the stem as the nose. Although the typeface is small, the information about pumpkin growing, history, and mythology will interest children. The twenty-four recipes from around the world, which suggest a remarkable number of ways to cook and eat pumpkin, will need adult participation. Be sure to see also the uncanny vegetable and fruit carvings in *How Are You Peeling?*, by the illustrators of this book.

Wilkes, Angela. *Children's Quick and Easy Cookbook.* **1997. Hardcover: DK. 96 pages. Ages 6–10. NONFICTION.**

Brightly colored photographs show the ingredients, steps, and finished products in this oversized basic cookbook. The more than sixty recipes, most with high child appeal, are fairly simple and fast. They go from lunch suggestions to entrées to desserts. Although the pages are a bit cluttered, younger children working with adults and older children with an adult in calling distance will find this glossy cookbook useful.

Conford, Ellen. *What's Cooking, Jenny Archer?* Illustrated by Diane Palmisciano. 1989. Hardcover and paperback: Little, Brown. 56 pages. Ages 7–10. FICTION.

In this short book, Jenny Archer starts making her own lunches when she gets tired of what the school serves. Her imaginative efforts appeal to her friends, so she goes into business preparing bagged lunches to order. But juggling her recipes, her friends' requests, and buying food present more problems than she ever imagined. An amusing story that takes place mostly in the kitchen, this is one in a popular series with large print, occasional pictures, and plenty of laughs.

Cunningham, Marion. *Cooking with Children: 15 Lessons for Children, Age 7 and Up, Who Really Want to Learn to Cook.* Illustrated by Emily Lisker. Photographs by Penina Meisels. 1995. Hardcover: Knopf. 172 pages. Ages 7 and up. NONFICTION.

After much thought and experience cooking with children, Cunningham has put together a progressive series of recipes to teach children all the basic skills they need to cook. Each of the fifteen lessons starts with a list of what will be learned, followed by the step-by-step recipe with illustrations, and sidebars with extra information. The recipes cover a wide range from appetizers to entrées to desserts. Occasional color photographs show children cooking and eating. A very good cooking primer.

Waters, Alice, with Bob Carrau and Patricia Curtan. *Fanny at Chez Panisse: A Child's Restaurant Adventures with 46 Recipes.* **Illustrated by Ann Arnold. 1992. Hardcover and paperback: Harper. 133 pages. Ages 7 and up. NONFICTION.**

Alice Waters of Chez Panisse, and her daughter, Fanny, share a love of food. In this inviting book, Fanny's voice describes the world-famous California restaurant as her second home where she tries new food and sees old friends. The second half of the book gives simple recipes. Older children who have begun cooking could handle most of the recipes on their own, while parents will find recipes to try with younger children. For those who love good food and restaurants.

Delacre, Lulu. *Salsa Stories.* **2000. Hardcover: Scholastic. 112 pages. Ages 8–11. FICTION.**

When Carmen Teresa's family gets together to celebrate New Year's, they hold a storytelling session hoping that she will write down their tales. In lively language laced with Spanish words (a glossary is at the back), the relatives and friends tell of their adventures growing up in Puerto Rico, Argentina, Cuba, and Guatemala. In the end, Carmen Teresa collects not stories but recipes from the many foods the storytellers describe. Recipes appear at the end of this enjoyable set of stories.

Whitmore, Arvella. *The Bread Winner.* **1990. Hardcover: Houghton. 138 pages. Ages 9–12. FICTION.**

Sixth-grader Sarah Puckett wants to help her parents survive the poverty brought on by the Great Depression, which forced them to move from the country to the city. She slowly starts making money with her bread-making knowledge, and learns enough about business to open a bakery with her family and restore their financial well-being. A moving story about a girl who takes risks and develops her baking and business skills.

Koertge, Ron. *Confess-O-Rama*. 1996. Hardcover: Orchard. Paperback: Laurel Leaf. 166 pages. Ages 12–14. FICTION.
Fifteen-year-old Tony has moved so often, because of the deaths of his father and three stepfathers, that he no longer bothers to make new friends. Now in Southern California, he seeks relief through cooking, his favorite hobby, and for once gets some encouragement for his interest. Meanwhile, he also gets pulled unexpectedly into romance through a telephone help line called "Confess-O-Rama." Dry, witty dialogue will have readers laughing at this story about art, love, and growing up. Highly recommended.

Mysteries, Detectives, and Criminals

Sharmat, Marjorie Weinman. *Nate the Great*. Illustrated by Marc Simont. 1972. Paperback: Dell. 64 pages. Ages 3–8. EASY READER.

Nate the Great has the narrative style of a hard-boiled detective, with short sentences and a tough manner. But he also likes pancakes and his dog, Sludge. His current case concerns his friend Annie, who is missing a picture of her dog, Fang. Nate starts by investigating Fang: "He sniffed me. I sniffed him back." In the end, Nate uses his knowledge of colors to solve the mystery. With sprightly, memorable illustrations, this is the first in a popular series.

Cushman, Doug. *Aunt Eater Loves a Mystery*. 1987. Hardcover and paperback: Harper. 64 pages. Ages 3–9. EASY READER.

In the first of four short mysteries, Aunt Eater, an anteater who loves to read mystery books, takes a train and has her luggage stolen—or was it? While visiting a friend at the end of her train journey, Aunt Eater solves a puzzle concerning a mysterious shadow. Back home, a strange note in her mailbox turns out not to be so strange after all. Finally, Aunt Eater cleverly recovers a cat she had lost. With humorous pictures on most pages, this book is aimed at beginning readers. Part of a series.

Yolen, Jane. *Piggins*. Illustrated by Jane Dyer. 1987. Paperback: Harcourt. 32 pages. Ages 4–8. PICTURE BOOK.

Contrary to the phrase "The butler did it," Piggins the butler solves mysteries. He works in a proper household of a wealthy fox family, the Reynards. When the Reynards give a dinner party, Mrs. Reynard wears her new diamond necklace, which has a curse on it. During the meal, the lights go out and the necklace disappears—or does it? Piggins announces that he has spotted three clues and knows who did it. Children and adults will enjoy this spoof, the first in a series.

Wisniewski, David. *Tough Cookie*. 1999. Hardcover: Lothrop. 32 pages. Ages 4–9. PICTURE BOOK.

Fans of adult hard-boiled detective stories will especially enjoy reading this to their children, who will miss many references but still find it funny. Detective Tough Cookie lives at the bottom of the cookie jar, where he protects the little crumbs from danger. When he hears that his archenemy Fingers has hurt a friend, the detective sets out for the top of the jar to confront Fingers. In the end, he gets some unexpected help to defeat the villain. Wisniewski's extraordinary cut-paper illustrations are the highlight of this creative mystery takeoff.

Landon, Lucinda. *Meg Mackintosh and the Case of the Missing Babe Ruth Baseball*. 1986. Paperback: Secret Passage Press. 48 pages. Ages 7–10. FICTION.

When Meg's grandfather was a boy, his cousin planted the clues leading to a hidden baseball signed by Babe Ruth, but Grandfather never found it. Now, detective Meg Mackintosh is hot on the trail, hoping to beat her older brother Pete to the baseball. The clues in the black-and-white pictures on every page include one in code and others that require familiarity with nursery rhymes. With large print, many pictures, and challenging clues, this is one in a popular series.

Schomp, Virginia. *If You Were a . . . Police Officer*. **1998. Hardcover: Benchmark. 32 pages. Ages 8–11. Of interest to younger children. NONFICTION.**

The idea of becoming a police officer attracts many children. This simple photo-essay provides a sense of an urban officer's duties, plus information on more specialized jobs. Color photographs, which vary in quality, show police on motorcycles and horses, helping children, handcuffing suspects, working on SWAT teams, and diving on search-and-rescue teams. The text pulls in readers with second-person narrative, like: "A missing skier? You roar to the rescue in your police snowmobile." A short overview of a high-interest topic.

Wright, Betty Ren. *Too Many Secrets*. **1997. Hardcover: Scholastic. 128 pages. Ages 8–12. FICTION.**

Chad agrees to look after Miss Beane's dog while she is hospitalized after tumbling down the stairs. When Chad and his friend Jeannie visit Miss Beane's house, they hear footsteps— perhaps the same burglar Miss Beane thought she heard. The kids stake out the house, hoping to catch the burglar and become heroes. Chad worries that they should tell the sheriff or even their parents, but he is angry at his father, so they keep the burglar a secret. Another suspenseful mystery from a popular children's writer.

Fleischman, Sid. *Bandit's Moon*. **Illustrated by Jos. A Smith. 1998. Hardcover: Greenwillow. Paperback: Yearling. 144 pages. Ages 9–12. FICTION.**

Newly arrived in California, orphaned twelve-year-old Annyrose gets separated from her brother and thrown into the company of a Mexican bandit, the feared Joaquín Murieta. Hoping to find her brother in Gold Rush country, Annyrose travels with the bandit and agrees to teach him to read. Hearing about the unlawful treatment of Mexicans, Annyrose starts questioning her notions of right and wrong. One thrilling episode follows another, with plenty of narrow escapes. A lively read about the life of a bandit in the Wild West.

Sobol, Donald J. *Encyclopedia Brown: Boy Detective.* **Illustrated by Leonard Shortall. 1963. Hardcover: Dutton. Paperback: Bantam. 112 pages. Ages 9–12. FICTION.**

In each chapter, readers can try to solve a short mystery, then check the answer in the back. Fifth-grader Leroy Brown, nicknamed Encyclopedia, is "like a complete library walking around in sneakers." Son of the town's police chief, he cleverly helps his father catch criminals and sets up his own detective agency. He puzzles out how a diamond necklace was stolen from under his father's eyes, and why a man must have robbed his own store. Many books follow in this series of minimysteries.

Byars, Betsy. *Tarot Says Beware.* **1995. Hardcover: Viking. Paperback: Puffin. 160 pages. Ages 9–13. FICTION.**

Herculeah Jones comes by her interest in crime naturally: Her mother is a private eye; her father, a police detective. Her best friend, Meat, does his best to hold her back from dangerous situations, but more often than not Herculeah drags him in, too. In this case, Herculeah finds the body of a murdered fortune teller, Madame Rosa. Following clues to a local flea market, Herculeah risks her own life to solve the mystery. One in a series about a smart, strong female detective.

Jackson, Donna M. *The Bone Detectives: How Forensic Anthropologists Solve Crimes and Uncover Mysteries of the Dead.* Photographs by Charlie Fellenbaum. 1996. Hardcover: Little, Brown. 48 pages. Ages 10–14. NONFICTION.

Crime detection and science merge in forensic anthropology, in which old bones are studied for clues to a crime. This book describes an investigation that began in 1987 when a skull, bones, and clothing fragments were uncovered on a Missouri ranch. A "bone detective" investigated, a process followed in detail in the text and photographs until the murderer is convicted. Sidebars discuss investigation techniques such as identifying fingerprints and analyzing teeth. While some readers will find the subject grisly, others will love it.

Jackson, Donna M. *The Wildlife Detectives: How Forensic Scientists Fight Crimes Against Nature.* Photographs by Wendy Shattil and Bob Rozinski. 2000. Hardcover: Houghton. 48 pages. Ages 10–14. NONFICTION.

When crimes are committed involving wild animals, only one crime lab in the world is equipped to analyze the crimes, the National Fish and Wildlife Forensics Laboratory in Oregon. This book describes how scientists aided in solving a case of an elk shot illegally in 1993 in Yellowstone. Rangers and other officers tracked down the criminal, while the forensic scientists analyzed DNA, identified cut-off antlers, and more. Sidebars add information about wildlife forensics and crimes. Well-written and absorbing.

Jones, Charlotte Foltz. *Fingerprints and Talking Bones: How Real-Life Crimes Are Solved.* **Illustrated by David G. Klein. 1997. Hardcover: Delacorte. Paperback: Yearling. 144 pages. Ages 10–14. NONFICTION.**

Bite marks, fingerprints, DNA, fibers, traces of soil—clues like these help police solve crimes. This undemanding book surveys all kinds of ways to detect crimes, including high-tech methods still under development. It briefly covers forensic anthropology, which entails getting clues from skeletons, and how animals like K-9 dogs help with detective work. Dozens of anecdotes about real crimes illustrate the facts. Sure to please future detectives.

Williams, Stanley "Tookie," with Barbara Cottman Becnel. *Life in Prison.* **1999. Hardcover: Morrow. 144 pages. Ages 12–14. NONFICTION.**

Anyone who thinks life in prison sounds even a bit glamorous should read this real-life report from a death-row inmate. Convicted killer Williams, who has been a prisoner at San Quentin for twenty years, wants to convey to kids how bad prison life is. He describes the bleak living conditions, humiliating treatment, tasteless food, and the omnipresent violence. Written in a conversational tone with stories from his own experience, he paints a chilling picture of life behind bars.

Holidays and Festivals

Howard, Elizabeth Fitzgerald. *Chita's Christmas Tree.* Illustrated by Floyd Cooper. 1989. Hardcover: Bradbury. Paperback: Aladdin. 32 pages. Ages 3–7. PICTURE BOOK.

Set in Baltimore in a time when families traveled by horse and carriage, this warm Christmas story tells how a girl named Chita and her father, a doctor, drive their horse out to the woods, where Chita picks out a Christmas tree. They return home for baking and Christmas Eve with relatives. Will the Christmas tree, with Chita's name carved in it, arrive at their house for Christmas morning? Glowing paintings convey a happy Christmas celebration by African-Americans long ago. Also see *Papa Tells Chita a Story.*

Silverman, Erica. *The Halloween House.* Illustrated by Jon Agee. 1997. Hardcover: Farrar, Straus & Giroux. Paperback: Sunburst. 32 pages. Ages 3–7. PICTURE BOOK.

In a rhyme based on the rhythm of "Over in the Meadow," this entertaining Halloween story follows two escaped prisoners into a haunted house. For each number from ten down to one, a group of fearsome creatures scares the prisoners, including werewolves, vampires, bats, ghosts, and more. The amusing pictures take the edge off the scariness, and add a twist at the end that will make readers laugh. Wonderful for reading aloud.

Stock, Catherine. *Thanksgiving Treat.* 1990. Paperback: Aladdin. 32 pages. Ages 3–7. PICTURE BOOK.

This gentle story about Thanksgiving will ring true to young children who feel left out during holiday preparations.

Although excited to be at his grandparents' house, the narrator is disappointed that no one wants his help. Soft watercolors show relatives peeling potatoes, rolling out pie dough, shucking corn, and chopping wood, but they all send him away. Finally, his grandfather invites him to help with a task that the others greatly appreciate. A warm, simple story.

Say, Allen. *Tree of Cranes*. 1991. Hardcover: Houghton. 32 pages. Ages 3–9. PICTURE BOOK.

In this unusually lovely book, a Japanese boy learns about Christmas. His mother, who grew up in California, surprises him by making origami cranes and digging up a small evergreen tree. What is she up to? Sick in bed, he watches and finally learns about the holiday she celebrated as a child. They celebrate together in a simple way and exchange gifts that mean a lot to them. The large-scale elegant watercolors help tell the touching story.

Van Allsburg, Chris. *The Polar Express*. 1985. Hardcover: Houghton. 32 pages. Ages 3–9. PICTURE BOOK.

On Christmas Eve, a boy boards a train of children going to the North Pole. They travel through dark woods, past wolves, and up mountains before they arrive at the lovely city where Santa chooses the boy to receive the first present of the year. He asks for and receives a bell from Santa's sleigh, but loses it before he gets home. Then the bell mysteriously appears as a present under the family's Christmas tree. Glorious paintings have made this a Caldecott Medal winner, a bestseller, and a family favorite.

Shaik, Fatima. *On Mardi Gras Day.* **Illustrated by Floyd Cooper. 1999. Hardcover: Dial. 32 pages. Ages 4–8. PICTURE BOOK.**

Soft-edged oil paintings evoke the festive feeling of Mardi Gras, seen through the eyes of children. The day begins with donning masks, then watching parades. Large pictures depict elaborate costumes and a float, while the simple poetic text adds flavor. A family celebrates together with food, and when evening falls, they savor the final parade before bedtime. The book highlights participants of African-American and Native American descent, who carry on old Mardi Gras traditions.

Teague, Mark. *One Halloween Night.* **1999. Hardcover: Scholastic. 32 pages. Ages 4–8. PICTURE BOOK.**

One Halloween night, friends Wendell, Floyd, and Mona have trouble from the start. Treats like Broccoli Chews and Eggplant Fizzlers are the least of their troubles once some nasty girls start chasing them. But luckily they are able to escape magically from every new problem, no matter how bad, and the bullies find the tables are turned on them. Large, stylized paintings express spookiness and magic.

Fishman, Cathy Goldberg. *On Rosh Hashanah and Yom Kippur.* **Illustrated by Melanie W. Hall. 1997. Hardcover: Atheneum. Paperback: Aladdin. 40 pages. Ages 4–9. NON-FICTION.**

Soft-edged, glowing paintings add a cozy note to this book about Rosh Hashanah and Yom Kippur. Narrated by a girl in a large family, the text explains the meaning and customs surrounding the Jewish New Year and Day of Atonement from a child's point of view. A glossary at the end gives definitions and pronunciations of words that may be unfamiliar. Appealing to those who celebrate the holidays and to those who want to learn more about them.

Kimmel, Eric. *Hershel and the Hanukkah Goblins.* **Illustrated by Trina Schart Hyman. 1989. Hardcover and paperback: Holiday House. 32 pages. Ages 4–9. PICTURE BOOK.**

In this tale, a man named Hershel enters a village on the first night of Hanukkah and finds no menorahs lit because goblins are haunting the synagogue. Hershel bravely offers to spend eight nights in the synagogue and light the Hanukkah candles. Each night a progressively scarier goblin shows up and Hershel outwits it. On the final night the horrific King of the Goblins comes, the greatest challenge of all. The excellent artwork is frightening yet comical in spots. A Caldecott Honor Book.

Pinkney, Andrea Davis. *Seven Candles for Kwanzaa.* **Illustrated by Brian Pinkney. 1993. Hardcover: Dial. Paperback: Puffin. 32 pages. Ages 4–9. PICTURE BOOK NONFICTION.**

Expressive scratchboard illustrations show a family during Kwanzaa, a holiday that celebrates African heritage and values. As the narrative explains, Kwanzaa has traditions that span the week of December 26 through January 1, with principles attached to each day. The first, for example, celebrates *umojo*, which means unity. The book goes through each day and its special meaning. An unusually attractive informational book about a joyful holiday.

Stevenson, James. *Mud Flat April Fool.* **1998. Hardcover: Greenwillow. 48 pages. Ages 4–9. PICTURE BOOK.**

The animals at Mud Flat are celebrating April Fools' Day in this installment of an amusing series. Ten very short chapters tell about the mild jokes that the animals play on each other. Squirrels, beavers, birds, dogs, foxes, and even snails, many dressed in human clothes, kid around with plastic roses that squirt water and similar pranks. The priceless, cartoonlike pen-and-watercolor drawings are humorous and cozy. Bravo for Mud Flat fun.

Polacco, Patricia. *Rechenka's Eggs.* **1988. Hardcover: Philomel. Paperback: Paper Star. 32 pages. Ages 4–10. PICTURE BOOK.**

Set in Russia, this holiday story tells of Babushka, an old woman living alone who excels at painting Ukranian-style eggs in wonderful detail. Out of kindness, she takes care of an injured goose. When the goose breaks the painted eggs that Babushka hoped to enter in a contest, the woman and pet are sad, but a miracle saves the day. The woman is twice-blessed by the goose, leading to a happy ending. A story of love and rebirth, beautifully illustrated.

Schotter, Roni. *Purim Play.* **Illustrated by Marylin Hafner. 1998. Hardcover: Little, Brown. 32 pages. Ages 4–10. PICTURE BOOK.**

Frannie and her brother always celebrate Purim by putting on a play for their relatives about Queen Esther saving her people. This year they need someone to play Haman, the villain. When their old neighbor Mrs. Teplitzky volunteers, the children are grumpy but cheer up when she turns out to be an effective villain. The play is a success, and Frannie has a new friend in Mrs. Teplitzky. This friendly tale includes the Purim story, information on how Purim is celebrated, and a recipe for hamantaschen.

Matthews, Mary. *Magid Fasts for Ramadan*. Illustrated by E. B. Lewis. 1996. Hardcover: Clarion. Paperback: Houghton. 48 pages. Ages 5–9. FICTION.

During the month of Ramadan, devout Muslims fast from sunrise to sunset. Magid, an eight-year-old in present-day Egypt, wants to be old enough to fast, like his twelve-year-old sister. He resolves to fast secretly and manages to go several days without his breakfast or lunch, but it is harder than he expected. Can he keep it up for the whole month? Light-filled watercolors add personality to Magid and his family in this engaging story that introduces an important part of Islamic life.

Ancona, George. *Fiesta Fireworks*. 1998. Hardcover: Lothrop. 32 pages. Ages 7–10. NONFICTION.

Glorious exploding fireworks set against a black sky fill many pages of this book about a Mexican fireworks display. The text starts with a girl whose grandfather is a master *pirotecíco*, a master fireworks maker shown at work with his sons in large, sharp photographs. The men are preparing fireworks for a local saint's festival, including huge painted animals with fireworks attached and wheels that go on a tall castlelike structure, a *castillo*. It discusses other aspects of the festival, then returns to the spectacular nighttime fireworks.

Rocklin, Joanne. *The Very Best Hanukkah Gift*. Illustrated by Catherine O'Neill. 1999. Hardcover: Delacorte. 114 pages. Ages 8–12. FICTION.

Children will relate to Daniel as he tries to overcome his fear of dogs and make his best gifts ever for his family. The book moves from the first day of Hanukkah, when Daniel's mother serves zucchini latkes, to everyone's surprise, to the final day when a power outage changes the family's traditional party. Funny, everyday incidents concerning Daniel, his know-it-all older brother, and his brave younger sister occur in each chapter, along with Hanukkah lore and customs. Lighthearted and charming.

Robinson, Barbara. *The Best Christmas Pageant Ever.* **Illustrated by Judith Gwyn Brown. 1972. Hardcover and paperback: Harper. 80 pages. Ages 9–12. FICTION.**

When the narrator's mother agrees to direct the church pageant, the six dreaded Herdman children try out and intimidate the other children into letting them have the best parts. One fiasco follows another as the incorrigible Herdmans put their own irreverent spin on the roles of Mary, Joseph, the Wise Men, and the Angel. Yet their fresh approach to the Christmas story, which they hadn't heard before, turns the performance into something special. One of the funniest books around, this is an outstanding read-aloud. Followed by *The Best School Year Ever.*

Van Draanen, Wendelin. *Sammy Keyes and the Skeleton Man.* **1998. Hardcover: Knopf. Paperback: Random House. 172 pages. Ages 9–12. FICTION.**

When seventh-grader Sammy and her two best friends go trick-or-treating, Sammy insists on stopping at an old house overgrown with bushes. On their way up the path, someone in a skeleton costume pushes past them. Sammy finds a fire and something worse in the house, which leads to a mystery for her to solve. Meanwhile, she has problems at school to work out, too. One in a series with a daring detective who never takes the easy way out.

Goldin, Barbara Diamond. *The Passover Journey: A Seder Companion.* Illustrated by Neil Waldman. 1994. Hardcover: Viking. Paperback: Puffin. 64 pages. Ages 9–13. Of interest to younger children. NONFICTION.

In this beautiful book about Passover, the magical pastel paintings and borders complement the engaging prose. It opens with the story of Moses and the Pharaohs, with each double-page spread adding a new incident in the saga from Moses's birth to the plagues to the parting of the Red Sea on the Israelite's journey to freedom. The second half explains the steps of a seder and how they correspond to the Passover story. Notes at the end from the author and illustrator add a personal touch.

Kindersley, Anabel. *Celebrations!: Festivals, Carnivals, and Feast Days from Around the World.* Photographs by Barnabas Kindersley. 1997. Hardcover: DK. 64 pages. Ages 10–13. Of interest to younger children. NONFICTION.

This oversized book shows children in many countries and the holidays they celebrate. For each holiday, a large photograph of a child dominates the page, with one paragraph that describes the holiday and another from the child's point of view. The rest of each page consists of smaller photos with long, descriptive captions about clothing, food, ceremonies, and other celebratory customs. The open design, excellent photographs, and personable children make this a good way to learn about holidays around the world.

Gardening

Azarian, Mary. *A Gardener's Alphabet*. 2000. Hardcover: Houghton. 32 pages. Ages 3–7. PICTURE BOOK.

For each letter of the alphabet, this beautiful book shows a wood-block print that celebrates gardening. Arbor, bulbs, and compost start the book off. Gardening tools, flowers and vegetables, and different gardening tasks provide most of the subjects. Many of the illustrations show a child, or a child and an adult gardening together. The gracefully composed prints by a Caldecott-winning artist feature rich colors and depict the pleasures of gardening in all seasons.

Ehlert, Lois. *Planting a Rainbow*. 1988. Hardcover and paperback: Harcourt. 32 pages. Ages 3–7. PICTURE BOOK.

Bold colors leap off the page in this tribute to flower gardens. Imaginative graphics show the beginnings of a flower garden and follow it as it grows. Greenery marked by labeled sticks soon turns into magnificently bright flowers. After the garden is blooming profusely, the book divides the flowers by color, with a series of pages that get progressively bigger. This unusually vibrant book will inspire some ideas for next year's flower garden.

Doyle, Malachy. *Jody's Beans*. Illustrated by Judith Allibone. 1999. Hardcover: Candlewick. 32 pages. Ages 3–8. PICTURE BOOK.

This charming British import will inspire readers to grow scarlet runner beans on teepeelike poles when they see young Jody's success. Jody's grandfather comes to visit and the two of them plant twelve beans in a circle. He advises her via telephone how to water and thin the beans, then visits again to construct the simple teepee. The splendid red flowers and delicious beans amply reward Jody's patience and work. Simple watercolors with details that children will enjoy show a close family and a happy young gardener.

Stewart, Sarah. *The Gardener.* **Illustrated by David Small. 1997. Hardcover: Farrar, Straus & Giroux. Paperback: Sunburst. 40 pages. Ages 3–8. PICTURE BOOK.**

Set during the Depression, this memorable story is told through Lydia Grace's letters to her family when financial reasons send her to stay with her uncle in the city. Quirky illustrations with an old-fashioned air create a bleak urban setting that Lydia Grace immediately improves with flowers everywhere. Although her baker uncle never smiles, she wins his heart while she also makes a paradise out of an empty rooftop. A tribute to flowers and the strength of the human spirit, this is a Caldecott Honor Book.

Lisle, Janet Taylor. *The Lost Flower Children.* **Illustrated by Satomi Ichikawa. 1999. Hardcover: Philomel. 122 pages. Ages 8–12. FICTION.**

After their mother dies, nine-year-old Olivia and five-year-old Nellie have to go live with their great-aunt Minty while their father travels for work. Aunt Minty's garden turns out to be the cure for Nellie's unreasonable behavior and understandable fears, which Olivia has been trying to help with on her own. As the summer progresses, the children solve a mystery among the flowers based on a story from the past. The fine writing and sympathetic characters will pull readers into this fine novel.

Lerner, Carol. *My Indoor Garden.* **1999. Hardcover: Morrow. 48 pages. Ages 8–14. NONFICTION.**

This attractive book will please plant lovers with its charming illustrations and useful advice. In clear, concise writing, the author explains everything a child needs to know to grow indoor plants, with detailed information on light, water, soil, fertilizer, potting, pests, and more. It also describes ways to start plants rather than buy them. The final two pages give a chart of common houseplants, their characteristics, and their needs. Outstanding nonfiction. Also see the author's *My Backyard Garden.*

Rosen, Michael J. *Down to Earth.* **1998. Hardcover: Harcourt. 64 pages. Ages 9–13. Of interest to younger children. NONFICTION.**

In this handsome volume, forty-one children's writers and illustrators reflect on gardens and nature. Each page has a reminiscence about a childhood garden or a reflection about a current one. Many well-known illustrators created the pictures to go with their writing, and Rosen illustrated the rest, resulting in a surprisingly harmonious variety of pictures. Twenty pages at the end present garden activities and recipes related to gardens. A pleasure to look at, read, and use for projects.

Watts, Claire, and Alexandra Parsons. *Plants: Make It Work!* **1993. Hardcover: World Book. Paperback: Aladdin. 48 pages. Ages 9–14. NONFICTION.**

Subtitled "A Creative, Hands-On Approach to Science," this experiment and crafts book explores the principles behind garden flowers and vegetables. It looks at classifying plants, how bulbs grow, measuring plant growth, how plants absorb water, and more. For each topic, it gives step-by-step directions for an informative project such as pressing flowers and making natural dyes. One in an excellent series that makes science enjoyable, this will give young gardeners a better understanding of their natural materials.

Lovejoy, Sharon. *Roots, Shoots, Buckets & Boots: Gardening Together with Children.* **1999. Hardcover and paperback: Workman. 158 pages. Ages 9–14. Of interest to younger children. NONFICTION.**

This lovely book, which can be used by children or parents or both together, has child-oriented projects and enticing illustrations. It explains the projects clearly, with information added by the watercolors. It opens with the "Top 20 Plants for Kids," then explains how to make relatively easy theme gardens including a sunflower house; a flower maze; a garden of giant vegetables, and six more wonderful small gardens. It closes with gardening basics and a list of resources with many Web sites. Also see the author's *Hollyhock Days* and *Sunflower Houses.*

Burnett, Frances Hodgson. *The Secret Garden.* **Illustrated by Tasha Tudor. 1911. Hardcover and paperback: Harper. 358 pages. Ages 10–13. Of interest to younger children. FICTION.**

Few gardens are as magical as the one in this classic children's book. When orphaned Mary Lennox moves from India to England to live with her uncle, her life is lonely until she finds a locked garden. The idea of bringing the neglected plants and trees back to life brings her to life as well. With her sickly cousin Colin, a local boy named Dickon, and some help from the gardener, Mary transforms the garden using her strong will and determination. An enduring favorite full of garden lore and plants.

Bauer, Joan. *Squashed*. 1992. Paperback: Laurel Leaf. 208 pages. Ages 10–14. FICTION.

Sixteen-year-old Ellie is devoting herself to raising a huge pumpkin to win the Rock River Pumpkin Weigh-In. But she faces hazards like pumpkin thieves, bad weather, and a father who thinks she should study more and garden less. Meanwhile, a new boy in town who grows champion corn catches Ellie's eye. Can Ellie and her pumpkin, Max, win? Can she attract the corn grower and convince her father that pumpkins matter? Ellie's hilarious voice and the eccentric citizens of Rock River make this a pleasure to read.

Fleischman, Paul. *Seedfolks*. Illustrated by Judy Pedersen. 1997. Hardcover and paperback: Harper. 80 pages. Ages 11–14. FICTION.

Brief vignettes introduce characters who live in the poor part of a city. One immigrant girl plants beans in an empty lot, attracting the help and attention of a few others. Slowly the lot becomes a community garden. The gardeners, who have moved to the city from around the world and around the United States, create a varied garden and rich social interaction, but also encounter a few problems to resolve. A slim but powerful book about building a community.

Games, Hobbies, Toys, and Magic Tricks

Freeman, Don. *Corduroy*. 1968. Hardcover: Viking. Paperback: Puffin. 32 pages. Ages 2–6. PICTURE BOOK.

The teddy bear Corduroy, who lives in a store's toy department, realizes one day that he is missing a button. He sets off after the store closes to find a replacement, leading to a series of funny adventures in the store. In the morning, Corduroy wakes up to the smiling face of a girl who has come to take him home. This simple story, with its apt scratchboard pictures, has captivated children for decades. Followed by the equally delightful *A Pocket for Corduroy*.

Stuve-Bodeen, Stephanie. *Elizabeti's Doll*. Illustrated by Christy Hale. 1998. Hardcover: Lee & Low. 32 pages. Ages 3–7. PICTURE BOOK.

In a story that celebrates the imagination, Elizabeti watches her mother with the family's new baby and wants a baby, too. She finds a baby-sized rock, which she names Eva, and imitates her mother's actions: washing the baby, feeding it, and carrying it on her back in a "kanga," a cloth. She even diapers it and is "very relieved to find that Eva's bottom was still clean." A small crisis near the end is happily resolved. Rich collages, with many colorful cloths, convey the Tanzanian setting.

Caudill, Rebecca. *The Best-Loved Doll.* **Illustrated by Elliott Gilbert. 1962. Paperback: Henry Holt. 64 pages. Ages 3–8. FICTION.**

In this old-fashioned book, Betsy loves all four of her dolls. When she gets a party invitation that says to bring one doll, it's a difficult choice. The invitation says that prizes will go to the oldest doll, the best-dressed, and the doll who can do the most things. Three of Betsy's dolls would be perfect, but after five years of love and play that have left her the worse for wear, all the fourth doll does is smile. Betsy's choice leads to a happy ending.

Clements, Andrew. *Workshop.* **Illustrated by David Wisniewski. 1999. Hardcover: Clarion. 32 pages. Ages 3–8. PICTURE BOOK.**

Extraordinary cut-paper illustrations and a short text pay tribute to old-fashioned hand tools. Each double-page spread focuses on one tool, personified in a poetic description: "Axe is a chopper, a splitter, a sudden rusher. / Axe finds the board that hides in the log. / Axe is the great divider." The large pictures show a boy apprentice helping a group of men build a merry-go-round whose ornate designs highlight the intricacy of the cut-paper artwork.

Kleven, Elisa. *The Puddle Pail.* **1997. Hardcover: Dutton. Paperback: Puffin. 32 pages. Ages 3–8. PICTURE BOOK.**

Two crocodile brothers amble to a beach where Sol, the practical brother, enthusiastically collects seashells and seaweed, and urges Ernst to join him. But the more creative Ernst makes imaginative collections of things like clouds and puddles, which Sol slowly comes to appreciate. Joyful collage illustrations express the spirit of the story with bright colors and a variety of textures, full of the sort of details that collectors will appreciate. A wonderful tribute to those who march to a different drummer.

Scruggs, Afi. *Jump Rope Magic.* **Illustrated by David Diaz. 2000. Hardcover: Scholastic. 32 pages. Ages 3–8. PICTURE BOOK.**

Exuberant paintings set the tone for this joyful story about a girl who loves to jump rope. Her friends turn the rope for Shameka as she shouts out rhymes and they answer in a call-and-response rhythm. The other girls flee at the sight of "Mean Miss Minnie," a crabby neighbor, but Shameka pulls her into jumping. Well-known rhymes such as "Cinderella dressed in yellow" and "Shimmy, shimmy ko ko bop" combine with an irresistible original rhyming text in this magical jump rope tale.

Wyler, Rose, and Gerald Ames. *Spooky Tricks.* **Illustrated by S. D. Schindler. 1994 Revised Edition. Hardcover and paperback: Harper. 64 pages. Ages 6–9. EASY READER.**

This newly illustrated version of an old favorite offers simple directions in an easy-to-read format for doing magic tricks. The tricks all have a spooky component, although they are not truly scary. Several rely on uncomplicated optical illusions, while others require basic sleight-of-hand. Many use strings, handkerchiefs, coins, and other common items. Only a few call for complicated props and helpers. With suggestions for patter and tips for performing, this is a fine starting point for aspiring magicians.

Silbaugh, Elizabeth. *Let's Play Cards: A First Book of Card Games.* **Illustrated by Jef Kaminsky. 1996. Hardcover: Simon & Schuster. Paperback: Aladdin. 48 pages. Ages 6–10. NONFICTION.**

Beginning readers will enjoy learning, or refreshing their memories of, five simple card games in this accessible book.

After an explanation of basic facts about cards, the short chapters describe War, Concentration, Go Fish, Crazy Eights, and Clock Solitaire. The rules are described clearly enough for novices to start playing. The cartoonish drawings feature a "card shark," a shark who gives advice and tells jokes in asides. A good way to learn a pastime that can lead to hours of fun.

Fox, Paula. *Maurice's Room*. Illustrated by Ingrid Fetz. 1966. Hardcover: Macmillan. Paperback: Aladdin. 64 pages. Ages 7–10. FICTION.

In this short, timeless novel, Maurice baffles his parents by collecting objects from the urban streets around their apartment. His small room brims over with an assortment of strange things: dead beetles, dried tar balls, pieces of colored glass, salamanders, cigar boxes, a rusty grater, and much more. In each chapter, collecting gets Maurice and his best friend into trouble, yet he likes it far more than getting new presents. The happy ending hints at far more collecting in the future.

Walker, Lester. *Carpentry for Children*. 1982. Hardcover: Consumers Union. 208 pages. Ages 7–14. NONFICTION.

In a series of careful explanations and projects, Walker guides children through the basics of carpentry. He opens with a description of each major tool, its purposes and how to use it, then provides instructions for building a workbench, toolbox, and saw horses. Each project starts with a list of tools and materials, then goes on to demonstrate the steps in line drawings plus photographs of children enjoying the work. Projects for seven-to-eleven-year-olds include blocks, a tugboat, and a lemonade stand, and for children eleven to fourteen, a raft, stilts, and a coaster car, among others. An excellent manual for would-be carpenters.

Cole, Joanna, and Stephanie Calmenson. *Marbles: 101 Ways to Play*. Illustrated by Alan Tiegreen. 1998. Hardcover: Morrow. Paperback: Beech Tree. 128 pages. Ages 8–12. NONFICTION.

Marbles are an old folk tradition, and rules vary by where the players learned their games. This lively guide compiles lots of versions of marble games from easy to difficult. First come the basics: kinds of marbles, shooting methods, ways to decide who goes first, and a glossary of marble terms. The rest of the book gives step-by-step directions for circle games, hole games, shooting games, and others. Humorous pictures make the rules and moves easy to understand.

Cook, Nick. *Roller Coasters, or I Had So Much Fun, I Almost Puked*. 1998. Hardcover: Carolrhoda. 56 pages. Ages 8–12. NONFICTION.

Who invented the roller coaster? How do modern roller coasters work? What are the different kinds? This entertaining book answers those questions and more, accompanied by photographs and illustrations of roller coasters old and new. It discusses their history, their effect on the human body, and modern design techniques. A sidebar gives "Top Ten Tips for a Scarier Ride." Roller-coaster fans will appreciate the details on specific roller coasters and Web sites for further research.

Gryski, Camilla. *Cat's Cradle, Owl's Eyes: A Book of String Games*. Illustrated by Tom Sankey. 1984. Paperback: Morrow. 80 pages. Ages 8–12. NONFICTION.

This careful guide explains how to play string games and form string figures with step-by-step directions. After a useful introduction about terminology and basic positions, it goes on to describe forty figures or games, some for two people, each depicted in detail with diagrams of the movements. Seventeen pages are devoted to the complicated game Cat's Cradle. A brief note with each game tells what it is called and where it originated. For more string games, try Gryski's other books.

Selznick, Brian. *The Houdini Box.* **1991. Hardcover: Knopf. 64 pages. Ages 8–12. FICTION.**

The black-and-white pen drawings on nearly every other page of this book lend it an old-fashioned, sometimes comic, air. The simple story concerns Victor, a ten-year-old boy who idolizes the magician Houdini and has the luck to meet him in a train station. Houdini bequeaths the boy a box, but only when Victor has grown up does he realize its importance through a strange coincidence. A good read-aloud, this captures children's interest, for what child wouldn't like to be more like Houdini?

Hahn, Mary Downing. *The Doll in the Garden: A Ghost Story.* **1989. Hardcover: Houghton. Paperback: Camelot. 128 pages. Ages 8–13. FICTION.**

When ten-year-old Ashley moves into an old house with her mother, she is drawn to the overgrown garden despite the crabby landlady's warnings to keep out. She and her new friend Kristi find an old doll there and encounter a mysterious white cat that has no shadow. It is the cat that leads Ashley, and then Kristi, into a strange ghostly adventure concerning the lovely old doll. One of many ghost stories by a popular author.

Friedhoffer, Bob. *The Magic Show: A Guide for Young Magicians.* **Illustrated by Linda Eisenberg. 1994. Hardcover: Millbrook. 80 pages. Ages 9–13. NONFICTION.**

This unusually useful book gives directions for eighteen magic tricks and explains in detail how to put on a show with a sense of theater. It describes how to create a stage personality, add music, publicize a show, and use a magician's table, with a diagram for constructing one. The tricks are divided into three categories: opening an act, the act's middle, and tricks for a strong finish. The author offers five routines composed of three tricks that work well together.

Needham, Kate. *Collecting Things*. Illustrated by David Eaton. 1995. Paperback: Usborne. 32 pages. Ages 9–13. NONFICTION.

Have you ever thought of starting a collection but don't know what to collect? This colorful book goes through fourteen types of collecting, including stamps, marbles, shells, rocks, fossils, autographs, coins, and more. For each topic, two or three pages suggest where to find the objects and give tips for displaying the collections. The final chapter briefly highlights eleven other collecting ideas. A good overview of collecting, although you will need more detailed books once you've chosen a hobby.

Bauer, Joan. *Sticks*. 1996. Hardcover: Delacorte. Paperback: Bantam. 182 pages. Ages 9–14. FICTION.

Geometry turns out to be a great way to plan pool strategy in this absorbing novel. Ten-year-old Mickey's family owns a pool hall and his long-dead father was a pool champion. When Mickey practices for the pool hall's Youth Tournament, he finds that the mathematical skill of calculating angles on the pool table improves his game. With help from an old family friend, his chances for winning look good, until he does something foolish. He still stands a chance, but it's not going to be easy.

Presto, Fay. *Magic for Kids*. 1999. Hardcover: Kingfisher. 72 pages. Ages 9–14. NONFICTION.

With a professional air, this book carefully describes twenty-five magic tricks and gives general tips for performing.

A symbol indicates how hard the trick is, with plenty of fairly simple tricks for beginners. Many use scarves, cards, coins, ropes, and paper tubes. Detailed instructions with drawings and photographs tell how to prepare the simple props and how to perform the tricks, with suggested patter for the performance.

Cassidy, John. *The Klutz Yo-Yo Book.* **Illustrated by Sara Boore. 1987. Paperback: Klutz Press. 80 pages. Ages 9 and up. NONFICTION.**

Most readers will spend their time on the first half of this book, which, after a few pages of basic technique, demonstrates yo-yo tricks. Illustrations combine with clearly written directions to explain each trick. The moves build on each other and get increasingly difficult, ending in two tricks that require a yo-yo in each hand. The rest of the book gives a history of the yo-yo, followed by a brief bibliography. If you buy the book, rather than check it out from the library, it comes with a wooden yo-yo.

Keene, Raymond. *The Simon & Schuster Pocket Book of Chess.* **1989. Paperback: Aladdin. 192 pages. Ages 11–14. NONFICTION.**

This excellent guide by an international chess grandmaster takes a thorough approach to the game with instructions for beginners and more advanced information for current players. After a short history, the book sets forth the basic rules and explains standardized chess notation, using many diagrams. Chapters discuss each piece and how it moves, opening moves, the middle game, and the endgame, with quizzes to check the reader's comprehension. Final sections, now out of date, discuss chess champions, and computers and chess.

Sign Language
and Secret Codes

Rankin, Laura. *The Handmade Alphabet*. 1991. Hardcover: Dial. Paperback: Puffin. 32 pages. Ages 3–8. PICTURE BOOK.

This is a beautifully illustrated introduction to the alphabet of ASL, American Sign Language. Soft, colored-pencil drawings move from A to Z, each with a hand that shows the sign for the letter, and an object or objects that start with that letter. The cleverly designed artwork uses young and old hands, and black and white ones. Thoughtful and elegant, this is an exceptional book on a subject that fascinates many children.

Wheeler, Cindy. *Simple Signs*. 1997. Hardcover: Viking. Paperback: Puffin. 32 pages. Ages 3–8. PICTURE BOOK NON-FICTION.

In this simple introduction to American Sign Language, each page displays a hand sign of interest to children, starting with "hello" and ending with "love." Color pictures show the object, emotion, or action described, such as a dog, a car, or eating. Next to the picture is a line drawing of a child signing the word, with arrows to show movement. A good launching pad for learning signs, accessible even to preschoolers. Also see the author's *More Simple Signs*.

Fain, Kathleen. *Handsigns: A Sign Language Alphabet.* **1993. Hardcover and paperback: Chronicle. 40 pages. Ages 3–9. PICTURE BOOK NONFICTION.**

Each page from A to Z shows the letter in upper and lower case large print, the hand sign in a box, and a large color illustration of an animal whose name begins with the letter. The hand signs are easy to understand and imitate. The introduction has a note on American Sign Language and a short history of manual speech; an appendix lists the animals' names with a short description of each. An attractive introduction to finger spelling with the American Manual Alphabet.

Millman, Isaac. *Moses Goes to a Concert.* **1998. Hardcover: Farrar, Straus & Giroux. 32 pages. Ages 5–9. PICTURE BOOK.**

Moses is deaf but he can feel vibrations from his new drum through his hands and feet. When he and his fellow students go to a concert, they sit up front and hold balloons, which help them feel the music. Afterward, the orchestra's stocking-footed percussionist, who is deaf, invites them to visit her onstage. Throughout, small frames show Moses signing sentences, and final pages show more signs for readers to try. An upbeat story that integrates sign language well. Followed by *Moses Goes to School.*

Patterson, Francine. *Koko-Love! Conversations with a Signing Gorilla.* **Photographs by Ronald H. Cohn. 1999. Hardcover: Dutton. 32 pages. Ages 5–10. NONFICTION.**

This updated introduction to Koko starts out with the gorilla at her own computer, where she answers questions in an online interview. Koko, who has her own version of sign language and recognizes more than two thousand words, demonstrates some of them in a series of photographs. This conversational essay, accompanied by many color photographs, presents an irresistible portrait of Koko, and her relationship with her fellow gorillas, her pet kitten, and her "adopted mom" Dr. Patterson.

Schwartz, Alvin. *The Cat's Elbow and Other Secret Languages*. Illustrated by Margot Zemach. 1982. Hardcover and paperback: Farrar, Straus & Giroux. 82 pages. Ages 9–14. NONFICTION.

Children are not the only ones who have invented and used secret languages, as this intriguing book makes clear. Folklorist Schwartz starts with the well-known language Pig Latin, then describes and demonstrates eleven more secret languages from around the world. Each is explained with examples, and readers can practice by using the clever exercises provided, with answers at the back of the book. Eat-gray Un-fay (great fun)!

Janeczko, Paul B. *Loads of Codes and Secret Ciphers*. 1984. Hardcover: Macmillan. 108 pages. Ages 10–14. NONFICTION.

This outstanding book on codes and ciphers gives readers dozens of ways to communicate in secret. It starts by introducing types of concealment, with fascinating examples such as hoboes' signs and other secret languages. It describes ways to conceal messages using grids, playing cards, and even carved wood. For complicated methods, examples and exercises let the reader practice. A book that will lead to hours of playing around with codes and ciphers.

Durrett, Deanne. *Unsung Heroes of World War II: The Story of the Navajo Code Talkers.* 1998. Hardcover: Facts on File. 120 pages. Ages 12–14. NONFICTION.

This engrossing book relates how Navajo Indians helped win World War II, specifically at Guadacanal and Iwo Jima. It gives background on Navajos, then describes the events that led to twenty-nine Navajos enlisting in the marines and creating a secret code based on their language. In the Pacific, they transmitted important messages in the code, which was never broken. A remarkable piece of history that will appeal to those interested in war, secret codes, and gripping true stories.

Visual Puzzles and Optical Illusions

Steiner, Joan. *Look-Alikes*. **1998. Hardcover: Little, Brown. 32 pages. Ages 3–8. PICTURE BOOK.**

This instant hit with children features large, double-page pictures in which everyday objects serve as building blocks. For example, in a playground scene, dominoes form steps, pencils serve as the poles on a swing set, and a tortilla chip is the sail on a small boat, to a name only a few of the hidden items. Children can simply enjoy the ingenuity of the pictures or search for specific objects from lists at the back. Hard to put down, this is the first in a series.

Johnson, Stephen T. *Alphabet City*. **1995. Hardcover: Viking. Paperback: Puffin. 32 pages. Ages 4–8. PICTURE BOOK.**

Extraordinary oil paintings that look like photographs illustrate this clever alphabet book. Each page has a painting of a letter formed by an urban object. "A" is the end of a sawhorse, "B" is created by twists in a fire escape, "C" is the curve of a cathedral window. Children love looking closely to find the letter, and then looking for letters in their own surroundings. This wonderful lesson in visual literacy is a Caldecott Honor Book.

Marzollo, Jean. *I Spy: A Book of Picture Riddles.* **Photographs by Walter Wick. 1992. Hardcover: Scholastic. 32 pages. Ages 4–8. PICTURE BOOK.**

For children who like to find things in pictures, this book hits the mark. Each large double-page spread presents a bright photograph crowded with small items, based on a theme, like nature or sports. A rhyme tells the reader what to look for: "I spy a shovel, a long silver chain / A little toy horse, a track for a train." Extra Credit Riddles challenge readers to find more listed objects. One in a very popular series.

Hoban, Tana. *Look Book.* **1997. Hardcover: Greenwillow. 32 pages. Ages 4–8. PICTURE BOOK NONFICTION.**

On the first page of this book, readers look through a hole and see a grainy yellow and brown fragment of a photograph. The challenge is to identify the whole object from the fragment. A turn of the page shows a color photograph of the object, and then, another photograph of the object set in a larger context. Then, on to the next challenge. Children love identifying the object and, after they have discovered the answers, stumping friends. Also see *Look Look Look* and *Look Again!*

Banyai, Istvan. *Zoom.* **1995. Hardcover: Viking. Paperback: Puffin. 64 pages. Ages 4–9. PICTURE BOOK.**

This wordless book takes the reader on a visual journey that has unexpected twists and turns throughout. Perspectives change constantly, keeping the viewer alert and surprised. Each picture shows the same scene from farther and farther away, yet that simple description does not convey the startling quality of the visual experience. The book will mesmerize children, who will want to share it with their friends. Also see the sequel *Re-Zoom.*

Handford, Martin. *Where's Waldo?* 1987. Hardcover: Candle-wick. 32 pages. Ages 4–9. PICTURE BOOK.

Children who like to lose themselves in detailed pictures enjoy this book and its sequels. Each large double-page spread shows a scene packed with small figures in a setting like the beach, a ski slope, or a train station. Instructions tell the reader what tiny figures to look for in every picture, with a choice of levels of difficulty. Besides searching, children may enjoy the incidents and humor packed into each scene. While not as popular as they once were, these books still appeal to many children.

Snape, Juliet and Charles Snape. *Marvelous Mazes.* 1994. Paperback: Abrams. 32 pages. Ages 5–9. PICTURE BOOK.

Make your way through a complicated castle to escape, or through an adobe city full of twists and turns. Twelve colorful mazes fill the large pages of this inviting book. Each maze works its way through a distinctive setting, including a pirate ship, troll world, and enchanted forest. Dead ends and deceptive turns will keep children busy trying to reach the appointed destination in the picture. Small versions in the back show possible solutions. Lots of fun.

Wick, Walter. *Walter Wick's Optical Tricks.* 1998. Hardcover: Scholastic. 45 pages. Ages 8–14. NONFICTION.

Be prepared to study the photographs in this visually challenging book from the photographer of the "I Spy" series. Each page illustrates an optical trick in a colorful photo, with comments and questions on the facing page to make you think about what you are seeing. An appendix supplies more information about the optical principles. This fine set of sharp photos offers an effective, enjoyable way for children to sharpen their powers of observation and thinking.

Jennings, Terry. *101 Amazing Optical Illusions: Fantastic Visual Tricks*. 1996. Hardcover and paperback: Sterling. 88 pages. Ages 8 and up. NONFICTION.

Readers can spend hours with this book, staring at the optical illusions and following directions to make visual crafts like flip books and kaleidoscopes. The large colorful pages offer a range of illusions: op art, aftereffects, pictures that shift shapes, illusions about perceived size, and much more. Although short on explanations, the book provides plenty of entertainment as well as an introduction to a popular subject.

N. E. Thing Enterprises. *Magic Eye III*. 1994. Hardcover: Andrews and McMeel. 32 pages. Ages 10 and up. NONFICTION.

A brief introduction gives instructions on the best ways to use your eyes to appreciate the artwork in this unusual collection of pictures. The rest of the nearly wordless book consists of colorful 3–D pictures, with a guide at the back to show the images the reader is looking for. Once you have the knack for looking at these 3-D pictures, which is not easy for most people at first, this and the other books in the series are hard to resist.

Science, Math, and Technology

Computers and Robots

Novak, Matt. *The Robobots.* 1999. Hardcover: DK Ink. 32 pages. Ages 3–7. PICTURE BOOK.

Colorful rounded illustrations, reminiscent of Mickey Mouse cartoons, show a robot family moving into a traditional neighborhood full of small frame houses and picket fences. The Robobots step out of their strange vehicle, excited to meet the neighbors, but everyone is afraid of them. When the neighbors band together to ask the new family to leave, the Robobots welcome them so merrily into their odd home, complete with walking television sets and flying easy chairs, that soon all are friends.

Pinkney, Brian. *Cosmo and the Robot*. 2000. Hardcover: Greenwillow. 32 pages. Ages 3–7. PICTURE BOOK.

Cosmo lives on Mars where his best friend is his robot Rex. But when Rex starts acting like a monster, Cosmo's parents insist on hauling him to an asteroid dump. They give Cosmo a belt of supersonic tools to cheer him up, which he wears one day when he and his sister, Jewel, go rock collecting. Out in the bleak landscape, Cosmo finds an abandoned terrain rover and takes it apart, then comes up with a way to fix Rex, too. Space suits, a space-age home, and terrain rovers augment the futuristic fun.

Brown, Marc. *Arthur's Computer Disaster*. 1997. Hardcover and paperback: Little, Brown. 32 pages. Ages 3–8. PICTURE BOOK.

Arthur loves to play the computer game Deep, Dark Sea more than anything. One morning he hopes to play but his mother needs the computer for her work. When she leaves for a little while, Arthur and his friend disobey her instructions not to touch the computer and start playing. Disaster strikes when the boys drop the keyboard and the screen goes blank. Nothing they do fixes it until Mom comes home and saves the day. Right on target in the usual amusing Arthur style.

Palatini, Margie. *Elf Help: http://www.falala.com*. Illustrated by Mike Reed. 1997. Hardcover: Hyperion. 32 pages. Ages 3–8. PICTURE BOOK.

Santa's list on a computer printout? The elf Alfred, "a wiz-of-a-won computer hacker," has put children's requests into a database. Santa is doubtful about the high-tech idea, but he relents and inserts Alfred's floppy disk into his new sleigh computer. But Alfred has input the wrong gift under each child's name, so a girl in the desert gets ice skates and a boy in

Alaska gets a surfboard. Luckily, they love their strange gifts and all is well. Bright acrylic paintings add sparkle to this cyber Christmas story.

Rodda, Emily. *Power and Glory.* **Illustrated by Geoff Kelly. 1994. Hardcover: Greenwillow. 32 pages. Ages 3–8. PICTURE BOOK.**

On the cover of this snappy book, a round-faced boy manipulates a video game remote control, while his glasses reflect villains from the video screen. "For my birthday, I get a video game: Power and Glory. Yes!" it opens. The boy begins playing and just as he gets into a dangerous spot, his mother calls him. Back at the game, he escapes that danger and encounters another, when his brothers interrupt. And so the engrossing game continues, shown in zany wild drawings, until a final twist.

Pilkey, Dav. *Ricky Ricotta's Giant Robot.* **Illustrated by Martin Ontiveros. 2000. Hardcover: Scholastic. 112 pages. Ages 6–9. FICTION.**

This zany book about a huge robot incorporates "flip" pages for readers to animate by flipping them back and forth. Ricky Ricotta, a small mouse, likes school but dreads the local bullies. Luckily, a huge robot created by a mad scientist comes to his rescue, defying the scientist's instructions to destroy the town and attaching himself to Ricky as a pet. In brief chapters, good overcomes evil more than once in comic book fashion. The boldly outlined pictures on every page are as silly and appealing as the story.

Kazunas, Charnan, and Tom Kazunas. *Personal Computers*. 1997. Hardcover and paperback: Children's Press. 48 pages. Ages 7–9. Of interest to younger children. NONFICTION.

This solid introduction to personal computers begins with a brief history of computers, then goes on to explain the most widely used computer terms. Two short chapters discuss different kinds of software, floppy disks, and CD-ROMs. The final chapter mentions the Internet but not in detail. An appendix recommends books and Web sites about computers. With frequent color photographs, unusually large typeface and lots of white space, this book will appeal to young readers.

Keller, Holly. *Angela's Top-Secret Computer Club*. 1998. Hardcover: Greenwillow. 64 pages. Ages 7–10. FICTION.

Who has infiltrated the computer system at Angela's school and messed up the report cards? It's the last day of school, and Angela vows that she and her computer club friends will solve the mystery before the summer is over. When her friend Albert starts getting mysterious e-mail messages, the club realizes they are clues and eventually Angela puts together the pieces of the puzzle. Large print and occasional pictures makes this lively computer mystery accessible to younger readers.

Sonenklar, Carol. *Robots Rising*. Illustrated by John Kaufmann. 1999. Hardcover: Henry Holt. 100 pages. Ages 8–12. NONFICTION.

This book about robots today begins by describing hazardous jobs robots do, like dealing with dangers at nuclear power plants and in police work. Black-and-white photographs and drawings, which are not as good as the text, show robots that look something like small tractors. One chapter looks at robots in the space program, followed by a fascinating overview of robots modeled on insects. A glossary, bibliography, and list of Web sites about building robots complete the picture.

Gralla, Preston. *Online Kids: A Young Surfer's Guide to Cyberspace*. 1999 Revised Edition. Hardcover and paperback: John Wiley. 278 pages. Ages 8–14. Of interest to younger children. NONFICTION.

This substantial book starts out with the basics: equipment, safety, search engines, chat groups, and e-mail. The remaining two hundred pages describe Web sites of interest to kids, covering a wide range of topics including astronomy, writing and reading, sports, pets, hobbies, games, and much more. Each Web site is described briefly and rated for usefulness and coolness. A fine tool for browsing, with practical applications. The last section explains how to create a home page.

Gutman, Dan. *Virtually Perfect*. 1998. Hardcover and paperback: Hyperion. 128 pages. Ages 9–12. FICTION.

Lucas Turner, known as Yip, comes from a family of F/X, or special effects, experts. Yip's father has state-of-the-art F/X software that he claims can create excellent virtual actors. Yip secretly tries it and, with help from his sister, ends up with a brilliant, handsome teenage actor named Victor. To their shock, Victor emerges from the computer, looking completely human. But Victor doesn't have a conscience, which begins an endless run of trouble. A quick, enjoyable read about technology getting out of hand.

Cooper, Susan. *The Boggart*. 1993. Hardcover: McElderry. Paperback: Aladdin. 196 pages. Ages 9–13. FICTION.

Computers and ancient magic share the stage in this outstanding fantasy about a boggart, a mischievous Celtic spirit, who disrupts the lives of two siblings. By accident, Jess and Emily bring the invisible boggart home to Canada from Scotland. When it starts playing sly tricks on the family, the children get blamed. But before they can send him home, the boggart encounters modern technology and jeopardizes his very existence. An original, compelling story. Followed by *The Boggart and the Monster*.

Wallace, Mark. *101 Things to Do on the Internet.* **Illustrated by Isaac Quayle and Zöe Wray. 1999. Hardcover: Usborne. Paperback: E D C. 64 pages. Ages 9–14. NONFICTION.**

This thoughtful guide opens with the basics like how to use search engines, send e-mail, and design an e-mail signature. It gives specific Web sites, most of which seem likely to endure, of interest areas that kids can explore on the Web: outer space, music, animals, sports, chess, race cars, and cooking, among others. Several paragraphs with helpful illustrations explain each Web activity. Safety tips appear throughout. A fine way to begin Web surfing.

Skurzynski, Gloria. *Cyberstorm: A Novel with a Virtual Reality Twist.* **1995. Hardcover: Macmillan. 138 pages. Ages 10–13. FICTION.**

What happens when virtual reality becomes more real than virtual? Set in 2015, this fast-paced novel revolves around a virtual reality machine that allows people to relive their favorite memories. They can hear, see, and smell the past as if they were there. But when eleven-year-old Darcy ends up in the machine experiencing an older woman's memories, something goes badly wrong and Darcy's life is threatened by dangers in the past. A page-turner about future technology gone wrong.

Hamilton, Jake. *Special Effects in Film and Television*. 1998. Hardcover: DK. 64 pages. Ages 10–14. NONFICTION.

In this oversized book about spectacular special effects, each double-page spread addresses one topic with a main paragraph plus many photographs accompanied by long captions. The book explains techniques behind fires, battles, explosions, storms, and tornadoes. It shows a step-by-step transformation of a man's head into a monster's and the digital creation of a dragon. Examples from well-known films illustrate effects from computer-generated imagery and old-fashioned methods.

Disasters

Beard, Darleen Bailey. *Twister*. Illustrated by Nancy Carpenter. 1999. Hardcover: Farrar, Straus & Giroux. 32 pages. Ages 3–7. PICTURE BOOK.

Enjoying a spring day, two children play on the porch and fool around with a wheelbarrow. Suddenly, such a strong storm hits that their mother sends the children into the cellar while she goes to get an elderly neighbor. When she doesn't come back, the children cope with their fear on their own. Afterward, they find their trailer worse for wear, but their mother and the neighbor are safe. Soft-focused pictures take off some of the edge but still communicate the danger and then the children's relief.

Jam, Teddy. *The Year of Fire*. Illustrated by Ian Wallace. 1992. Hardcover: McElderry. 32 pages. Ages 4–8. PICTURE BOOK.

With more text than most picture-story books, this tells of a brush fire in 1919 that burned a forest near the narrator's home in Canada. Since the family did not have a phone, the father rode for help when they saw the smoke. The narrator and his brother pitched in with the neighbors to fight the fire. Detailed pen-and-watercolor illustrations show the drama and danger of fighting the fire, and its effects on the countryside years later.

Kurtz, Jane. *River Friendly River Wild.* **Illustrated by Neil Brennan. 2000. Hardcover: Simon & Schuster. 32 pages. Ages 5–9. PICTURE BOOK.**

In 1997, the Red River flooded Grand Forks, North Dakota, displacing families and ruining homes. In unrhymed poems told in a girl's voice, readers feel her love of the river as well as the disaster's impact. Lovely glazed oil paintings reinforce the feelings in each poem. The girl's family leaves their house as the river rises, then their neighborhood. The flood ruins their possessions, but that is not the end of their troubles. An unusually moving portrait of a disaster and its effects.

Polacco, Patricia. *Tikvah Means Hope.* **1994. Hardcover: Doubleday. 32 pages. Ages 5–9. PICTURE BOOK.**

This moving story about a disastrous fire in urban California hills starts the day before the fire, when two children help an older neighbor build a sukkah to celebrate the harvest festival of Sukkoth. The children spend the night in the sukkah, a hut made from cloth, palm branches, and fruit. But the next day, the fire starts and although their families are safe, their houses burn. Stark pictures of the burned neighborhood depict the tragedy but the story ends on a hopeful note.

Simon, Seymour. *Earthquakes.* **1991. Hardcover: Morrow. Paperback: Mulberry. 32 pages. Ages 5–10. NONFICTION.**

This photo-essay, which will capture children's attention, explains the geological causes of earthquakes in clear terms, with informative diagrams and maps. It features dramatic photographs of earthquake damage, including pictures from the 1906 and 1989 San Francisco quakes. It explains the Richter scale and concludes with advice on what to do if an earthquake strikes. One in a terrific series about geological events and weather that includes *Volcanoes*, *Storms*, and *Icebergs and Glaciers*.

Ransom, Candice F. *Fire in the Sky*. Illustrated by Shelly O. Haas. 1997. Hardcover: Lerner. Paperback: Carolrhoda. 72 pages. Ages 8–11. FICTION.

Stenny knows all about the giant airship the *Hindenburg*, which lands at the Naval Air Station near his house in New Jersey. He dearly hopes that his older brother, a navy man, will get him a tour of the German dirigible. But when Stenny rides his bike to watch the *Hindenburg* land, he witnesses one of the greatest disasters of the century. The airship catches on fire, mayhem reigns, and Stenny, who has always longed to be a hero, has his chance to prove his courage. A short exciting novel.

Kehret, Peg. *The Volcano Disaster*. 1998. Hardcover: Pocket. Paperback: Minstrel. 136 pages. Ages 8–12. FICTION.

Sixth-grader Warren has to do a project on the volcano Mount St. Helens, which erupted in Washington State in 1980. But he would rather try to complete his deceased grandfather's invention, the "Instant Commuter," which theoretically sends the user to a place by aiming a pointer at a map. Warren mistakenly points it at a photograph of Mount St. Helens just before it erupted and sends himself there. A swift story based on a real disaster. One in a fiction series about disasters.

Kramer, Stephen. *Eye of the Storm: Chasing Storms with Warren Faidley*. Photographs by Warren Faidley. 1997. Hardcover: Putnam. Paperback: Paper Star. 48 pages. Ages 8–14. NONFICTION.

How did Warren Faidley shoot the breathtaking photographs of lightning, tornadoes, and hurricanes that fill this book? The author answers that question by describing several of Faidley's experiences in taking his amazing weather photographs. First, the photographer follows tornadoes in Oklahoma and Texas, then he photographs lightning in Arizona, and finally he goes to Florida for a major hurricane. Spectacular photographs illustrate the fascinating true story about an unusual career.

Vogel, Carole Garbuny. *Shock Waves Through Los Angeles: The Northridge Earthquake.* **1996. Hardcover: Little, Brown. 32 pages. Ages 8–14. NONFICTION.**

The dust jacket of this book will pull readers in with its photographs of earthquake damage: a house sliding down a cliff, a broken freeway, and a building collapsing in on itself. More photographs throughout the short book show similar damage as well as fires, burst pipes spouting water, and rescue teams at work. Diagrams help explain how earthquakes occur. The lively, concise narrative makes the Los Angeles earthquake feel real and frightening.

Lauber, Patricia. *Hurricanes: Earth's Mightiest Storms.* **1996. Hardcover: Scholastic. 64 pages. Ages 9–13. Of interest to younger children. NONFICTION.**

In 1938, a massive hurricane swept across Long Island, through New England, and on to Canada. The ocean surged into walls of water forty feet high. Less-sophisticated forecasting meant far less warning than people get today. This fine book compares the hurricane of 1938 with Hurricane Andrew in 1992, which also left massive destruction. It describes the causes of hurricanes and new developments in tracking them. Many photographs show the power of these amazing natural forces.

Ballard, Robert, and Rick Archbold. *Ghost Liners: Exploring the World's Greatest Lost Ships.* Illustrated by Ken Marschall. 1998. Hardcover: Little, Brown. 64 pages. Ages 9–14. NONFICTION.

Robert Ballard, known for finding the sunken *Titanic* in 1986, writes about the *Titanic* and four other huge ships that sank, including the *Andrea Doria*. First he reviews each event, then talks about his underwater exploration of the ship. Effective underwater photographs, artistic renderings, and other visual information fill the pages. When possible, he profiles a child who was aboard the ship. Certain to engage those who are mesmerized by past tragedies and sunken ships.

Ballard, Robert D. *Exploring the* Titanic. Illustrated by Ken Marschall. 1988. Hardcover and paperback: Scholastic. 64 pages. Ages 9–14. NONFICTION.

This popular volume reviews the tragic voyage of the *Titanic* and describes the recent exploration of its remains. The historical section uses vivid accounts from survivors, cross-section diagrams, photographs, and paintings to convey the 1912 tragedy. Oceanographer and adventurer Ballard then discusses his expeditions to find the ship and photograph its remains. Diagrams depict the equipment and vehicles used, and eerie underwater photographs show their findings.

Beil, Karen Magnuson. *Fire in Their Eyes: Wildfires and the People Who Fight Them.* 1999. Hardcover and paperback: Harcourt. 64 pages. Ages 9–14. NONFICTION.

To deal with a wilderness wildfire, a fire management officer can call in a ground or helicopter crew, a team of smoke jumpers, a crew of "hotshots," or all of them. Smoke jumpers parachute into wildfires; hotshots take on big fires, digging fire lines, setting backfires, and laying explosives. This dynamic book vividly recounts a hotshot's dangerous experience in an Idaho fire, then describes how smoke jumpers are trained. Excellent photographs show more about this challenging, wild work.

Bunting, Eve. SOS Titanic. 1996. Hardcover and paperback: Harcourt. 246 pages. Ages 9–14. FICTION.

Fifteen-year-old Barry is crossing the ocean on the *Titanic* to reunite with the parents he seldom sees. Although Barry is traveling first class, the other Irish passengers he knows are in steerage class. Two of them, Jonnie and Frank Flynn, have it out for Barry, but their sister Pegeen does him a kind turn. When the ship begins to sink, Barry has to choose between saving himself quickly and trying to help the others. Full of details about the lavish ship and its demise, likely to interest fans of the movie.

Tanaka, Shelley. *The Disaster of the* Hindenburg: *The Last Flight of the Greatest Airship Ever Built*. 1993. Hardcover: Scholastic. 64 pages. Ages 9–14. NONFICTION.

Before the *Hindenburg* went up in flames in 1937, German zeppelins had logged more than a million miles as the quickest, most convenient way to fly long distances. Far larger than modern jumbo jets or today's blimps, the *Hindenburg* was unusually expensive and luxurious. The author weaves facts into a narrative about two teenagers on the ill-fated flight, one who died and one who survived. A gripping story with a variety of well-chosen photographs, graphs, and other visual sidebars.

Cottonwood, Joe. *Quake!* 1995. Hardcover and paperback: Scholastic. 146 pages. Ages 10–13. FICTION.

Based on a 1989 earthquake in Northern California, this quick-moving novel centers on fourteen-year-old Franny and her friend Jennie, who are baby-sitting Franny's younger brother when the earthquake strikes. With no adults around, Franny proves her courage as she turns off dangerous gas mains in her house and others. The children help rescue a trapped neighbor, cope with scary aftershocks, and worry about the fate of their parents. A suspenseful modern-day survival story.

Murphy, Jim. *The Great Fire*. 1995. Hardcover and paperback: Scholastic. 144 pages. Ages 10–14. NONFICTION.
Murphy re-creates the Great Fire of 1871, which burned for thirty-one hours and destroyed central Chicago. He uses the vivid writings of four people who encountered the fire firsthand: a twelve-year-old girl who almost died, a newspaper reporter, a visitor from New York, and the *Chicago Tribune* editor in chief. Through their eyes, the reader experiences the sounds and sights of the burning city. Maps, etchings, photographs, and numerous quotes from primary sources create a sense of immediacy in this excellent Newbery Honor Book.

Ecology

Cowcher, Helen. *Rain Forest.* 1988. Hardcover: Farrar, Straus & Giroux. Paperback: Sunburst. 32 pages. Ages 3–7. PICTURE BOOK.

Striking paintings show colorful rain forest animals losing their habitat when machines start chopping down the trees in which they live. Humans are invading the homes of macaws, howler monkeys, blue morpho butterflies, sloths, and more. The animals panic, first because of the cutting and then from another danger: a flood. The flood drives out those destroying the rain forest, but how much longer will the animals be safe? An effective story about rain forest creatures and the dangers they face.

Glaser, Linda. *Our Big Home: An Earth Poem.* Illustrated by Elisa Kleven. 2000. Hardcover: Millbrook. 32 pages. Ages 3–8. PICTURE BOOK.

"We share air, water, soil, sky, sun, rain and being alive. And we all share one home, here on Earth. Our precious living home"—so concludes this poetic celebration. The lyrical text names animals, plants, and other elements of the earth as it reviews the things we all share. Sunny, mixed-media illustrations show children around the world enjoying its beauty and bounty. The message that all should care for the earth comes across not as a heavy-handed lesson but as a reminder of what we could lose.

Seuss, Dr. *The Lorax.* **1971. Hardcover: Random House. 64 pages. Ages 4–8. PICTURE BOOK.**

In this story about ecological dangers, a character called the Once-ler describes how he destroyed a beautiful country-side. He recalls arriving in a place with green grass, blue skies, and brightly colored Truffula trees. But inspired by greed, the Once-ler chops down all the trees to make useless but sellable products. The wise Lorax begs the Once-ler to cease but to no avail. At the end, in bleak surroundings, the Once-ler gives a child a seed to plant, the only hope for the future. This tale uses Seuss's characteristic jaunty text and illustrations to deliver its important message.

Cherry, Lynne. *A River Ran Wild: An Environmental History.* **1992. Hardcover and paperback: Harcourt. 32 pages. Ages 5–10. PICTURE BOOK NONFICTION.**

The Nashua River in New England has had a rich history of interaction with humans. This attractive short book takes the reader on a historical and environmental journey of the river from the 1400s to the present. It focuses on the changes in the river and its banks, the heavy pollution it suffered from factories and then its clean-up thanks to citizen action. Watercolor and colored-pencil illustrations give a feel for the beautiful region, while borders around the text show artifacts from each age.

Rand, Gloria. *Fighting for the Forest.* **Illustrated by Ted Rand. 1999. Hardcover: Henry Holt. 32 pages. Ages 6–9. PICTURE BOOK.**

In this beautiful book, the narrator and his dad love to hike in a huge ancient forest. They cannot believe it when they find the trees marked for clear-cutting. Both fight against the cutting by organizing volunteers, writing letters, and picketing, but it is too late to save that forest, shown devastated after the lumbering operation. In the end, they find another place to hike and resolve to keep fighting for other forests. A thoughtful story about a child who cares about saving the environment.

Lasky, Kathryn. *The Most Beautiful Roof in the World: Exploring the Rain Forest Canopy*. Photographs by Christopher G. Knight. 1997. Hardcover and paperback: Harcourt. 48 pages. Ages 9–12. NONFICTION.

Meg Lowman, a scientist who specializes in the relationships between plants and insects, often climbs one hundred feet into the Central American rain forest to do her work. Clear, colorful photographs show the animals and plants Lowman finds in the canopy. In one section, her school-aged sons accompany her on a night walk, an expedition full of interesting sights. The vivid photo-essay integrates information about the rain forest and its importance with fascinating details about Lowman's studies.

George, Jean Craighead. *The Fire Bug Connection: An Ecological Mystery*. 1993. Paperback: Harper. 148 pages. Ages 9–13. FICTION.

Maggie, who loves insects, is thrilled to receive fire bugs from Czechoslovakia for her twelfth birthday. She is less thrilled that Mitch Waterford, computer whiz and practical jokester, will be joining her family at the camp in Maine where her parents are doing science research. But when the fire bugs start dying, Mitch proves a valuable ally in trying to solve the ecological mystery about what is killing them. A fast-moving puzzle full of nature lore and scientific principles.

Maynard, Caitlin, Thane Maynard, and Stan Rullman.
Rain Forests and Reefs: A Kid's View of the Tropics. **1996.**
Hardcover: Watts. 64 pages. Ages 9–14. NONFICTION.

In this trip to the rain forest through the eyes of a teen-ager, a middle-schooler describes her expedition with seventeen other teenagers and seven adults to the Central American rain forest and coral reefs of Belize. She conveys her excitement in journal entries, while the main text describes the area's ecology. Sidebars profile people who work to preserve the environment, and add more facts and terminology. With many color photographs, the multifaceted text reads like an engaging scrapbook.

Patent, Dorothy Hinshaw. *Fire: Friend or Foe.* **Photographs by William Muñoz. 1998. Hardcover: Clarion. 80 pages. Ages 9–14. NONFICTION.**

For many years, wildfires were automatically fought in parks and other wilderness places, but recently that practice has changed. Patent explains how fire can provide benefits to grasslands and forested areas, creating nutrients that result in new and different growth. She discusses the effects of fires, focusing on the 1988 Yellowstone fires and their aftermath. She also describes wilderness firefighting and controlled burning. Excellent color photographs augment this attractive, highly readable book.

Smith, Roland, and Michael J. Schmidt. *In the Forest with the Elephants.* **1998. Hardcover: Harcourt. Paperback: Gulliver. 64 pages. Ages 9–14. NONFICTION.**

A third of the 35,000 remaining Asian elephants live in the southeast Asian country Myanmar, where half work as timber elephants. This intriguing essay, generously illustrated with color photographs, explains the elephants' work and their relationship with their *oozies*, the men who work with them harvesting timber. It discusses their training and the ecological advantages of having elephants instead of machinery work in this carefully harvested forest. A fascinating glimpse into an unusual animal-human relationship.

Swinburne, Stephen R. *Once a Wolf: How Wildlife Biologists Fought to Bring Back the Gray Wolf.* **Photographs by Jim Brandenburg. 1999. Hardcover: Houghton. 48 pages. Ages 9–14. Of interest to younger children. NONFICTION.**

This is at once a powerful story about ecology and a stunningly beautiful photo-essay about wolves. Although at one time wolves roamed much of North America, the coming of settlers put bounties on the animals' heads and succeeded in killing most of them. This well-told narrative describes the changing view of these mammals and the slow process of getting them reintroduced into Yellowstone Park. A balanced account illustrated with exquisite photographs.

Skurzynski, Gloria, and Alane Ferguson. *Wolf Stalker.* **1997. Hardcover: National Geographic. 128 pages. Ages 10–13. FICTION.**

In this first book of the "National Parks Mystery" series, three children act to rescue a wolf accused of killing a dog. At Yellowstone, Jack, his younger sister, Ashley, and their family's new foster child, Troy, follow a wounded wolf into the wilderness. Although adolescents Jack and Troy clash at first, they soon realize that only by working together can they save the wolf and themselves, and solve the mystery of the dog's killing. A suspenseful wilderness mystery with lots of adventure.

Thomas, Rob. *Green Thumb*. 1999. Hardcover: Simon & Schuster. Paperback: Aladdin. 192 pages. Ages 11–14. FICTION.

Thirteen-year-old Grady excels at science but has no friends. When he is invited to spend a summer working for a scientist in the Amazonian rain forest, he jumps at the chance. He loves the rain forest and its amazing vegetation, but he slowly realizes that the scientist's experiments have a dark side to them that may harm the local tribes. Grady uses his computer skills and draws on his courage to battle the mad scientist. An action-packed, improbable, but entertaining tale.

Klass, David. *California Blue*. 1994. Hardcover and paperback: Scholastic. 199 pages. Ages 12–14. FICTION.

High school junior John doesn't fit into his family or his small lumbering town in Northern California. He runs track instead of playing football, and cares more about natural history than his peers do. When he encounters a butterfly that he has never seen before, John is excited and worried. If it is a new kind of butterfly, the discovery will send the town into turmoil when environmentalists find out. Vivid characters, a strong pace, and excellent writing will keep readers hooked until the final dramatic scenes.

Human Body and Sexual Reproduction

Gomi, Taro. Translated by Amanda Mayer Stinchecum. *Everyone Poops*. 1993. Hardcover: Kane/Miller. 27 pages. Ages 2–7. PICTURE BOOK NONFICTION.

In this refreshingly straightforward book that opens with the words "An elephant makes a big poop. A mouse makes a tiny poop," simple watercolors on bright backgrounds show lots of animals and several humans. Popular with young children, it asks questions such as "What does whale poop look like?" A clever design and touches of humor characterize this Japanese import that has sold enormously well in the United States. Also look for the similar *The Gas We Pass* by Shinta Cho.

Cole, Joanna. *The Magic School Bus Explores the Senses*. Illustrated by Bruce Degen. 1999. Hardcover: Scholastic. 48 pages. Ages 3–10. PICTURE BOOK NONFICTION.

Help! It's not Ms. Frizzle at the controls of the Magic School Bus, it's the new assistant principal, taking readers on an exciting field trip through the five senses. The bus shrinks and enters a police officer's eye, a little boy's ear, a dog's nose, and the taste buds and skin of Ms. Frizzle herself, the most enthusiastic science teacher around. Sidebars and illustrations add lots of information; an afterword separates fact from fantasy in this enjoyable way to learn about the senses.

Berger, Melvin. *Why I Cough, Sneeze, Shiver, Hiccup & Yawn*. Illustrated by Holly Keller. 1983. Hardcover: Harper. 34 pages. Ages 4–8. PICTURE BOOK NONFICTION.

What causes you to sneeze even when you don't want to? This simple text clearly explains reflexes like sneezes, shivers, and hiccups, and how they work their way through the nervous system. Colorful pictures show children and their physical reactions, while diagrams illustrate nerves and the pathways of a sneeze, hiccup, and yawn. This is one of many books about the human body in the excellent "Let's-Read-and-Find-Out Science Books" series, which includes *My Five Senses, Germs Make Me Sick, A Drop of Blood, Sleep Is for Everyone, What Happens to a Hamburger*, and more.

Brown, Laurie Krasny, and Marc Brown. *What's the Big Secret? Talking about Sex with Girls and Boys*. 1997. Hardcover and paperback: Little, Brown. 32 pages. Ages 4–9. NONFICTION.

Cheerful pictures by the creator of the "Arthur" series establish the relaxed mood of this useful book about sex and development. It discusses similarities and differences between girls and boys, shows and describes the reproductive systems, and answers many questions that younger children have about sex, but with only a brief mention of puberty. The tone is warm and reassuring, with plenty of humor for children and their parents in the pictures and balloon dialogue. It stresses the importance of family and love and being at home with one's body. A very good resource.

Harris, Robie H. *It's So Amazing: A Book about Eggs, Sperm, Birth, Babies, and Families.* **Illustrated by Michael Emberley. 1999. Hardcover: Candlewick. 82 pages. Ages 8–11. Of interest to younger children. NONFICTION.**

Cozy pictures of real-looking children and adults (naked and clothed), and many funny asides between a bird and bee make this fine book on where babies come from accessible to children. The text moves from looking at human bodies and genitals to detailed descriptions of eggs and sperm and how they get together. It briefly discusses sexual abuse and AIDS, but the emphasis is on how families are created, including adoption, with an overall spirit of celebration. Highly recommended.

Simon, Seymour. *Muscles: Our Muscular System.* **1998. Hardcover: Morrow. Paperback: Harper. 32 pages. Ages 8–11. Of interest to younger children. NONFICTION.**

Each double-page spread in this well-designed nonfiction book has a large photograph, drawing, or diagram on one page, opposite a few paragraphs of large-print text. It describes the muscles, how they work, and their relationship to exercise, relating the explanations to the photographs. Simon addresses the reader to make the information more immediate, such as "There are muscles that you control, and muscles, like those in your heart, that work without your even knowing it." One in a recommended series that also includes *The Heart* and *The Brain*.

Gravelle, Karen, and Jennifer Gravelle. *The Period Book: Everything You Don't Want to Ask (But Need to Know).* **Illustrated by Debbie Palen. 1996. Hardcover and paperback: Walker. 117 pages. Ages 8 and up. NONFICTION.**

This book covers most questions girls have about menstruation, including some that are hard to ask. The conversational text discusses the physical and emotional changes puberty brings, and goes into great detail about menstruation and how to deal with it. One chapter describes visiting a gynecologist. Humorous pictures set a light tone and supply information through diagrams. The book does not cover boys' changes, birth control, or sexual activity, but it fulfills its limited goals very well.

Blume, Judy. *Are You There God? It's Me, Margaret*. 1970. Hardcover: Bradbury. Paperback: Yearling. 149 pages. Ages 9–12. FICTION.

Twelve-year-old Margaret worries about her body and her lack of religion. She is waiting to get her period and start developing breasts like her friends. She tells God her problems, asks for help, and goes to temple and church with friends to explore religion. As a sixth grader, Margaret attends her first dance, gets her first kiss, and buys her first bra. While Blume's writing is short on character development, its strength is an openness about subjects children wonder about but can't always discuss. Although thirty years old, this novel holds up well in terms of children's concerns.

Parker, Steve. *The Human Body: An Amazing Look Inside at You!* 1996. Hardcover: Abrams. 128 pages. Ages 9–12. Of interest to younger children. NONFICTION.

This unusually clear and accessible introduction to the human body uses clever computer paintings that appear to show a real child with a cut-away to see inside his body. This technique makes it surprisingly easy to understand where body parts are located and how they relate to each other. The large, uncluttered pages supply a lot of information without overwhelming the reader, explaining all the body systems and much more. A wonderful resource on a topic that intrigues many children.

Jukes, Mavis. *Expecting the Unexpected.* **1996. Hardcover: Delacorte. Paperback: Yearling. 144 pages. Ages 9–13. FICTION.**

When Mrs. Furley sponsors a "Pad Fest" in their Human Interactions Class, showing different types of menstrual pads, the sixth graders know that nothing embarrasses this teacher. They have all signed a pledge to take the class seriously, but can they keep it? Meanwhile, River and her friends are playing tricks on their classroom teacher every day just to keep him in line. One funny incident after another, interspersed with some realistic worries, keeps this novel zipping along.

Harris, Robie H. *It's Perfectly Normal: Changing Bodies, Growing Up, Sex & Sexual Health.* **Illustrated by Michael Emberley. 1994. Hardcover and paperback: Candlewick. 90 pages. Ages 9–14. Of interest to younger children. NONFICTION.**

For parents who want their children to feel comfortable with their bodies and sexuality, this is an outstanding book. In a conversational voice, it discusses many aspects of sexual development and sexuality including puberty, sexual intercourse, birth, birth control, abortion, STDs, sexual abuse, and more. The clear explanations reflect a knowledge and understanding of children and adolescents. The book offers more than one viewpoint on controversial subjects and emphasizes the importance of being ready for a sexual relationship. Humorous cartoons, many of nude figures, lighten the tone and add diagrams. Highly recommended.

Gravelle, Karen, with Nick and Chava Castro. *What's Going on Down There? Answers to Questions Boys Find Hard to Ask.* Illustrated by Robert Leighton. 1998. Hardcover and paperback: Walker. 150 pages. Ages 10 and up. NONFICTION.

Gravelle, with the help of two boys, has assembled a lot of information about the changes a boy's body goes through at puberty, answering questions that might be embarrassing to ask. After explaining the male reproductive system and changes at puberty, the book discusses girls' bodies, sexual intercourse, birth control, and STDs. Goofy illustrations add some information and humor. Although the book doesn't cover sexual abuse and doesn't discuss homosexuality adequately, it is a solid, reassuring introduction.

Math and Money

Hutchins, Pat. *The Doorbell Rang.* **1986. Hardcover: Greenwillow. Paperback: Mulberry. 24 pages. Ages 3–7. PICTURE BOOK.**

This is a cheerful picture-story book that incorporates a math lesson. Ma has made twelve cookies, six each for Victoria and Sam—until the doorbell rings and they have to share them with two friends. Just as they are about to eat, the doorbell rings again and more friends appear. With each ring, the total of twelve must be divided again. When you read this, have some cookies on hand to divide and then eat.

Grossman, Bill. *My Little Sister Ate One Hare.* **Illustrated by Kevin Hawkes. 1996. Hardcover: Crown. Paperback: Random House. 32 pages. Ages 3–8. PICTURE BOOK.**

"My little sister ate one hare. We thought she'd throw up then and there" is how this riotously funny counting book opens. With a perfect match of writer and illustrator, it bounces the reader along from one to ten. Two through nine describe increasingly disgusting foods that the sister eats, mostly rodents, reptiles, and insects. The punch line is hilarious. Children may learn their numbers from this book, if they aren't laughing too hard.

Wells, Rosemary. *Bunny Money.* **1997. Hardcover: Dial. Paperback: Viking. 32 pages. Ages 3–8. PICTURE BOOK.**

This wonderful combination of humor and math begins "Max's sister, Ruby, saved up a wallet of money for Grandma's birthday present." Ruby has ten one-dollar bills and one five-dollar bill when she and the incorrigible Max take the bus—one dollar—to shop. Readers can follow along counting how the dollars and change get spent, some on unexpected purchases like vampire teeth. The book's endpapers have bunny money that can be photocopied and colored for pretend shopping. One in a great series.

Schwartz, David M. *If You Hopped Like a Frog.* **1999. Hardcover: Scholastic. 32 pages. Ages 3–9. PICTURE BOOK NONFICTION.**

"If you hopped like a frog, you could get from home plate to first base in one mighty leap!" This clever introduction to ratio and proportion reads like a picture-story book. A large, comical picture accompanies each comparison to an animal's traits: the strength of an ant, the length of a giraffe's neck, and more. Notes at the back give additional information and suggest questions to take the comparisons further. A fine combination of math and fun.

Axelrod, Amy. *Pigs Will Be Pigs: Fun with Math and Money.* **Illustrated by Sharon McGinley-Nally. 1994. Hardcover: Four Winds. Paperback: Aladdin. 40 pages. Ages 4–9. PICTURE BOOK.**

One evening, the Pig family decides to go out to eat, if they can find some cash around the house. Humorous pictures show the family throwing their possessions about higgledy-piggledy as they scour the house for money. They slowly dig out enough money, a little at a time, for their Mexican dinner. A final page shows the money they found and poses questions about what they spent and what else they could have spent. A comical combination that is mostly story and some math.

Leedy, Loreen. *Measuring Penny*. 1997. Hardcover and paperback: Henry Holt. 32 pages. Ages 5–9. PICTURE BOOK NONFICTION.

When Lisa's math teacher instructs his students to measure something in standard and nonstandard units, Lisa chooses her dog, Penny. She measures Penny and other dogs in lots of imaginative ways: the length of their noses in inches, the length of their tails in dog biscuits, how high they can jump relative to her own body, their relative weight on the seesaw, and much more. A creative and enjoyable math book with jaunty pictures.

Tompert, Ann. *Grandfather Tang's Story*. Illustrated by Robert Andrew Parker. 1990. Hardcover: Crown. Paperback: Dragonfly. 32 pages. Ages 6–10. PICTURE BOOK.

Grandfather Tang tells Little Soo a story about two fox fairies that change themselves into a series of different animals, a game that turns dangerous for the fox friends. Each new animal is illustrated with tangrams, geometric shapes explained on the last page. A tangram template is given for readers to trace, cut the shapes out, and make the designs in the story. An unusual book that combines a story with geometrical concepts.

Scieszka, Jon, and Lane Smith. *Math Curse*. 1995. Hardcover: Viking. 32 pages. Ages 8–12. PICTURE BOOK.

When the narrator's teacher says one Monday, "*You know, you can think of almost everything as a math problem,*" daily life suddenly seems to be filled with numbers, fractions, geometry, and much more. Jokes mingle with serious math problems in a frantic pace. Collage pictures incorporate geometric shapes, charts, numbers, money, and monsters, while the text includes boxed math problems, equations, and multiple choice tests. Although too frenzied for some, this is a highly original picture book that adds up to a lot of fun.

Merrill, Jean. *The Toothpaste Millionaire*. 1972. Hardcover and paperback: Houghton. 90 pages. Ages 9–12. FICTION.
Rufus is an unusual twelve-year-old boy who loves to figure things out, including math problems. On a shopping trip, Rufus can't believe the cost of toothpaste and decides he could make it for far less. So he does, with the help of friends, and sells it for pennies. But as business grows, he faces some of the difficulties of running a successful enterprise. Real-life math problems and topics like stocks and competition are woven into a lively, surprisingly timeless story about a young entrepreneur.

Juster, Norton. *The Phantom Tollbooth*. Illustrated by Jules Feiffer. 1961. Hardcover and paperback: Knopf. 256 pages. Ages 9–13. FICTION.
Milo drives his electric car through a phantom tollbooth to a strange land where he visits the cities of Dictionopolis and Digitopolis, the Forest of Sight, and the Island of Conclusions (to which many people jump). Accompanied by the dog Tock, Milo tries to bring the princesses Rhyme and Reason back from the Castle in the Air. Along the way he also encounters the math-loving Dodecahedron and the Mathemagician. Anyone who enjoys playing with words or numbers will love this clever novel.

Markle, Sandra. *Discovering Graph Secrets: Experiments, Puzzles, and Games Exploring Graphs*. 1997. Hardcover: Atheneum. 40 pages. Ages 9–14. NONFICTION.
The first graph in this enthusiastic book shows the "Average Number of M&Ms per Bag by Color." As the book demonstrates over and over, graphs make information easy to grasp.

Using subjects of interest to kids like food and roller derbies, the author presents experiments that encourage readers to examine different kinds of graphs closely. Short mysteries accompany some of the graphs, with answers at the back. Readers will conclude that graphs are both useful and fun.

Sachar, Louis. *Sideways Arithmetic from Wayside School*. 1989. Hardcover: Scholastic. Paperback: Avon. 118 pages. Ages 9–14. FICTION.

"Everyone take out your spelling books," says the teacher at Wayside School. "It's time for arithmetic." The new student Sue doesn't understand the first problem, which is to add "elf" and "elf." Her bafflement increases throughout this clever, brain-teasing book full of strange math problems. Although some of the chapters open with scenes of students interacting, the bulk of the pages give problems to solve, with the solutions at the back. A novel with entertaining challenges for those who like math.

Enzensberger, Hans Magnus. Translated by Michael Henry Heim. *The Number Devil: A Mathematical Adventure*. Illustrated by Rotraut Susanne Berner. 1998. Hardcover and paperback: Henry Holt. 262 pages. Ages 9 and up. FICTION.

In this unusual novel, a little red devil appears to Robert in his dreams for twelve nights and teaches him mathematics in a playful way. The sometimes cranky devil introduces infinite numbers, prime numbers, square roots, factorials, and more. Along with Robert, the reader learns techniques that seem almost like magic tricks to make numbers easier to use and understand. Richly colored pictures illustrate principles and add a bit of humor. Fun for those who love math *and* for those who don't.

Burns, Marilyn. *Math for Smarty Pants*. **Illustrated by Martha Weston. 1982. Paperback: Little, Brown. 128 pages. Ages 10–14. NONFICTION.**

Five kids who are "smart" in math in different ways try lots of approaches to the subject in this collection of math problems, tricks, anecdotes, jokes, and visual puzzles. Readers can try the challenges and find the answers on later pages. Line drawings on every page illustrate problems and questions. Children who don't think they are good in math may become excited about one of the approaches, while those who already love math will plunge in for multiple ways to extend their excitement.

Godfrey, Neale S. *Neale S. Godfrey's Ultimate Kids' Money Book*. **Illustrated by Randy Verougstraete. 1998. Hardcover: Simon & Schuster. 128 pages. Ages 10–14. NONFICTION.**

This book by a financial expert lays out many aspects of the financial world in ways that young readers can understand. It discusses the history of money and trading, talks about coins and paper money, and addresses practical topics like making a budget and using a bank. It covers saving and checking accounts, ATMs, credit cards, taxes, and investing. The design is lively and colorful, with cartoonlike illustrations, sidebars, and financial brain-teasers. A good introduction to finance for kids.

Science Experiments
and Inventions

Gans, Roma. *Let's Go Rock Collecting*. Illustrated by Holly Keller. 1997. Hardcover and paperback: Harper. 32 pages. Ages 4–8. PICTURE BOOK NONFICTION.

This "Let's Read and Find Out" science book is actually more about rocks than collecting. It opens with two children who are interested in finding rocks, but quickly moves to a history and description of types of rocks. A diagram of a volcano and another of rock layers below a city set the scientific tone. Although most of the pictures are colorful pen-and-watercolor, photographs show granite, quartz, and other rocks. Like the other books in this fine series, this gives a strong introduction to its topic.

Selsam, Millicent E. *Greg's Microscope*. Illustrated by Arnold Lobel. 1963. Hardcover and paperback: Harper. 64 pages. Ages 4–8. EASY READER.

Although more than thirty-five years old, this book will appeal to children interested in science and the natural world. Greg is so excited about his friend's microscope that his father buys him a used one. Greg immediately looks at salt and sugar crystals, then thread and hair. His father explains some scientific concepts, while his mother, depicted in a very traditional role, also starts getting excited about the microscope. Lobel's pencil illustrations expand on the scientific information while adding dimensions to the characters.

Wiesner, David. *June 29, 1999.* **1992. Hardcover and paperback: Clarion. 32 pages. Ages 4–8. PICTURE BOOK.**

For a school science assignment, a girl plants seedlings and sends them into space on cardboard trays carried by helium balloons. When gigantic vegetables start appearing in the sky all over the country, she clips newspaper articles and keeps a chart of sightings, wondering if they are her seedlings grown huge. Eventually she realizes that they can't be, but only the reader sees the explanation, which involves space aliens. Superb illustrations full of details and humor make this a pleasure to read.

Martin, Jacqueline Briggs. *Snowflake Bentley.* **Illustrated by Mary Azarian. 1998. Hardcover: Houghton. 32 pages. Ages 5–10. PICTURE BOOK BIOGRAPHY.**

Wilson Bentley loved snow "more than anything else in the world." Born in 1865, he spent his life on a farm in Vermont, where he taught himself all about snowflakes. He only went to school for a few years, yet he conducted experiments, drew hundreds of snow crystals, and took remarkable photographs of snowflakes. He became an authority on the topic and left a significant legacy of photographs and knowledge. Charming woodcuts, which won the Caldecott Medal, show his life and work.

Duffey, Betsy. *The Gadget War.* **Illustrated by Janet Wilson. 1991. Hardcover: Viking. Paperback: Puffin. 76 pages. Ages 7–10. FICTION.**

Eight-year-old Kelley Sparks, who plans to be a "Gadget Whiz" when she grows up, has already created forty-three inventions, for which she followed a careful note-taking process. When a new boy at school also claims to be an inventor, a rivalry springs up and they try to out-invent each other. Kelley invents a food-fight catapult, but when she uses it to launch an orange in the school cafeteria, both inventors get into trouble. A breezy story that makes inventing look like fun.

Ardley, Neil. *The Science Book of Gravity.* 1992. Hardcover: Harcourt. 32 pages. Ages 8–11. NONFICTION.

Rarely do science experiment books do such a good job as this one. Each page or double-page spread contains a thoughtfully conceived experiment using mostly common household materials. The twelve experiments illustrate the principles of gravity in ways that will appeal to children, such as sending a toy car down a ramp made from a shoe box. Clear directions are reinforced by color photographs of each material and step. One in a recommended series, which covers electricity, magnets, machines, energy, and more.

Auch, Mary Jane. *I Was a Third Grade Science Project.* Illustrated by Herm Auch. 1998. Hardcover: Holiday House. Paperback: Bantam. 104 pages. Ages 8–11. FICTION.

When the third-grade teacher assigns a science project, Josh happily teams up with his smart friend Brian. Brian's idea, which Josh has his doubts about, is to hypnotize his dog into thinking he's a cat. Brian approaches the project scientifically with a hypothesis and careful notes, but he never expects the strange results. Readers will realize before the characters do what the funny outcome will be—a hilarious final scene. A funny book with lots of references to science projects.

Simon, Seymour. *The Howling Dog and Other Stories.* Illustrated by S. D. Schindler. 1997. Hardcover: Morrow. 96 pages. Ages 8–12. FICTION.

The first in the "Einstein Anderson, Science Detective" series, this collection of mini-mysteries relies on scientific principles to decipher each puzzle. Adam Anderson, known as "Einstein" because of his skill in science, encounters ten problems and solves them with his knowledge of gravity, solvents, friction, and other aspects of science. Einstein trades science tricks with his friend Margaret and outwits a local bully by using his brains. The reader can try to unravel each mystery, too, then check the answer.

Lang, Susan S. *Nature in Your Backyard: Simple Activities for Children.* **Illustrated by Sharon Lane Holm. 1995. Hardcover and paperback: Millbrook. 48 pages. Ages 8–12. Of interest to younger children. NONFICTION.**

This outstanding book describes twenty-one simple projects for learning more about nature. Sections include insects and worms, birds, backyard animals, seeds, plants, and soil. The first activity involves distributing bread soaked in sugar water around the yard, then seeing which ones attract ants, how quickly, and where they carry it. Clear instructions are followed by thoughtful questions and more facts. The activities require only a backyard, common materials, and an interest in nature.

Cobb, Vicki. *Science Experiments You Can Eat.* **Illustrated by David Cain. 1994 Revised Edition. Hardcover: Harper. 214 pages. Ages 9–13. NONFICTION.**

Dozens of experiments use food to demonstrate scientific principles in this lively book. For example, making ice pops illustrates the freezing points of solutions. Other topics are gases and liquids, microbes, enzymes, plants and how they function, proteins, and more. Clear instructions lead to end products that include grape jelly, meringues, Sally Lunn bread, and many other foods. Line illustrations show the steps and help explain concepts. See also *More Science Experiments You Can Eat.*

Mills, Claudia. *Standing Up to Mr. O.* 1998. Hardcover: Farrar, Straus & Giroux. Paperback: Hyperion. 160 pages. Ages 9–13. FICTION.

Maggie, a seventh-grader who excels at science, values the friendship of her biology teacher Mr. O., especially because she hasn't seen her father since she was four. But when the class starts performing dissections on live worms, Maggie refuses to participate and persists in her decision despite Mr. O.'s anger. Maggie starts spending time with Jake, a sullen rebel who sides with her, but she also finds her lab partner, Matt, increasingly attractive as they argue about the ethics of dissection. Sympathetic characters and an exploration of an important science issue result in a compelling novel.

Tucker, Tom. *Brainstorm! The Stories of Twenty American Kid Inventors.* 1995. Hardcover: Farrar, Straus & Giroux. Paperback: Sunburst. 144 pages. Ages 9–14. COLLECTIVE BIOGRAPHY.

Over the years, teenagers and preteens have invented some surprising products. This book profiles twenty such inventors and how they went about creating something new. For example, an eleven-year-old made the first popsicle. More recently, a seventh-grade girl concocted a colored car wax that disguises scratches on cars. The list goes on, each with a story worth reading. A final short chapter gives advice to young inventors.

Llewellyn, Claire. *The Big Book of Bones: An Introduction to Skeletons.* 1998. Hardcover: Peter Bedrick. 48 pages. Ages 10–13. Of interest to younger children. NONFICTION.

This eye-catching, thoughtful introduction explores many aspects of human and animal skeletons. Large, color photographs show skeletons and the animals they come from, while the text makes apt comparisons and gives easy-to-understand explanations about how bones function. Small sidebars labeled "Bone Up!" add interesting facts. The large format and clear layout make the book a pleasure to read, while the subject matter will draw in many eager readers.

Muller, Eric. *While You're Waiting for the Food to Come: A Tabletop Science Activity Book.* **Illustrated by Eldon Doty. 1999. Hardcover and paperback: Orchard. 96 pages. Ages 10–13. Of interest to younger children. NONFICTION.**

"Experiments and tricks that can be done at a restaurant, the dining room table, or wherever food is served" is one of the subtitles of this terrific book. When science educator Muller was driving cross-country, he devised more than thirty scientific activities involving napkins, straws, silverware, and more. The book gives clear step-by-step instructions, "Food for Thought" about the concepts, and "More to Chew On," to add information. This playful guide makes science an enjoyable part of everyday life. Don't miss it.

Zubrowski, Bernie. *Blinkers and Buzzers: Building and Experimenting with Electricity and Magnetism.* **Illustrated by Roy Doty. 1991. Paperback: Beech Tree. 112 pages. Ages 10–14. Of interest to younger children. NONFICTION.**

This outstanding book of well-chosen experiments starts with the creation of a flashlight out of a soda can, batteries, and other simple materials. Step-by-step directions with unusually helpful diagrams explain each experiment on a range of topics, including switches and electromagnets. The projects, which tend to use easily obtained materials, will tempt even those not usually interested in science. Also see Zubrowski's other excellent science books.

Gardner, Robert. *Make an Interactive Science Museum: Hands-On Exhibits!* Illustrated by Kris Kozak. 1996. Hardcover: TAB Books. Paperback: McGraw-Hill. 182 pages. Ages 11–14. NONFICTION.

In the opening pages, Gardner gives specific advice for setting up a science museum at home, school, or in a public building like a library. The chapters give step-by-step directions for making hands-on exhibits, interactive ones, optical puzzles, and more. The fascinating projects include building a sundial, analyzing fingerprints, trick photography, and underwater candles. While this is perfect for science buffs, it may also convince those who don't like science that it can be fun.

Space Exploration
and Astronomy

Getz, David. *Floating Home*. Illustrated by Michael Rex. 1997. Hardcover and paperback: Henry Holt. 40 pages. Ages 4–8. PICTURE BOOK.

When eight-year-old Maxine gets an assignment to look at her home in a new way and draw what she sees, she heads to Cape Canaveral to draw Earth as seen by an astronaut. With details that would-be astronauts will appreciate, the text and pictures follow the process of getting into her pressure suit and getting strapped into the shuttle's orbiter. It blasts off and travels faster then the speed of sound. Finally, in free fall, she sees Earth and draws it. An upbeat story of a space shuttle journey.

Fraser, Mary Ann. *One Giant Leap*. 1993. Paperback: Henry Holt. 40 pages. Ages 4–9. PICTURE BOOK NON-FICTION.

What was it like in Apollo 11 as the three astronauts headed for the first walk on the moon? This excellent book starts with the launch, takes readers into orbit and then blasting toward the moon, where they change to the landing module and make the tense final landing. The author weaves in NASA history but focuses mainly on the exciting moon landing. The front endpapers show the rocket and modules in detail, while the back endpapers track the trip, show a labeled spacesuit, and provide a glossary.

Crew, Gary. *Bright Star*. **Illustrated by Anne Spudvilas. 1997. Hardcover: Kane/Miller. 32 pages. Ages 5–9. PICTURE BOOK.**

In the 1860s, amateur Australian astronomer John Tebbett discovered two comets. In this fictional story, a hardworking farm girl who excels in school catches Tebbett's attention. Impressed with her quick mind, he invites her to visit his observatory. There, she peers through the huge telescope and talks to Tebbett about space. The conclusion implies that she'll be back and will perhaps pursue studies in astronomy. Impressionistic paintings enhance the sense of wonder about the night sky.

Yolen, Jane. *Commander Toad and the Voyage Home*. **Illustrated by Bruce Degen. 1998. Hardcover and paperback: Putnam. 64 pages. Ages 6–8. Of interest to younger children. EASY READER.**

One in the "I Can Read" series, this story of Commander Toad and his spaceship will amuse young space fans. Commander Toad captains the *Star Warts*, a green spaceship whose mission is to find new worlds and explore galaxies. As the funny pictures reveal, Commander Toad's mission is not entirely serious. He decides to head back to Earth one day, past constellations and black holes, but ends up on a strange planet where the crew has an unlikely adventure. Silly and amusing.

Kline, Suzy. *Horrible Harry Goes to the Moon*. **Illustrated by Frank Remkiewicz. 2000. Hardcover: Viking. 64 pages. Ages 7–10. FICTION.**

When Harry's third-grade class starts to collect facts about the moon, they turn to books and the Internet. Harry proposes that they also try to buy a used telescope for the class. The students plan a bake sale with a moon theme. If they succeed in raising enough money, they will host an evening of moon-viewing with their new telescope, an event for which Harry has a special scheme. A lighthearted school story full of information about the moon. One in a popular series.

Bredeson, Carmen. *Our Space Program*. 1999. Hardcover and paperback: Millbrook. 48 pages. Ages 8–12. Of interest to younger children. NONFICTION.

This overview looks at the U.S. space program from its beginning through current plans for the international space station. Lots of photographs illustrate the program's stages: the first astronauts; the Mercury, Gemini, and Apollo programs; the space stations and shuttles; the Mars Pathfinder and other probes; and more. Sidebars add detailed information on topics like Skylab, space junk, and the *Challenger* disaster. This fine introduction will inspire some readers to seek out longer books about different parts of the space program.

Rey, H. A. *Find the Constellations*. 1976 Revised Edition. Hardcover and paperback: Houghton. 70 pages. Ages 8–12. Of interest to younger children. NONFICTION.

Although this book is dated in a few aspects, it remains an excellent way to get to know the night sky. Rey, creator of Curious George, makes it easy to recognize the constellations and provides star-map quizzes to check the reader's new knowledge. The book also has sky views that show the summer, fall, spring, and winter stars. Small talking characters throughout the book add humor and information. An effective introduction to the constellations and other features of the night sky.

Scott, Elaine. *Close Encounters: Exploring the Universe with the Hubble Space Telescope.* **1998. Hardcover: Hyperion. 64 pages. Ages 8–14. NONFICTION.**

After a brief history of telescopes, this book focuses on the new information that the Hubble Space Telescope has provided about astronomy. Splendid color photographs of planets, stars, galaxies, and more will mesmerize the reader. The lucid text simplifies complicated information about how stars are born, the distances in outer space, black holes, and other topics about space. An exciting glimpse into the universe and the future.

Jones, Diana Wynne. *Dogsbody.* **1977. Hardcover: Greenwillow. 224 pages. Ages 9–13. FICTION.**

What if the stars were alive and resembled people? In this inventive novel, the star Sirius, the Dog Star and brightest star in the heavens, is alive and has been accused of committing a crime. His heavenly peers punish him by sending him to Earth in the form of a dog, the pet of a girl named Kathleen. As Sirius grows from a puppy to an adult dog, he starts remembering who he is and talking with Sol, the sun. Now he needs to prove that he is innocent, but his enemies hope to destroy him first. An excellent fantasy.

Klause, Annette Curtis. *Alien Secrets.* **1993. Hardcover: Delacorte. Paperback: Yearling. 240 pages. Ages 9–13. FICTION.**

Science fiction mixes with a murder mystery in this suspenseful story that takes place on a spaceship. Puck, who seemingly witnesses a murder before boarding, is sure that someone on the ship is a criminal. The only person she trusts is the alien Hush, who has been robbed of a precious artifact. Together they try to recover the sacred treasure and expose the criminals. Futuristic slang adds humor, while the final, uplifting scene offers a message about understanding between different cultures.

Heinlein, Robert A. *Red Planet*. 1949. Paperback: Ballantine. 190 pages. Ages 10–13. FICTION.

In this quick-paced novel, people from Earth have colonized Mars. When teenager Jim Marlowe starts boarding school in a Martian city far from his colony, he insists on taking along his pet, Willis, a small Martian creature who can talk. Because of Willis, Jim learns of a plot that could endanger his home, a crisis that leads to the question of whether Mars is ready for independence from Earth. Except for the traditional roles of females, this engaging story has held up well over the years.

Wunsch, Susi Trautmann. *The Adventures of Sojourner: The Mission to Mars That Thrilled the World*. 1998. Hardcover and paperback: Mikaya. 64 pages. Ages 10–13. Of interest to younger children. NONFICTION.

This enthusiastic account of the Sojourner rover conveys the excitement of the NASA staff who designed, tested, and controlled it. Sojourner was merely two feet long and one foot high, and far less costly than other ventures, yet it proved a remarkable success. With many color photographs, paintings, and diagrams, these well-designed pages proceed from the idea stage through Sojourner's performance on Mars taking photographs and gathering scientific data. Space fans shouldn't miss this one.

Becklake, Sue. *The Visual Dictionary of the Universe.* **1993. Hardcover: DK. 64 pages. Ages 11–14. NONFICTION.**

This oversized volume concentrates on astronomy with a few forays into space exploration. Each double-page spread looks at one topic, starting with "The Universe," "Galaxies," and "The Milky Way," then each of the planets. The format has a main paragraph of text plus photographs, drawings, and diagrams. Although each page presents a lot of information, the clean design keeps it from being overwhelming. Appendixes supply factual details. Sure to appeal to anyone interested in our galaxy and beyond. One in a popular series.

Collins, Michael. *Flying to the Moon: An Astronaut's Story.* **1994 Revised Edition. Paperback: Farrar, Straus & Giroux. 162 pages. Ages 12–14. NONFICTION.**

Collins, the Apollo 11 astronaut who piloted the command module while Armstrong and Aldrin took the first moon walk, describes his path to that mission from his air force career as a pilot to his training as an astronaut. This well-written account looks at the technology of space launches as well as his flights. Collins conveys the suspense of the Apollo 11 flight and a genuine enthusiasm for space exploration. A great read.

Sports for
Everyone

Baseball

Stadler, John. *Hooray for Snail!* **1984. Hardcover and paperback: Harper. 32 pages. Ages 3–7. PICTURE BOOK.**
Very simple language recounts a ball game in which Snail plays unexpectedly well. Snail gets up to bat with a bat considerably bigger than he is and, to everyone's surprise, slams the ball. Snail makes his slow way around the bases while the ball flies far out of the stadium and into outer space. Tension mounts as the ball zooms back and, after a nap, Snail heads for home. Hilarious pictures add to the appeal of this baseball story for the young.

Quindlen, Anna. *Happily Ever After.* **Illustrated by James Stevenson. 1997. Hardcover: Viking. Paperback: Puffin. 48 pages. Ages 4–9. FICTION.**

Kate, a baseball-loving fourth-grader, gets a magical baseball mitt for her birthday, but when she uses it to wish to be a princess, she's surprised at the results. After an encounter with a boring prince and an interesting witch, Kate arrives at a castle where she teaches the ladies-in-waiting and serving maids baseball and the chatter that goes with it. A funny, clever story accompanied by funny, clever pictures.

Zagwyn, Deborah Turney. *Apple Batter.* **1999. Hardcover: Tricycle. 32 pages. Ages 4–9. PICTURE BOOK.**

Eight-year-old Delmore longs to be a better baseball player, and his mother, Loretta, longs to have her three apple trees bear fruit. Both approach their goals with determination and hard work, as the richly colored watercolors show. Soon each tree puts forth a tiny apple. Then Delmore starts to connect with the ball, and eventually hits it straight. Unexpectedly, their goals conflict until Loretta comes up with a clever solution. A warm, beautifully illustrated story.

Rappaport, Doreen, and Lyndall Callan. *Dirt on Their Skirts: The Story of the Young Women Who Won the World Championship.* **Illustrated by E. B. Lewis. 2000. Hardcover: Dial. 32 pages. Ages 5–9. PICTURE BOOK NONFICTION.**

During World War II, women started playing professional baseball in a national league. This fine book recounts the 1946 world championship game between the Racine Belles of Wisconsin and the Rockford Peaches of Illinois. Through the eyes of a girl and her family, the reader watches the final inning during overtime when Sophie Kurys of the Belles hits a single, steals second base, and slides in for the winning run. Large, light-filled watercolors give the feel of the crowd and their emotions in this terrific book.

Shannon, David. *How Georgie Radbourn Saved Baseball*. 1994. Hardcover: Blue Sky. Paperback: Scholastic. 32 pages. Ages 6–10. PICTURE BOOK.

In this picture-story book for older children, Boss Swaggert, a bitter former baseball player, becomes powerful enough to eliminate the game of baseball. As a result, the sun won't shine and warm winds won't blow. Dark, scary pictures show his evil rise to power and the bleak world he creates after banning ball. But young Georgie Radbourn, born spouting baseball chatter, loves the game enough to challenge the Boss. A strange tale with an ending that will have baseball fans cheering.

Hall, Donald. *When Willard Met Babe Ruth*. Illustrated by Barry Moser. 1996. Hardcover: Harcourt. 48 pages. Ages 8–11. FICTION.

Those who love the history of baseball will love this novella about a boy who meets Babe Ruth. Lovingly illustrated with watercolors on every other page, the story concerns a baseball-loving father and son in New Hampshire who help Babe Ruth pull his car out of a ditch, then later seek him out at a game. A generation later, the boy has grown up and his daughter is the one to meet the great player. Written in simple, lyrical prose by poet Donald Hall, this book is a tribute to the game.

Gutman, Dan. *Honus & Me: A Baseball Card Adventure*. 1997. Hardcover and paperback: Avon. 144 pages. Ages 8–12. FICTION.

Joe "Stosh" Stoshack loves baseball and collecting baseball cards. But despite practicing, he doesn't turn into a strong player until he meets the famous shortstop Honus Wagner, who played in the first half of the twentieth century. A magical baseball card makes it possible for Joe to travel back in time, where the time he spends with Honus changes him forever. A book with plenty of baseball excitement and some serious ideas about what's important in life.

Horenstein, Henry. *Baseball in the Barrios.* 1997. Hardcover and paperback: Harcourt. 36 pages. Ages 8–12. NONFICTION.

Young baseball players in the United States may be surprised to learn how popular the sport is in countries like Venezuela. In this genial photo-essay, a Venezuelan fifth-grader named Hubaldo shares his enthusiasm about baseball and talks about its importance in his life since he started playing at age four. He discusses his country's teams and most famous players, but mainly focuses on his own experiences. Expressive color photographs on each page bring Hubaldo's surroundings home to the reader.

Kasoff, Jerry. *Baseball Just for Kids: Skills, Strategies and Stories to Make You a Better Ballplayer.* 1996. Hardcover: Grand Slam Press. 159 pages. Ages 8–14. NONFICTION.

This well-designed book gives detailed advice on base running, batting, playing the infield and outfield, pitching, and catching. It offers an excellent review for current players who will pick up tips and ideas. For new players, it gives a solid introduction with many demonstrations in black-and-white photographs, plus interesting bits of folklore, baseball history, and stories about great players. Judging from the photos and text, the book is aimed primarily at boys, but girls can learn a lot from it, too.

Egan, Terry, Stan Friedmann, and Mike Levine. *The Good Guys of Baseball: Sixteen True Sports Stories*. 1997. Hardcover: Simon & Schuster. Paperback: Aladdin. 112 pages. Ages 9–12. COLLECTIVE BIOGRAPHY.

Dedicated baseball fans are the most likely to appreciate these sixteen stories about players and teams. The authors, who wax sentimental about the game, overdo the sports clichés but also convey their enthusiasm for everything good about baseball. They describe players who overcame obstacles, such as Jim Abbott, who has only one hand yet pitched a no-hitter. In other stories, baseball players value doing the right thing above all else.

Adelson, Bruce. *Grand Slam Trivia: Secrets, Statistics, and Little-Known Facts About Pro Baseball*. Illustrated by Harry Pulver, Jr. 1999. Hardcover and paperback: Lerner. 64 pages. Ages 9–13. NONFICTION.

This lively book, illustrated with photographs and cartoonlike drawings, gives a history of baseball and an introduction to baseball statistics. Each page combines straight text with extras like trivia quizzes, factual questions and answers, and sidebars labeled "Did You Know?" The overview covers the major leagues, Negro leagues, and women's professional teams, while the chapter on statistics shows how to calculate earned run averages (ERAs) and batting averages. Fun for baseball fans.

Mackel, Kathy. *A Season of Comebacks*. 1997. Hardcover: Putnam. Paperback: Paper Star. 112 pages. Ages 9–13. FICTION.

The Burrows household revolves around twelve-year-old Allie, the best young softball pitcher in California. Mr. Burrows coaches the Blazers, Allie's team, and spends little time with ten-year-old Molly. Molly has a good time playing short-stop for another team. But when the Blazers need her to be their catcher, softball stops being fun. In the end, Allie makes a surprising choice and Molly's father rethinks his approach to sports and his family. Filled with softball action, this is an absorbing sports novel.

McKissack, Patricia C., and Fredrick McKissack, Jr. *Black Diamond: The Story of the Negro Baseball Leagues.* 1994. Hardcover and paperback: Scholastic. 192 pages. Ages 10–14. NONFICTION.

Until 1947, when Jackie Robinson integrated the Brooklyn Dodgers, talented black players joined the Negro Leagues. This readable book introduces such great players as Josh Gibson, "Smoky" Joe Williams, Satchel Paige, and many others as it describes the different Negro Leagues and the problems they faced. Although social history is woven into the story, the main focus is baseball, with enough details to satisfy fans.

Wolff, Virginia Euwer. *Bat 6.* 1998. Hardcover and paperback: Scholastic. 228 pages. Ages 10–14. FICTION.

In this outstanding novel set in 1949, two small-town baseball teams gear up for their fiftieth-anniversary game. Most of the girls have looked forward to their chance to play for years. But World War II has left painful memories that start to interfere with the coming game. The text, which switches among the players' voices, builds up tension between a newcomer whose father was killed at Pearl Harbor and a girl of Japanese descent whose family spent the war in a detention camp. A challenging, original book that mixes baseball and deeper issues.

Johnson, Scott. *Safe at Second.* 1999. Hardcover: Philomel. 245 pages. Ages 11–14. FICTION.

High school senior Todd is a remarkably talented pitcher who is being wooed by colleges and major league teams. His best friend Paulie, who loves baseball more than anything else but is not very good at it, is Todd's biggest fan. When a tragedy interferes with Todd's playing, Paulie feels as adrift as Todd does. They are still on the team, but both need to look for more than baseball to pull them through. Lots of sports action woven into a compelling story.

Basketball

Maccarone, Grace. *The Gym Day Winner.* Illustrated by Betsy Lewin. 1996. Hardcover: Scholastic. Paperback: Cartwheel. 32 pages. Ages 3–7. EASY READER.

In this easy-to-read book, Sam finds himself the least skill-ful athlete in running and gymnastics. But luckily, he is wide open during a basketball game, receives a pass, and makes a winning shot. A very short text uses simple words to tell this story many children will relate to. Bright pictures show boys and girls, including one in a wheelchair, enjoying sports. A re-assuring story for children who don't excel in sports.

Barber, Barbara E. *Allie's Basketball Dream.* Illustrated by Darryl Ligasan. 1996. Hardcover and paperback: Lee & Low. 32 pages. Ages 4–8. PICTURE BOOK.

Allie takes her new basketball to the playground one morning, where some older boys laugh at her. Even her friend Keisha proclaims, "My brother says basketball's a boy's game." But Allie argues that her cousin Gwen has won more than ten trophies on her high school basketball team. Allie finally con-vinces her friends to shoot baskets with her, and when she swishes one through, even the older boys applaud. Plenty of basketball plus a strong girl.

Martin, Bill, Jr., and Michael Sampson. *Swish!* Illustrated by Michael Chesworth. 1997. Hardcover and paperback: Henry Holt. 32 pages. Ages 4–8. PICTURE BOOK.

In this fast-paced picture book, a basketball game has come down to the final minute. The rhyming text gives a play-by-play, and when the Cardinals tie the game with a basket, a huge "SWISH" crosses the page. Then "44 to 44, / only 16 seconds more. / Blue Jays rushing, / gotta score." With another "SWISH," the Blue Jays make their jump shot, and the Cardinals take a time out. Will they try a three-point shot to win? Energetic watercolors capture the drama and the fierce concentration of the players.

Burleigh, Robert. *Hoops*. Illustrated by Stephen T. Johnson. 1997. Hardcover: Harcourt. 32 pages. Ages 4–9. PICTURE BOOK.

Poetic language captures the excitement and beauty of a pickup basketball game. "The smooth, skaterly glide and sudden swerve. / The sideways slip through a moment of narrow space." With only a sentence or two per page, the dramatic paintings dominate the book. The game's tension comes across in the close-ups of male and female players giving it all they have. An unusual, evocative celebration of basketball as it's played on the streets of America's cities.

Coy, John. *Strong to the Hoop*. Illustrated by Leslie Jean-Bart. 1999. Hardcover: Lee & Low. 32 pages. Ages 5–9. PICTURE BOOK.

When ten-year-old Jason gets into a pickup basketball game with older boys, it takes all his skill, determination, and self-confidence to keep playing. Initially he's intimidated to find himself guarding a stronger boy, but he quickly finds his own pace and even makes the winning shot. Collage illustrations combining photographs and scratchboard art convey the intensity of the game and the players. An unusual picture-story book about neighborhood basketball.

Marzollo, Jean, and Dan Marzollo. *Basketball Buddies*. Illustrated by True Kelley. 1998. Hardcover and paperback: Scholastic. 32 pages. Ages 6–10. FICTION.

In this novel for early readers, a tall but unskilled basketball player named Paul benefits from the support of his friends. "Too Tall Paul" would rather be playing with action figures than missing basketball shots, but with the help of his teammates—boys and girls—he develops his strengths in blocking and rebounds. A good-natured story with lots of basketball, shown in colorful pictures.

Christopher, Matt. *Center Court Sting*. 1998. Hardcover and paperback: Little, Brown. 160 pages. Ages 8–12. FICTION.

When anything goes wrong in his life, Daren blames someone else. He brings his negative attitude onto the basketball court, where his accusations end up dividing the team into two camps. Even his best friend sometimes seems to think that Daren is unreasonable. Can he learn to compete hard without making others mad at him? Basketball permeates every chapter of this novel by the most popular sportswriter for children.

Christopher, Matt. *On the Court with Lisa Leslie*. 1998. Paperback: Little, Brown. 112 pages. Ages 8–13. BIOGRAPHY.

This biography of basketball great Lisa Leslie starts with her childhood, then moves enthusiastically through her basketball career. Important, close games get special attention, including NCAA games and the 1996 Olympics. The athlete's willingness to work long, hard hours is emphasized. Unimpressive black-and-white photographs show Leslie playing for the L.A. Sparks. This is part of a welcome trend toward more children's biographies of female athletes.

Weatherspoon, Teresa. *Teresa Weatherspoon's Basketball for Girls*. 1999. Paperback: Wiley. 120 pages. Ages 8–14. NONFICTION.

Basketball great Teresa Weatherspoon of the New York Liberty has put together a fine resource for basketball players with the help of two sportswriters. It covers all the basketball basics in detail: shooting, passing, dribbling, defense, and more. Weatherspoon adds personal information and motivational comments in frequent sidebars. Black-and-white photos demonstrate the moves and also show the Liberty's workout routine. An inspiring, informative guide for young players.

Lovitt, Chip. *Michael Jordan*. 1999 Revised Edition. Paperback: Scholastic. 224 pages. Ages 9–13. BIOGRAPHY.

This updated biography describes the childhood and career of Michael Jordan, through his college days and his starring role with the Chicago Bulls to his 1999 retirement from basketball. Beginning with an introduction by Coretta Scott King, the book combines personal and professional details and anecdotes. The insert of color photographs is disappointing, but Jordan's myriad fans will nevertheless enjoy this biography of the player many consider the best ever.

Mullin, Chris, with Brian Coleman. *The Young Basketball Player*. 1995. Hardcover: DK. 48 pages. Ages 9–14. NONFICTION.

Each double-page spread in this popular book uses color photographs of kids playing to explain "Shooting," "Rebound Play," "Fast Break," and much more. Step-by-step instructions, detailed captions, and diagrams expand the information. Included are a short history of the game and a page on "Leagues," written before the current women's professional leagues started. Useful for beginning and slightly advanced players, this is one in an attractive series that includes many other sports.

Moore, Elaine. *Who Let Girls in the Boys' Locker Room?* 1994. Hardcover and paperback: Troll. 128 pages. Ages 10–13. FICTION.

Michelle loves basketball. She has a Michael Jordan poster in her room and plays on a community-center team. She hopes to try out for the junior high girls' team, but finds that budget cuts have created a co-ed team instead. She and two other girls make the team, but the boys treat them as if they are fragile. Determined to be a full-fledged player, Michelle helps the coach solve the problem. Despite a few clichés, the story will appeal to sports fans.

Soto, Gary. *Taking Sides*. 1991. Hardcover and paperback: Harcourt. 138 pages. Ages 11–14. FICTION.

A star basketball player on his junior high team, Lincoln Mendoza has moved from San Francisco's Mission District to a safer but mainly white suburb. Despite Lincoln's excellent playing, his new coach is biased against him. To add to his troubles, he quarrels with his best friend. Lots of dialogue, including Spanish words defined in a glossary, convey Lincoln's sympathetic character, his good relationship with his mother, and his growth as he tackles problems on and off the basketball court.

Stewart, Mark. *Basketball: A History of Hoops*. 1998. Hardcover: Watts. 160 pages. Ages 11 and up. NONFICTION.

Many photographs combine with well-organized information and lively writing in this history of a popular sport. Lots of details and anecdotes enliven the coverage of both college and professional basketball since the sport's beginning. Sidebars add information on topics like Olympic basketball and the three-point shot, with profiles of famous players and coaches. This history pays only slight attention to women's basketball, but otherwise it does a thorough job.

Brooks, Bruce. *The Moves Make the Man.* **1984. Hardcover and paperback: Harper. 280 pages. Ages 12–14. FICTION.**

Jerome loves basketball but isn't welcome on the team when he is the only black student to integrate a junior high. So he perfects his moves by playing on his own. When his mother falls ill, Jerome takes home ec to learn to cook, and meets Bix. Narrated in Jerome's distinctive voice, this is the story of their friendship, which they solidify through basketball, and the story of Bix's struggle with his family's problems. Beautifully written and full of basketball, this is a memorable Newbery Honor Book.

Deuker, Carl. *On the Devil's Court.* **1988. Paperback: Flare. 192 pages. Ages 12–14. FICTION.**

Seventeen-year-old Joe Faust would do anything to make the varsity basketball team before the end of high school. Surprisingly, he suddenly plays well enough to make the team and just as suddenly starts getting straight As. Everything is going so well that he has to face the question: Has he sold his soul to play basketball? The intriguing plot incorporates a lot of basketball in this suspenseful, high-quality sports novel.

Irwin, Hadley. *Sarah with an H.* **1996. Hardcover: McElderry. 134 pages. Ages 12–14. FICTION.**

The LaMond High School basketball team has a chance of winning the all-state finals if all goes well for Marti, the team's

captain, and her teammates. Newcomer Sarah Irvine, an outstanding player, may even break a tournament scoring record.
They just have to stick to their game plan and play as a team.
But the fact that Sarah is one of the first Jews in their small
town raises problems Marti had never expected. A realistic, if
sometimes painful, sports story.

Figure Skating

Blackstone, Margaret. *This Is Figure Skating.* Illustrated by John O'Brien. 1998. Hardcover: Henry Holt. 32 pages. Ages 3–7. PICTURE BOOK.

With a very simple text, this picture book introduces figure skating, its equipment, and some of its movements. Pen-and-watercolor illustrations feature skaters whirling around a city rink, demonstrating specific moves like the camel, sit spin, and scratch spins, and jumps including a loop, a double lutz, and a triple flip. Several images of the same person in different positions show the steps in the spins and jumps. The enthusiasm of the skaters gives this short book a sense of celebration about skating.

Isadora, Rachel. *Sophie Skates.* 1999. Hardcover: Putnam. 32 pages. Ages 3–8. PICTURE BOOK.

Eight-year-old Sophie takes lessons five mornings a week at five o'clock and three afternoons after school. A double-page spread shows her clothing and equipment, then shows and describes different moves and jumps on the ice. One section compares movements from ballet, which Sophie also studies, with movements in skating. The illustrations incorporate an unusual amount of information for such a short, attractive book.

O'Connor, Jane. *Kate Skates*. **Illustrated by DyAnne DiSalvo-Ryan. 1995. Paperback: Grosset & Dunlap. 32 pages. Ages 6–8. Of interest to younger children. EASY READER.**

When Kate gets new single-blade figure skates, she gives her younger sister, Jen, her old double-bladed ones. Kate plans to teach Jen to skate but it turns out Jen does well while Kate keeps falling, as she gets used to single skates. Pleasant, sometimes funny pen-and-watercolor illustrations show the girls and their mother at a public rink where Kate's favorite skating star Diana Lin is visiting. To Kate's embarrassment, she falls and Diana helps her up. The skating star is so kind that all turns out well. A cheerful, encouraging book for young readers and young skaters.

Brimner, Larry Dane. *Figure Skating*. **1997. Hardcover: Children's Press. 48 pages. Ages 7–9. Of interest to younger children. NONFICTION.**

Large typeface, color photographs, and an open design make this an appealing introduction to figure skating for younger readers. It opens with a short history of the sport told with well-chosen details and graphics. Chapters look at Olympic figure skating events, giving the distinguishing features of each and explaining the differences between pair skating and ice dancing. The "Stars on Ice" section highlights Oksana Baiul, Elvis Stojko, and Torvill and Dean. An appendix refers readers to other books, figure skating organizations, and Web sites.

Maifair, Linda Lee. *Go Figure, Gabriella Grant!* **1997. Paperback: Zondervan. 56 pages. Ages 8–11. FICTION.**

When Gabriella starts middle school and makes new friends, they don't understand her commitment to skating, why she wouldn't prefer going to football games and dances with them than practice skating six days a week. Their attitude starts to undermine Gabriella's self-confidence until her coach suggests inviting the friends to a competition. But now Gabriella is worried she will make mistakes in front of them. Gabriella's occasional references to her Christianity will appeal to some readers but they don't dominate the simple story. A quick read with plenty of references to spins and jumps.

Tripp, Valerie. *Samantha's Winter Party*. Illustrated by Dan Andreasen. 1999. Hardcover: Pleasant. 48 pages. Ages 8–11. FICTION.

In this short story made into a tiny book, nine-year-old Samantha and her friends enjoy skating together on a nearby pond. Set in 1904, this simple story revolves around Samantha's friendship with Nellie, a servant girl who lives next door. When Samantha suggests a skating party with presents, Nellie comes up with an unexpectedly magical gift for the whole group of girls. An afterword gives a brief but fascinating look at the history of skating, with some useful pictures. Very slight but sure to please "American Girl" fans and those who like skating.

Lowell, Melissa. *In the Spotlight*. 1993. Paperback: Bantam. 130 pages. Ages 9–12. FICTION.

One in the "Silver Blades" series about a group of figure skaters, this novel focuses on Danielle, who has the only solo in an upcoming ice show. Although a fine skater, Danielle lacks confidence and pressures herself to be perfect. Vowing to slim down for the show, she nearly quits eating and loses her energy. Luckily, she realizes her mistake and reaches the exciting event in good shape. Although the writing lacks depth, the issues and details about the sport seem real and will appeal to skating fans.

Morrissey, Peter. *The Young Ice Skater: A Young Enthusiast's Guide to Ice Skating.* 1998. Hardcover: DK. 37 pages. Ages 9–14. Of interest to younger children. NONFICTION.

This attractive book focuses on step-by-step photo sequences of figure skating jumps and spins. Although readers cannot expect to learn these movements from a book, would-be skaters and beginners will enjoy the demonstrations of the salchow, lutz, camel spin, and more. Other pages combine photographs and long captions to tell the history of the sport, show equipment, and explain basic moves such as stopping and skating backward. An appealing overview for those newly interested in figure skating.

Boitano, Brian, with Suzanne Harper. *Boitano's Edge: Inside the Real World of Figure Skating.* 1992. Hardcover: Simon & Schuster. 144 pages. Ages 10–14. Of interest to younger children. NONFICTION.

This large, glossy book really does take the reader inside the skating world. It effectively combines Boitano's own story as a top skater with interesting details about his fellow skaters, tips on skating and performing, and information about costumes, skates, choreography, judging, and much more. Well-known skaters such as Katarina Witt and Oksana Baiul contribute sidebars about Brian and their friendships with him. Many large color photos of Brian and others add a glamorous note. While some may find it a bit too focused on Boitano, this is nevertheless an unusually fine book about the sport.

Boo, Michael. *The Story of Figure Skating.* 1998. Hardcover: Morrow. Paperback: Beechtree. 224 pages. Ages 10–14. NONFICTION.

This solid volume will attract those with a serious interest in figure skating. It takes the reader through the history of the sport in detail from its beginning, then reviews the stars and key events decade by decade starting with the 1960s. One chapter discusses the practical side and professionals that keep the sport going, such as coaches, choreographers, and even the ice-making process. The author, who writes for *American Skating World*, uses a chatty, enthusiastic tone. The small, black-and-white photos are disappointing, but the book offers much more information than most.

Football

Sampson, Michael. *The Football That Won.* Illustrated by Ted Rand. 1996. Hardcover and paperback: Henry Holt. 32 pages. Ages 3–7. PICTURE BOOK.

Action-packed pictures are the highlight of this picture-story book about football. Players sprawl and crash across the pages—running, passing, and celebrating. Cheerleaders, the coach, fans, and even the Goodyear blimp make an appearance as the Cowboys win the Super Bowl, beating Kansas City. The cumulative rhyme, modeled on "The House That Jack Built," is awkward in spots, although it improves as the book goes on. Young football fans will enjoy the excitement.

Kessler, Leonard. *Kick, Pass, and Run.* 1966. Hardcover and paperback: Harper. 64 pages. Ages 6–9. Of interest to younger children. EASY READER.

What is the strange brown object that comes hurtling into the woods? Neither the rabbit, duck, cat, dog, nor owl recognizes it as a football. When a boy retrieves it, they follow him to the football field to see how he plays with it. Excited after a touchdown, the animals organize their own football game, but without a ball. Will an apple or a paper bag do as well? A diagram explains football basics for new fans in this cheerful easy reader.

Berenstain, Stan, and Jan Berenstain. *The Berenstain Bears and the Female Fullback.* **1993. Hardcover: Random House. 102 pages. Ages 7–11. Of interest to younger children. FICTION.**

In this chapter book about the popular bear family, Papa is excited that Brother is going out for football, but takes little interest in Sister's cheerleading plans. At school, the kids assume that Brother will be elected Class President until a girl bear named Queenie enters the election. Finally, Brenda, an athletic new girl tries out for the football team—until the coach objects. Suddenly, everyone in Bear Country is talking about what girls can and can't do, culminating in the biggest football game of the year.

Patey, R. L. "Buddy." *The Illustrated Rules of Football.* **Illustrated by Patrick T. McRae. 1995. Paperback: Ideals. 32 pages. Ages 8–11. NONFICTION.**

This slim book written by an experienced football official provides a basic understanding of football. It starts with a diagram and explanation of the playing field, then describes the ball, goalposts, yardage chain, down marker, and required clothing and equipment. In simple language with useful and attractive illustrations, the book covers players' positions, officials, scoring, formations, fouls, and more. The author stresses good sportsmanship in his final note.

Christopher, Matt. *Great Moments in Football History.* **1997. Hardcover and paperback: Little, Brown. 90 pages. Ages 8–12. NONFICTION.**

Each of nine chapters tells a remarkable story about a professional football player. One recounts Joe Namath's guarantee that his team, the New York Jets, would win the Super Bowl in 1969, with extended descriptions of the game's major plays.

Similarly, details of plays abound in the story of how 49ers' quarterback Steve Young made his reputation in a 1988 game against the Vikings, taking the place of an injured Joe Montana. Football fans will enjoy these accounts of exciting games.

Korman, Gordon. *Running Back Conversion: I Was Barry Sanders*. 1997. Hardcover and paperback: Hyperion. 96 pages. Ages 8–12. FICTION.
Three friends who hold a sleepover during every televised Monday night football game also have a magic jersey that transports one of them into the game. This time, Elliot finds himself in the body of Barry Sanders, the Detroit Lions' running back, while Sanders wakes up as a fifth-grader, watching himself on television. Elliot is starting to enjoy his role on the team, when something unexpected distracts him that could cost the game. Silly in parts, but with plenty of football. One in a series.

Christopher, Matt. *Undercover Tailback*. Illustrated by Paul Casale. 1992. Hardcover and paperback: Little, Brown. 146 pages. Ages 9–12. FICTION.
Twelve-year-old Parker works hard on the football field but his teammates tease him about making up stories. When he sees someone sneak out of the coach's office with a camera, no one believes him. He believes that someone has stolen the team's plays, but putting his energy into solving the mystery starts detracting from his schoolwork. He must find out who stole the plays and get his grades back up, or the season will be a disaster. A mystery with many football scenes.

Buckley, James, Jr. *America's Greatest Game: The Real Story of Football and the NFL*. 1998. Hardcover: Hyperion. 64 pages. Ages 9–13. Of interest to younger children. NONFICTION.

Enthusiasm for professional football saturates this book from the introduction by Jerry Rice to the coverage of the 1998 Super Bowl. Football fans will enjoy the many full-page color photographs, often action shots of favorite players. One page shows all the NFL helmets, while another lists the champions and Super Bowl winners since 1920. The emphasis is on the NFL, past and present, which produced the book.

Dygard, Thomas J. *Second Stringer*. 1998. Hardcover: Morrow. 192 pages. Ages 10–14. FICTION.

Almost all the scenes in this novel take place on the football field during practice or high school games. Kevin has been the second string quarterback for his high school career, watching as Rob won game after game. But now Rob has hurt his knee and may be out for the season. With his best friend's encouragement and some coaching from Rob, Kevin steps up and starts to play well. But will it be well enough to win the championship? A well-written sports novel sure to satisfy football fans.

Sullivan, George. *Quarterbacks*. 1998. Hardcover: Atheneum. 80 pages. Ages 11–14. Of interest to younger children. COLLECTIVE BIOGRAPHY.

This book profiles Brett Favre, Troy Aikman, Steve Young, Dan Marino, and many more popular quarterbacks. Three or four pages describe the eighteen quarterbacks with a brief personal history, recap of their careers, detailed descriptions of important games, and colored photos. Quotes from the players emphasize their determination, hard work, and ambition. Starting with recent players and moving back, the book also gives a sense of football history. Well-written and appealing.

Gymnastics

Brown, Marc. *D.W. Flips!* 1987. Hardcover and paperback: Little, Brown. 32 pages. Ages 2–5. PICTURE BOOK.

D.W., younger sister of the better-known Arthur, thinks she's too old for her "baby" gymnastics class but finds out that it is more of a challenge than she expected. Determined to excel, she practices her forward roll all week long, everywhere in the house, to her family's annoyance. During the next class, she performs as well as she had hoped and impresses everyone. But she is taken aback to realize that now she needs to learn a backward roll. One in a series about a determined, energetic young aardvark.

Hoban, Lillian. *Arthur's Birthday Party.* 1999. Hardcover and paperback: Harper. 64 pages. Ages 6–8. Of interest to younger children. EASY READER.

Arthur and his younger sister, Violet, are chimpanzees and so natural gymnasts. Arthur is showing off on a swing one day when he decides that his birthday party will include prizes for the best gymnasts. Violet and her friend practice on the swing set all week, and Arthur's pal Norman works on his trampoline skills. Everyone does well at the party, performing tricks most parents would not allow their human children to try. Not to be confused with the aardvark Arthur and his sister, D.W., these two chimps also star in a series about everyday problems and fun.

Ransom, Candice F. *Third Grade Stars*. 1994. Hardcover: Troll. 128 pages. Ages 8–11. FICTION.

Amber loves to cook up new ideas and do new craft projects. She enjoys being one of the most popular girls in her class along with her friend Delight. But when the third grade starts gymnastics in gym class, Amber envies Delight's prowess at the sport. Her divorced parents cannot afford gymnastics lessons so Amber starts her own gymnastics school on the theory that teaching children will help her learn. Nothing turns out the way she had hoped, yet in the end it looks like Amber will have gymnastics in her future. Aspiring gymnasts will relate to Amber's sudden passion for the sport.

Slater, Teddy. *Dana's Competition*. Illustrated by Wayne Alfano. 1996. Paperback: Scholastic. 77 pages. Ages 8–11. FICTION.

The first in the "Junior Gymnasts" series, this opens with a letter from Dominique Dawes about her gymnastics training that led ultimately to the Olympics. Like the novel itself, she stresses the importance of teamwork. The main character, Dana, is excited about her first competition in gymnastics, along with the other girls from Coach Jody's gym. Dana has always been the best of her group, but just before the competition, Amanda joins the gym and proves to be significantly better than Dana. Dana's jealousy of Amanda threatens the team's likelihood of winning the cup. Descriptions of gymnastics play a large role in this light series book.

Readhead, Lloyd. *The Fantastic Book of Gymnastics*. 1997. Hardcover: Copper Beech. 40 pages. Ages 8–12. Of interest to younger children. NONFICTION.

This attractive book gives a fine overview of gymnastics, with color photographs of regular children and world famous gymnasts. It describes equipment and how it is used, demonstrates warm-up exercises, and shows many step-by-step movements and positions for female and male gymnasts. Fold-out pages provide a large spread on competition events, with an explanation of scoring and much more. For safety reasons, the book advises learning gymnastics in a supervised setting, but this introduction will get readers excited about performing or watching the sport.

Charbonnet, Gabrielle. *Competition Fever*. 1996. Paperback: Bantam. 118 pages. Ages 9–12. FICTION.

Kelly's mother, a widow who owns a gymnastics academy, has married a Russian gymnastics coach who has a daughter, Maya, Kelly's age. At first, Kelly is excited, but when Maya doesn't respond to her friendliness, Kelly's excitement turns to doubt. A devious older girl at the gym feeds Kelly's doubts, which is easy when it turns out that Maya is as talented a gymnast as Kelly. Will the two of them put aside their differences enough to work together on a team event? Light on character development but with many descriptions of gymnastics, this will appeal to fans of the sport.

Rutledge, Rachel. *Women of Sports: The Best of the Best in Gymnastics*. 1999. Hardcover and paperback: Cronopio. 64 pages. Ages 9 and up. Of interest to younger children. NONFICTION.

After an introduction to the sport and its history, sportswriter Rutledge highlights the careers of eight gymnasts. Each profile describes the athlete's strengths as a gymnast and how she got involved in the sport, with plenty of action photographs. Sidebars give personal details and key career achievements. The gymnasts from the United States are Shannon Miller, Dominique Dawes, Kris Maloney, Dominique Moceanu, and Vanessa Atler. Russian gymnasts Svetlana Khorkina, Simona Amanar from Romania, and Ling Jie from China round out the picture. A final few pages look at concerns about the sport and its future.

Gutman, Dan. *Gymnastics*. 1996. Hardcover: Viking. Paperback: Puffin. 186 pages. Ages 10–14. NONFICTION.

The solid overview of gymnastics gives a brief history, then singles out Olga Korbut, Nadia Comaneci, Kurt Thomas, and Mary Lou Retton to discuss as the first superstars. One chapter goes through each of the men's and women's events in detail, another looks at judging and scoring, and yet another follows a girl through her day as a high school student and top gymnast. After a look at stars of the 1990s, Gutman adds a sobering chapter on the dangers and drawbacks of the sport. Lots of information, with many small black-and-white photos and an inset of color ones.

Jackman, Joan. *Gymnastics*. 2000. Hardcover: DK. 48 pages. Ages 10 and up. Of interest to younger children. NONFICTION.

In this "Superguide," which looks like an "Eyewitness" book, young male and female gymnasts demonstrate gymnastic moves in step-by-step photo sequences. Rolls, headstands and handstands, cartwheels and round-offs, flic flacs and walkovers are among the featured skills. Other double-page spreads show gymnasts vaulting, using the balance beam, and doing rhythmic gymnastics and sports acrobatics. With crisp color photographs, this is an attractive introduction that will inspire readers to try gymnastics.

Ice Hockey

Brownridge, William Roy. *The Moccasin Goalie*. 1995. Hardcover and paperback: Orca. 32 pages. Ages 3–8. PICTURE BOOK.

In a story that reads like a memoir, a group of kids in Canada devote all their free time to hockey. The narrator, Danny, has a crippled leg but plays goalie in his moccasins. He is heartbroken when a local man starts a real team but keeps Danny off, as well as Anita because she's a girl and Petou because he's small. Weeks later, though, the coach needs Danny to play goalie in the toughest game of his life. Stiff but colorful pictures create a prairie setting and convey the children's emotions.

Stevenson, James. *Sam the Zamboni Man*. Illustrated by Harvey Stevenson. 1998. Hardcover: Greenwillow. 32 pages. Ages 3–8. PICTURE BOOK.

Everyone who goes to hockey games knows the seemingly magical Zamboni machine that turns scuffed ice into a glistening surface. When Matt visits his grandfather in the city, he goes to a hockey game in a large stadium and watches proudly while his grandfather drives the Zamboni. After the game when they have the rink to themselves, Grandfather plays a little one-person hockey and then lets Sam drive the Zamboni with him. A wish-fulfillment fantasy for young hockey fans.

Maloney, Peter, and Felicia Zekauskas. *The Magic Hockey Stick*. 1999. Hardcover: Dial. 32 pages. Ages 4–8. PICTURE BOOK.

The narrator, who loves hockey, is thrilled when her parents buy Wayne Gretsky's hockey stick at a charity auction. She cannot resist using it in hockey games and finds she has magically become a great player. But when she reads that the Great One has hit a slump, she knows she must get the stick back to him. Humorous pictures and a jaunty rhyming text add to the fun.

Kramer, S. A. *Hockey Stars*. Illustrated by Mitchell Heinze. 1997. Hardcover and paperback: Grosset & Dunlap. 48 pages. Ages 6–9. COLLECTIVE BIOGRAPHY.

Large print and frequent pictures make this an accessible sports book for younger readers. Each of the four chapters focuses on a famous hockey player. It opens with the 1994 game in which Wayne Gretsky became the all-time highest scorer, then recaps his childhood and career. Next comes Mario Lemieux, his battle with cancer, and his determination to play again. Eric Lindros's road to becoming a team player and Patrick Roy's comeback as a goalie round out the collective biography.

Marzollo, Jean, and Dan Marzollo. *Hockey Hero*. Illustrated by True Kelley. 1998. Hardcover and paperback: Random House. 32 pages. Ages 7–10. Of interest to younger children. EASY READER.

Hal assumes he'll be the best player on his new hockey team, but nothing seems to be going right. Hoping to be a hero, Hal tries to take control and doesn't pass when his coach tells him to. After several losses, the coach switches Hal from center to defense, over the boy's objections. Cheerful pictures, mostly of hockey action, show that Hal's new position pays off in goals by his teammates. Hal, too, gains team spirit and new friends.

McFarlane, Brian. *Hockey for Kids: Heroes, Tips, and Facts.* **Illustrated by Bill Slavin. 1996. Hardcover: Morrow. Paperback: Kids Can. 64 pages. Ages 8–13. NONFICTION.**

Instructions, equipment, great players, history, hockey terms—this book provides a wide range of interesting material about ice hockey. It gives both an overview and small, surprising facts such as records for longest and shortest overtimes. Special sections look at a day in the life of a professional, give an interview with a referee, and discuss the history and role of women in hockey. Color photographs, drawings, and diagrams expand on the text in this enthusiastic manual and tribute to the game.

Christopher, Matt. *Penalty Shot.* **1997. Hardcover and paperback: Little, Brown. 128 pages. Ages 9–12. FICTION.**

Jeff sat out last year's season due to poor grades, so he is more determined than ever to play on the middle school ice hockey team. His hockey skills are good, but he is still struggling with English class. Meanwhile, he is trying to overcome his longtime fear of dogs. His life gets really complicated when someone starts sabotaging his homework and friendships by imitating his handwriting. An enjoyable combination of a mystery and lots of hockey.

Korman, Gordon. *The Chicken Doesn't Skate.* **1996. Hardcover and paperback: Scholastic. 208 pages. Ages 9–13. FICTION.**

What does a baby chick have to do with a hockey team? For some reason, the South Middle School Rangers cannot win unless the chicken Henrietta is at their games. But Henrietta is a part of a science experiment and is destined to end up cooked unless someone saves her. Told from different students' points of view, this amusing story includes hockey action, scenes from horror movies, and a dedicated scientist, all brought together by a chicken.

Brooks, Bruce. *Woodsie*. 1997. Hardcover and paperback: Harper. 144 pages. Ages 10–14. FICTION.

Eleven-year-old Woodsie has not played much hockey before he tries out for the Wolfbay Wings. Because the Wings have just lost their best players, Woodsie makes the team. Most of the novel describes team practices and how Woodsie learns to understand and play hockey. It ends with the team's first game of the season, in which Woodsie finds out just how different practice is from the real thing. The first in a series, an unusually well-written sports novel steeped in the game.

Rossiter, Sean. *Hockey the NHL Way: The Basics*. 1996. Paperback: Sterling. 92 pages. Ages 10–14. Of interest to younger children. NONFICTION.

With clear instructions, this book explains basic skills that hockey players must master. Color photographs show top players as well as young players, including a few girls, demonstrating skills. The topics include skating, offense, defense, goaltending, equipment, and fitness, with descriptions of specific maneuvers and practice drills for gaining skills. Tips and quotes from stars appear frequently. The author's excitement comes across in this useful guide to learning and improving hockey skills.

Sullivan, George. *All About Hockey*. 1998. Hardcover and paperback: Putnam. 145 pages. Ages 10–14. NONFICTION.

This thorough book on hockey lays out the basic rules and skills of the popular game, then discusses the lineup, offense, and defense in some detail. The second half of the book looks at national and international professional hockey and profiles a handful of hockey superstars. Back matter includes a glossary, all-time records, a list of organizations with addresses, and reading suggestions. A fine overview that uses black-and-white photographs and diagrams.

More Sports

Pinkney, Brian. *JoJo's Flying Side Kick.* 1995. Hardcover: Simon & Schuster. Paperback: Aladdin. 32 pages. Ages 3–7. PICTURE BOOK.

A resourceful African-American girl named JoJo needs to perform a flying side kick to win her yellow belt in tae kwon do. She gathers advice from family and friends on how to succeed, then puts it all together her own way. A splendid, energetic illustration captures her moment of triumph. The powerful scratchboard artwork suits the story perfectly. A highly recommended book on the ever popular topic of martial arts.

Mammano, Julie. *Rhinos Who Surf.* 1996. Hardcover: Chronicle. 32 pages. Ages 3–8. PICTURE BOOK.

Get ready for a dose of surfing slang in this jazzy book. "Rhinos who surf have no fear of MONDO waves. They SHRED! They DROP IN!" Each wave-filled page has a few sentences of text and a stylized picture of a rhino on a surfboard. Intricate patterns reminiscent of Hawaiian shirts fill the illustrations with beach colors. The book bursts with enthusiasm for surfing. The slang, defined in a glossary, will make future surfers feel very cool.

Luby, Thia. *Children's Book of Yoga: Games & Exercises Mimic Plants & Animals & Objects.* 1998. Hardcover: Clear Light. 96 pages. Ages 3–12. NONFICTION.

This thoughtful approach to children doing yoga draws on the natural world to explain each pose. Each of the dozens of positions is clearly explained and illustrated with a color photograph of children holding the pose along with a photograph of the object after which the pose is named. The book moves from simpler to more difficult levels, as do the poses within each chapter. An outstanding book that is both helpful and unusually beautiful. Also see author's *Yoga for Teens*.

Atkins, Jeannine. *Get Set! Swim!* Illustrated by Hector Viveros Less. 1998. Hardcover: Lee & Low. 32 pages. Ages 4–8. PICTURE BOOK.

It's time for Jessenia's first swim meet during her first year on the team. Their opponents live in a wealthier neighborhood and practice at a bigger pool, but her coach tells his team to focus on their own performances. In her first race, Jessenia gets distracted, but she has a second chance and makes the most of it. With support from her teammates and her family, Jessenia feels good about the meet even though they lose. An upbeat story about a young athlete and her first big competition.

Moran, George. *Imagine Me on a Sit-Ski*. Illustrated by Natalie Bernard Westcott. 1995. Hardcover: Albert Whitman. 32 pages. Ages 4–8. PICTURE BOOK.

Who would think that a boy in a wheelchair could ski? The narrator, who has cerebral palsy, cannot use his legs but he can use his arms a little and communicates with a wordboard. He is excited and scared about going with his classmates to a ski resort. The ski instructors put him in a sit-ski, which looks like a zippered kayak, give him short poles, and help him learn to steer by shifting his weight. Westcott's cheery pictures show the fun he and his classmates have in this refreshing book.

Antle, Nancy. *Staying Cool.* **Illustrated by E. B. Lewis. 1997. Hardcover: Dial. 32 pages. Ages 4–9. PICTURE BOOK.**

More than anything, Curtis wants to be a boxer, so he spends lots of time after school at the gym his grandfather has opened in a boarded-up grocery store. Light-filled watercolors show the warm interactions between Curtis and his firm but loving grandfather. Curtis, who struggles with his temper when he fights, knows he must conquer the problem before he can enter the local Golden Gloves boxing tournament. An unusual topic, effectively portrayed in this fine story and excellent illustrations.

Witt, Alexa. *It's Great to Skate: An Easy Guide to In-Line Skating.* **Illustrated by Nate Evans. 2000. Hardcover: Random House. Paperback: Aladdin. 32 pages. Ages 6–9. NONFICTION.**

Here is a guide to the popular sport of in-line skating that strong beginning readers can read themselves. With large print and plenty of illustrations, it lays out the basics of in-line skating, such as equipment, how to brake, and where to start. It gives tips on learning to balance and how to skate fluidly, conveying that in-line skating is not especially easy to learn but that it can be a lot of fun. The comical pictures expand on information in the enthusiastic text.

Hoyt-Goldsmith, Diane. *Lacrosse: The National Game of the Iroquois.* **Photographs by Lawrence Migdale. 1998. Hardcover: Holiday House. 32 pages. Ages 8–12. NONFICTION.**

North American Indians have played a game similar to lacrosse for hundreds of years, for pleasure, exercise, and as part of their religion. This photo-essay introduces the sport and discusses its history by focusing on thirteen-year-old Iroquois Monte Lyons and his father and grandfather, who all love lacrosse. Other pictures show lacrosse skills, a diagram of the field, and a demonstration of how wooden lacrosse sticks are made. A welcome overview of an increasingly popular sport.

Macy, Sue, and Jane Gottesman, editors. *Play Like a Girl: A Celebration of Women in Sports*. 1999. Hardcover: Henry Holt. 32 pages. Ages 8–12. Of interest to younger children. NONFICTION.

This inspiring book brings together powerful photographs and moving words about women's sports. Each double-page spread has crisp color photos of athletes in an array of sports: tennis, skiing, swimming, track, soccer, skateboarding, and more. Quotes from athletes or writers express the excitement and emotion of competing. So many images of strong women provide a welcome contrast to the many media images of women chosen for their conventional looks. A great gift book, too.

Christopher, Matt. *Spike It!* 1998. Hardcover and paperback: Little, Brown. 160 pages. Ages 9–12. FICTION.

Jamie is an intense volleyball player whose view is, "Go for the kill and spike it down their throats!" Her middle school team will make the state play-offs if they can win their next few games, but Jamie's personal life starts distracting her. Her father's sudden remarriage and Jamie's new stepsister, Michaela, an ace volleyball player, are more than she can handle. Will their problems at home keep the two girls from playing their best? A fast-paced sports novel.

Bailey, John. *The Young Fishing Enthusiast: A Practical Guide for Kids.* 1999. Hardcover: DK. 48 pages. Ages 9–14. NONFICTION.

This guide to fishing, which covers a new subject every few pages, uses many color photographs to help provide information on fish, equipment, and techniques. For example, one large double-page spread shows many kinds of fishing tackle, with captions and short paragraphs to explain the photographs. Other topics include basic casting, fly-fishing, bait fishing, lure fishing, and surf fishing, with step-by-step illustrations of casting. An enthusiastic, instructive book.

Creech, Sharon. *The Wanderer.* 2000. Hardcover: Harper. 306 pages. Ages 10–14. FICTION.

A storm-tossed ocean voyage presents a metaphor for life, a theme beautifully explored in this novel. Sophie, her cousins Cody and Brian, and her three uncles set off from Connecticut to sail to Ireland, a trip that nearly kills them. Sophie and Cody record their inner journeys and details of ship life in short journal entries. The relationships among the six change during the weeks, and Sophie especially feels reborn after the dangerous crossing. This elegantly designed book is another fine work by a Newbery Medalist.

Rafkin, Louise. *The Tiger's Eye, the Bird's Fist: A Beginner's Guide to the Martial Arts.* Illustrated by Leslie McGrath. 1997. Hardcover: Little, Brown. 133 pages. Ages 10–14. NONFICTION.

This excellent overview of martial arts combines history, descriptions of different martial arts and types of training, profiles of current practitioners and past masters, traditional stories concerning martial arts, and more. For readers who are deciding whether to take up a martial art, this is a useful place to start. It will also interest those who have seen martial arts in the movies or on television, and want to know more. Female martial artists get unusually good coverage in this enjoyable book.

Rouse, Jeff. *The Young Swimmer: A Young Enthusiast's Guide to Swimming.* **1997. Hardcover: DK. 40 pages. Ages 11–14. Of interest to younger children. NONFICTION.**

This overview of swimming, which covers a different subject on each double-page spread, describes specific skills and strokes, each illustrated in a series of clear photographs, sometimes showing the swimmer from different angles. It also includes a history of the sport, useful equipment, suggestions for warm-ups, and other useful tips. A good introduction to swimming or review of past lessons. One in a sports series similar to the "Eyewitness" books.

Lipsyte, Robert. *The Brave.* **1991. Paperback: Harper. 195 pages. Ages 12–14. FICTION.**

Seventeen-year-old Sonny Bear is a good boxer who could be great, but when rage overcomes him, he acts carelessly and loses fights. Fate keeps giving him new chances, though. His uncle Jake, who lives on the Moscondaga Reservation, gets Sonny in shape, and policeman Albert Brooks, from Lipsyte's book *The Contender*, tries to help Sonny in New York City. But Sonny struggles with himself and the biases he encounters. A fine, suspenseful novel, not just for boxing fans. Followed by *The Chief*.

Wallace, Rich. *Wrestling Sturbridge.* **1996. Hardcover and paperback: Knopf. 133 pages. Ages 12–14. FICTION.**

High school senior Ben takes wrestling seriously, as does everyone in his small town. But he is frustrated because he wrestles in the same weight class as Al, a better wrestler. Ben believes he has a chance at displacing Al, and it all comes down to one key match. But his single-minded focus may jeopardize his relationship with his girlfriend, and he knows the sport doesn't offer a way out of the stifling town that almost nobody leaves. A perceptive novel with well-drawn characters and plenty of sports action.

Soccer

Gibbons, Gail. *My Soccer Book*. 2000. Hardcover: Harper. 24 pages. Ages 3–6. PICTURE BOOK NONFICTION.

This small book explains soccer through a simple text and useful pictures. In several labeled illustrations, it shows the field and its parts, soccer equipment, and roles of specific players. It also discusses points, fouls, and time segments. Cheerful pictures of boys and girls playing together add information and portray the game as fun. Although it does not teach technique, this is a fine basic introduction for young children to a popular sport.

McNaughton, Colin. *Preston's Goal!* 1998. Hardcover: Harcourt. 32 pages. Ages 3–6. PICTURE BOOK.

Preston is a happy young pig obsessed with soccer. When his mother sends him on an errand, he kicks and dribbles his soccer ball the whole way. He keeps up a running commentary as if he were starring in a game, and leaves a path of destruction from kicks that hit various other animals. But a wolf that is following Preston, intent on eating him, gets blamed for the damage and fails to get his prey. Great fun for young soccer fans.

London, Jonathan. *Froggy Plays Soccer*. Illustrated by Frank Remkiewicz. 1999. Hardcover: Viking. 32 pages. Ages 3–7. PICTURE BOOK.

The Dream Team, Froggy's soccer team, could win the city cup if they beat the Wild Things. They just need to remember a cardinal rule: "Don't use your hands." Although Froggy in his usual funny way spaces out during the game, he manages to make some good plays anyway. But at a crucial moment, he uses his hands. Can the Dream Team still win? A felicitous combination of picture, story, and likable hero, like the other books in the series.

Browne, Anthony. *Willy the Wizard*. 1995. Hardcover: Knopf. Paperback: Dragonfly. 32 pages. Ages 3–8. PICTURE BOOK.

Willy is a small gorilla who loves soccer but never gets picked for a team in games with larger gorillas. One evening he sees a ghostly figure playing soccer who gives Willy some much-needed soccer boots. Willy is suddenly a terrific player. But when he gets to the field for an important game, he finds he has left the mysterious boots at home. Will it keep him from excelling? An entry in a popular series with strange, wonderful illustrations.

Saltzberg, Barney. *The Soccer Mom from Outer Space*. 2000. Hardcover: Crown. 32 pages. Ages 4–8. PICTURE BOOK.

The night before Lena's first soccer game, her father tells her about his first game on the Atomic Pickles team, when his normally well-behaved mother started screaming "like a human siren." From there, it only got worse, as the hilarious deadpan pictures reveal. After her pickle hat gives way to an entire pickle costume, the boy begs her to be like the other parents but comes to regret his request. One funny twist after another will keep children and parents laughing through this wonderful, zany tribute to soccer moms.

Marzollo, Jean. *Soccer Sam*. Illustrated by Blanche Sims. 1987. Hardcover and paperback: Random House. 48 pages. Ages 5–9. FICTION.

In this simple story, Sam's cousin, who is visiting from Mexico, feels ill at ease. He can barely speak English, and doesn't know how to play basketball or kickball. But when he gets his hands (and feet) on a soccer ball, everything changes. His skill intrigues the other second-graders, so he teaches them to play and they end up challenging the third graders. The cousins' affection for each other adds a good feeling to this sports story. The sequel is *Soccer Cousins*.

Edom, Helen, and Mike Osborne. *Starting Soccer*. Illustrated by Norman Young. 1993. Hardcover: E D C. Paperback: Usborne. 32 pages. Ages 5–11. NONFICTION.

This upbeat introduction to soccer uses watercolor illustrations of children playing the game to demonstrate skills and drills. Each move is clearly delineated in step-by-step pictures, using arrows and close-ups of feet to clarify instructions. Sidebars offer even more tips and information. It ends with suggested stretches for warming up and cooling down. Useful and well-designed.

Greene, Stephanie. *Owen Foote, Soccer Star*. Illustrated by Martha Weston. 1998. Hardcover: Clarion. 96 pages. Ages 7–10. FICTION.

Second-grader Owen, who is finally old enough to join the town soccer league, has persuaded his best friend, Joseph, to join, too. But a few kids in the league are bigger and better at soccer than Owen, and not always too friendly. Joseph, not a strong player, needs Owen's encouragement and understanding, another challenge for Owen. All comes out right in the end, though, in this warm soccer tale. One in a delightful series.

SOCCER

Avi. *S.O.R. Losers*. 1984. Hardcover: Simon & Schuster. Paperback: Avon. 90 pages. Ages 8–12. FICTION.

Because all students at South Orange River School have to play a team sport, Ed and his friends, who don't care about sports, end up on a soccer team with a kind but unskilled coach. They resign themselves to losing by huge margins and just enjoy each other's company and interests. But the rest of the school hates losing, so suddenly the team is under pressure to win at least one game. How these witty friends deal with the pressure results in a wonderful, unexpected conclusion.

Christopher, Matt. *On the Field with Mia Hamm*. 1998. Paperback: Little, Brown. 128 pages. Ages 9–12. BIOGRAPHY.

Mia Hamm started playing organized soccer at age five, and also played baseball as a child and football on her middle school team. This readable biography follows her stellar career in college and the Olympics, incorporating information on recent changes for girls and women in sports. Hamm's hard work and tenacity will inspire girls and boys alike in their athletic pursuits. Written before the 1999 World Cup championship, this is still of great interest to soccer fans.

Costello, Emily. *Foul Play*. 1998. Paperback: Skylark. 152 pages. Ages 9–12. FICTION.

The first in the "Soccer Stars" series, this novel starts with the season's first practice. Three of the new girls have not played soccer before, to the disappointment of Tess, an ambitious, talented player who can't understand why no one, including the coach, cares as much about winning as she does. As the season progresses, with many detailed descriptions of games, Tess comes to appreciate how her friends view the team. A light, fast read about a girls' team with plenty of soccer action.

331

Coleman, Lori. *Fundamental Soccer.* **Photographs by Andy King. 1995. Hardcover: Lerner. 64 pages. Ages 10–14. NONFICTION.**

After a short history of soccer, this book turns to basics like dribbling, passing, shooting, and more. A series of clear, color photographs shows enthusiastic teenagers executing each move or skill, and several pages describe a specific game in some detail. Conditioning exercises, drills and skills training, and rules and fouls are covered, followed by "razzle dazzle" moves like sliding tackles and scissors kicks. Useful as a detailed introduction to soccer or as a review for experienced players.

Scott, Nina Savin. *The Thinking Kid's Guide to Successful Soccer.* **Illustrated by Anne Canevari Green. 1999. Hardcover: Millbrook. 96 pages. Ages 10–14. NONFICTION.**

This perceptive book addresses what goes on in players' heads as they pursue a sport. Rather than coaching on technique, the author has gathered useful advice on how to approach soccer: getting into the "zone"; dealing with mistakes and success; and handling difficult teammates, opponents, coaches, and parents. With quotes from major players and coaches, the peppy advice talks about how to overcome bad nerves and enjoy the game. A welcome approach that every sport could use.

Transportation and Engineering

Airplanes and Ships

McPhail, David. *First Flight*. 1987. Hardcover: Little, Brown. 32 pages. Ages 2–7. PICTURE BOOK.

The younger narrator, holding a toy airplane and teddy bear, announces that he is about to take his first flight. Pen-and-watercolor illustrations show him arriving at the airport, going through security, and boarding the plane, while a large picture shows workers readying his plane. The teddy bear, grown magically huge, sits with the boy and provides comic relief throughout the flight. A meal, a movie, some turbulence, and a nap round out the trip. A perfect introduction to air travel for young children.

Crews, Donald. *Sail Away.* **1995. Hardcover: Greenwillow. Paperback: Harper. 32 pages. Ages 3–7. PICTURE BOOK.**

In this eye-catching account of a day sailing, a family sets out in their boat on a clear morning, first motoring, then hoisting the sails. Watercolors applied with brush and airbrush sweep across the pages as the wind picks up and sails billow, decorated with the word *whoosh*! The innovative typeface changes the size and slant of words as the boat weathers a storm and returns to port. With only a few sentences on a page, the illustrations tell most of the story about an exciting time on the water.

Pallotta, Jerry, and Fred Stillwell. *The Airplane Alphabet Book.* **Illustrated by Rob Bolster. 1997. Hardcover and paperback: Charlesbridge. 32 pages. Ages 3–8. PICTURE BOOK NONFICTION.**

From A for Aviation Trainer Six, or AT-6, to Z for Zero, the nickname for a Mitsubishi A6M fighter plane, this alphabet book shows many aircraft and describes each in a short paragraph or two. They range from the historic Wright Flyer to the modern ultralight, and from bombers to small personal planes like the Piper Cub. The brief information may raise questions that require further research, but this is a good starting place for young airplane buffs.

Brown, Don. *Ruth Law Thrills a Nation.* **1993. Hardcover: Ticknor & Fields. Paperback: Houghton. 32 pages. Ages 4–8. PICTURE BOOK BIOGRAPHY.**

In November 1916, Ruth Law set a new distance record flying in an open cockpit plane from Chicago to upstate New York. Appealing watercolors show her elaborate preparations, which included sleeping on a hotel roof to acclimate herself to the cold. With maps strapped to her legs, she flew until darkness made it impossible to navigate. Brown conveys the excitement and challenge of the flight, after which Law was hailed as a hero. A memorable story from the early days of flying.

Borden, Louise. *The Little Ships: The Heroic Rescue at Dunkirk in World War II*. Illustrated by Michael Foreman. 1997. Hardcover: McElderry. 32 pages. Ages 6–10. PICTURE BOOK.

In this fine book, a girl from a British fishing village accompanies her father to evacuate soldiers at Dunkirk in 1940. The girl knows enough about boats to help her father sail their fishing boat across the English Channel to the beach where half a million British and French soldiers are waiting to escape the Germans. The boat is a fictional part of a real armada in which little ships ferried soldiers from beaches to bigger ships. A thrilling story, graced with sweeping watercolors full of action.

Byars, Betsy. *Coast to Coast*. 1992. Paperback: Yearling. 164 pages. Ages 9–13. FICTION.

Birch's grandfather is selling his small plane although he had always hoped to fly from his home in South Carolina to California. Thirteen-year-old Birch persuades him to go on the trip and take her along. The talkative girl, her quiet grandfather, and his dog, Ace, spend their days in the tiny plane and their nights at small-town motels near tiny airports. Birch gets comfortable flying the plane, while she and her grandfather form a quirky, solid friendship. Lots of airplane information and two likable characters.

Hughes, Carol. *Jack Black & the Ship of Thieves*. 2000. Hardcover: Random House. 240 pages. Ages 9–13. FICTION.

In this rip-roaring adventure, Jack joins the crew of the *Bellerophon*, the largest airship ever built. He overhears a plot to sabotage the dirigible but falls out of the ship before he can warn his father, the captain. Fortunately, Jack lands on a sailing ship. Unfortunately, it is a pirate ship with a strange crew and a stranger mission: to put an end to an automated warship that destroys everything in its path. With lots of cliff-hangers and a cast of larger-than-life characters including a female flying ace, this is a rousing tale that plunges from one peril to the next.

Mikaelsen, Ben. *Sparrow Hawk Red.* **1993. Hardcover and paperback: Hyperion. 192 pages. Ages 9–13. FICTION.**

Thirteen-year-old Ricky is making his first solo loop in the small plane his father has taught him to fly even though he is legally too young. Shortly after, Ricky learns that drug smugglers killed his mother. Vowing to revenge her death by stealing a specially equipped airplane from the Mexican smugglers, he runs away to Mexico, disguises himself as a homeless kid, and concocts a plan. An action-packed and suspenseful novel with heart-stopping flight scenes.

Szabo, Corinne. *Sky Pioneer.* **1997. Hardcover: National Geographic. 64 pages. Ages 9–13. BIOGRAPHY.**

Numerous black-and-white photographs dominate this biography of the first woman to fly solo across the Atlantic. Earhart, who bought her first plane in 1922, was also the first woman to make a solo round-trip flight across the United States. In 1930, she set three women's world speed records. She often challenged herself, and like many early aviators, died during a challenge, trying to fly the longest route ever taken around the world. This slim biography emphasizes Earhart's air feats and spirit of adventure.

Simon, Seymour. *The Paper Airplane Book.* **Illustrated by Byron Barton. 1971. Hardcover and paperback: Viking. 48 pages. Ages 9–13. Of interest to younger children. NONFICTION.**

In this popular book, clear prose explains airplane dynamics such as drag, lift, thrust, and more, and step-by-step directions show how to make a basic paper airplane. The instructions then suggest modifications to the basic paper plane that illustrate principles of flight. Another section shows how to make several other models. Except for the scarcity of girls, the illustrations have stood the test of time, adding information and action to the text. An unusually enjoyable combination of science and crafts.

Macaulay, David. *Ship.* **1993. Hardcover and paperback: Houghton. 96 pages. Ages 9–14. NONFICTION.**

Divided into two parts, this tall, narrow book first describes a maritime archaeological crew recovering a sunken ship from the Caribbean. Large drawings show the divers, their finds, and how they conduct their careful excavation. When an archivist finds a sixteenth-century diary, the focus switches to a step-by-step account of how the ship was built in Spain in 1504, using diagrams and diary entries to make the process easy to understand. An interesting combination of past and present.

Kentley, Eric. *Boat.* **1992. Hardcover: Knopf. 64 pages. Ages 9 and up. Of interest to younger children. NONFICTION.**

Starting with simple crafts like sealskin kayaks and progressing to luxurious liners and racing yachts, this "Eyewitness" book provides a wide range of information on different kinds of boats. The double-page spreads will catch the reader's eye with the colorful photographs of graceful boats and occasional diagrams and sketches. For readers interested in history, many sections discuss boats from the past, showing artifacts as well as ships in the photos, and offering interesting historical details in the narrative and captions. One delightful page shows figureheads and other ornaments, while another shows equipment for modern sailing. A visual treat.

Yep, Laurence. *Dragonwings.* **1975. Hardcover and paperback: Harper. 248 pages. Ages 10–13. FICTION.**

In 1909, a Chinese flier flew an airplane over the California hills, having improved on the design of the Wrights' plane. Inspired by that story, this novel tells of a Chinese boy named Moon Shadow, whose father, Windrider, builds a plane. New to San Francisco at age eight, Shadow slowly becomes familiar with a father he had never met. When Shadow is fourteen, the father and son move to the Oakland hills where Windrider hopes to launch his plane. A Newbery Medal winner with memorable characters and a vivid setting.

Avi. *The True Confessions of Charlotte Doyle.* **1990. Hardcover: Orchard. Paperback: Avon. 232 pages. Ages 10–14. FICTION.**

It's 1832, and Charlotte Doyle expects a quiet, chaperoned trip from England to America; instead, she finds her life drastically changed by the perilous voyage. She must choose sides between a furious crew and a cruel captain, and then prove her worth as a sailor. But her unconventional choice and actions almost cost Charlotte her life when she is tried for a murder she didn't commit. A Newbery Honor Book, this seafaring adventure is highly recommended.

Freedman, Russell. *The Wright Brothers: How They Invented the Airplane.* Illustrated with original photographs by Wilbur and Orville Wright. 1991. Hardcover and paperback: Holiday House. 130 pages. Ages 10–14. BIOGRAPHY.

As amateur photographers who knew they were making history, the Wright brothers documented their progress with extraordinary photographs, which are used to great effect in illustrating this biography. The text provides fascinating details about the brothers and their work, as well as background about aviation and their contributions to it. A sense of their personalities, and their intense enjoyment in inventing comes across clearly. Even those not interested in aviation will be pulled in by the well-told story and the starkly beautiful photographs. A Newbery Honor Book not to be missed.

Paulsen, Gary. *The Voyage of the* Frog. 1989. Hardcover: Orchard. Paperback: Yearling. 142 pages. Ages 10–14. FICTION.

When his uncle dies, David inherits Owen's sailboat, the *Frog.* He takes the boat out beyond sight of the California coast to scatter his uncle's ashes and gets caught unprepared in a storm. By the time the storm subsides, David is lost in the Pacific on the twenty-two-foot boat. The fourteen-year-old must remember everything his uncle Owen taught him about sailing if he is to survive. But nothing could have prepared him for the dangers and the magical moments he encounters alone at sea. A suspenseful adventure full of beauty and fear.

Ingold, Jeanette. *Airfield.* 1999. Hardcover: Harcourt. 160 pages. Ages 11–14. FICTION.

Fifteen-year-old Beatty is staying in a small Texas town with her aunt and uncle during the Depression. Her uncle works at a tiny airport where Beatty helps out, while her father, a small-time pilot, visits only occasionally. To her shock, Beatty learns that her mother, who died when Beatty was young, was also a pilot. Slowly Beatty pieces together a picture of her daring mother, which makes her want to fly, too. A fast-moving story with a lot about planes and a low-key romance.

Docherty, Paul. *The Visual Dictionary of Flight.* 1992. Hardcover: DK. 64 pages. Ages 12 and up. Of interest to younger children. NONFICTION.

From the Wright brothers' planes to the Concorde and ultralights, this oversized book provides a detailed look at air vehicles. Each large double-page spread covers one topic, such as biplanes and triplanes, World War II aircraft, jetliners, helicopters, gliders, and much more. Typically, one or two photographs dominate the page, with each individual feature of the photograph labeled. Readers who love airplanes can spend hours poring over the intricate information on different aspects of flight.

Buildings, Bridges, and More

Gibbons, Gail. *How a House Is Built*. 1990. Hardcover: Holiday House. 32 pages. Ages 3–8. PICTURE BOOK NONFICTION.

This simple text with its cheerful pictures follows the steps of building a wood-frame house from an architect drawing plans to a family moving in. The bright pages show dozens of workers including heavy equipment operators, well drillers, carpenters, plumbers, masons, and more, including some women. Names of machines, parts of the house, and materials are labeled, and some pages are split into panels to show several stages of an operation such as laying the foundation. This is easy to understand and packed with information that interests younger children.

Sturges, Philemon. *Bridges Are to Cross*. Illustrated by Giles Laroche. 1998. Hardcover: Putnam. 32 pages. Ages 4–9. PICTURE BOOK NONFICTION.

Exquisite cut-paper illustrations depict bridges from all over the world in this elegant book. Each double-page spread shows a well-known bridge with a few lines of text plus the bridge name, location, description, and date it was built. The bridges vary from a rope suspension bridge in the Andes to the Segovia Aqueduct in Spain built by the Romans to the Sydney Harbor Bridge in Australia, an intricate bowstring arch bridge. The details in the illustrations are remarkable as are many of the structures pictured. An outstanding combination of information and artwork.

Fisher, Leonard Everett. *The Great Wall of China.* **1986. Hardcover: Macmillan. Paperback: Aladdin. 32 pages. Ages 5–10. PICTURE BOOK NONFICTION.**

Large black-and-white acrylic paintings dominate this history of a massive building feat. The story opens 2,200 years ago when King Cheng of Ch'in united many kingdoms and standardized money, weights, and more. In order to keep Mongol horsemen from conquering his kingdom, the ruler ordered that a wall be built across the top of China. One million workers marched north to begin the ten-year project. Dramatic illustrations show the backbreaking work and the harsh conditions involved in constructing the 3,750-mile-long wall. An extraordinary story told succinctly.

Mann, Elizabeth. *The Brooklyn Bridge.* **Illustrated by Alan Witschonke. 1996. Hardcover: Mikaya. 48 pages. Ages 8–11. NONFICTION.**

In this well-written story about the Brooklyn Bridge, readers learn how suspension bridges work and follow the process of building the longest bridge of its time. John Roebling initiated the engineering feat by designing the bridge, but died and left the construction to his son Washington. When Washington was confined to his bed with illness caused by the project, his wife, Emily, had to supervise the workers. Black-and-white photographs and color illustrations convey the massive undertaking, its dangers, and the excitement it generated. Sure to satisfy engineering and history buffs.

Lourie, Peter. *Erie Canal: Canoeing America's Great Waterway.* **1997. Hardcover and paperback: Boyds Mill. 48 pages. Ages 8–12. NONFICTION.**

This attractive photo-essay follows the author as he canoes the Erie Canal from Lake Erie to the Hudson River. The book opens with a helpful map of the canal including the cities and locks that he passes through. The first-person narrative combines history with observations about the canal today. The many black-and-white historical photographs make the past come alive, while the sharp color photos show operating locks, abandoned sections of the canal, and the beauty of the waterway. Lourie explains how the canal was built, how locks work, and where the Erie Canal fits in the history of transportation.

Doherty, Craig A., and Katherine M. Doherty. *Hoover Dam.* **1995. Hardcover: Blackbirch. 48 pages. Ages 9–13. NONFICTION.**

The Hoover Dam, which took five years to build, weighs 6.6 million tons and stands 726.4 feet high. Its construction during the 1930s was an impressive engineering feat, as this slim book emphasizes. The chapters describe some of the historical context and political negotiations that led to the dam, but focus mainly on how it was built. Black-and-white photographs from the time show aspects of the project with its dangers and its creative solutions to problems. A final chapter enthusiastically describes the dam today but ignores ecological and other controversies instead of giving a more even-handed account.

Johmann, Carol A., and Elizabeth J. Rieth. *Bridges! Amazing Structures to Design, Build & Test.* **1999. Paperback: Williamson. 96 pages. Ages 9–13. NONFICTION.**

This paperback full of information explains how bridges work and presents activities and experiments to clarify the concepts. Arches, beam bridges, suspension bridges, and more become easy to understand with the help of the many thoughtfully designed projects, small and large. Illustrated with black-and-white photographs, useful diagrams, and some comic drawings, the book incorporates history as well as engineering in a way children will enjoy. A great way to learn about a fascinating subject.

Macaulay, David. *Cathedral: The Story of Its Construction.* **1973. Hardcover and paperback: Houghton. 80 pages. Ages 9–13. Of interest to younger children. NONFICTION**

This remarkable book broke ground in the field of children's nonfiction with its elegant design and attention to detail. With large black-and-white pen drawings filling each page, it tells the story of how a fictional medieval cathedral was built, from quarrying stone to hanging the final banners and lighting the candles. The many diagrams and the well-written text explain the complicated process clearly. A must for readers interested in construction. Also see Macaulay's other books, including the 1999 book *Building the Book Cathedral*, about the writing, illustrating, and editing process.

Adkins, Jan. *The Art and Industry of Sandcastles.* **1971. Hardcover: Houghton. 32 pages. Ages 9 and up. Of interest to younger children. NONFICTION.**

This hand-lettered book, illustrated with pencil drawings, delves into the topic of castles as well as sandcastles. For those looking to build a sandcastle, Adkins offers clear instructions on making towers, walls, moats, parapets with crenelations, and other features, using simple tools like buckets and trowels. Drawings of increasingly complicated castles provide more ideas for the sandcastle builder. Other facts of castle life describe inhabitants, customs, weapons, and more. An unusually creative approach to the topics, beautifully presented.

Hewett, Joan. *Tunnels, Tracks, and Trains: Building a Subway.* **Photographs by Richard Hewett. 1995. Hardcover: Lodestar. 48 pages. Ages 10–12. Of interest to younger children. NONFICTION.**

How does a subway get built today under a large city? This photo-essay gives some answers to that complicated question by looking at the construction of the Los Angeles subway, which will take twenty years to complete. After a short overview, the book introduces the chief engineer and his current project, one of the subway stations. The most intriguing photographs and descriptions show the sixty-foot-deep, sixty-foot-wide cut; the huge machine that bores tunnels; and various workers underground. Short profiles portray the project manager, the station designer, a miner, an artist, and a driver. Readers will only wish the book were longer.

Platt, Richard. *Stephen Biesty's Incredible Cross-Sections.* **Illustrated by Stephen Biesty. 1992. Hardcover: Knopf. 48 pages. Ages 10 and up. Of interest to younger children. NONFICTION.**

This popular volume shows cross-sections of the insides and structural details of a castle, cathedral, car factory, oil rig, jumbo jet, ocean liner, the Empire State Building, and more. A general paragraph describes each structure, while the rest of the text comprises small paragraphs with connecting lines to parts of the picture. The detailed pictures often show a tiny figure using a toilet—in a castle, for example—a sight that interests children. For those fascinated by structures and vehicles, this oversized volume and Biesty's other cross-section books will provide hours of entertainment.

Severance, John. *Skyscrapers: How America Grew Up.* **2000. Hardcover: Holiday House. 112 pages. Ages 11–14. NONFICTION.**

Although this serious approach to the history of buildings lacks the glossy color photographs found in other books, it compensates with a more thoughtful text. Severance's overview of skyscrapers for the last century and a half goes beyond the surface to make important social and technological connections. For example, he discusses how skyscrapers were only possible with the invention of steam elevators and the brakes that made them safe, and the advanced plumbing that could accommodate high floors. He links early skyscrapers to the personalities behind them, and surveys important recent buildings throughout the world. Black-and-white photographs illustrate the insightful history.

Bortz, Fred. *Catastrophe! Great Engineering Failure—and Success.* **1995. Hardcover and paperback: W.H. Freeman. 80 pages. Ages 12–14. NONFICTION.**

A hotel sky-walk that collapses, a bridge that twists apart in the wind, a space shuttle that explodes—these monumental engineering disasters and others are analyzed in this absorbing book. The author takes readers through analyses of the disasters, using helpful diagrams and photographs. For example, he compares the 1965 electrical blackout in the Northeast to potential problems on the information superhighway, because both systems rely on interconnections. A stimulating look at catastrophes, large engineering projects, and the uses of failure, written by a knowledgeable, enthusiastic guide.

Cars, Trucks, and Trains

Collicutt, Paul. *This Train.* 1998. Hardcover: Farrar, Straus & Giroux. 32 pages. Ages 3–7. PICTURE BOOK NONFICTION.

Train lovers will immediately be sidetracked by the endpapers of this picture book, which show clearly labeled trains from around the world. A train fills each page, with a few words that contrast the pictures opposite each other: "This train is long. This train is short." The bright paintings show trains in all their glory, in all different settings. Easy enough for beginning readers and packed with enough trains to satisfy train fanatics.

Kuklin, Susan. *Fighting Fires.* 1993. Paperback: Aladdin. 32 pages. Ages 3–8. NONFICTION.

Colorful photographs introduce a company of firefighters, including some women, and show them at work. Each job within the group is pictured and explained, with new words highlighted and defined. Readers learn about the different clothing worn to protect the firefighters and the different parts of fire trucks. A final page gives fire prevention tips and advice on what to do in case of a fire. An attractive volume by a well-respected author/photographer, this is certain to appeal to many children.

Pinkwater, Daniel. *Tooth-Gnasher Superflash.* 1981. Hardcover: Macmillan. 32 pages. Ages 3–8. PICTURE BOOK.

Is there anything better in life than a car that can turn into a flying chicken? Well, maybe a car that can turn into a dinosaur. When Mr. Popsnorkle, his inane wife, and their five children go looking for a new car, they test-drive the Tooth-Gnasher Superflash, accompanied by the salesman Mr. Sandy. To Mr. Sandy's shock and the children's delight, Mr. Popsnorkle keeps pushing buttons on the dashboard that make the car transform into animals. The bright, childlike pictures go hand-in-hand with the zany story of a car any child would love to have.

Pluckrose, Henry. *Building a Road.* **1998. Hardcover and paperback: Watts. 32 pages. Ages 3–8. NONFICTION.**
 Simple text and color photographs explain the process of building a road. The book describes in broad terms each step in preparing the road and the equipment that accomplishes it. The photographs show how excavators dig and move the soil, spreaders level it, and dump trucks carry the soil away. Then the addition of asphalt requires a dump truck and road roller. Children fascinated by machinery and interested in how things are made will enjoy this introduction to road building.

Robbins, Ken. *Trucks: Giants of the Highway.* **1999. Hardcover: Atheneum. 32 pages. Ages 3–8. PICTURE BOOK NONFICTION.**
 This is a wonderful combination of big-rig facts and stunning photographs. The brief text describes different aspects of tractor-trailers: purpose, size, details about the cab and tractor, and more. The wide format gives room for many full-page photographs that add information and beauty. The composition and color raise these photos far above those usually found in transportation books. Highly recommended.

Tunnell, Michael O. *Mailing May*. Illustrated by Ted Rand. 1997. Hardcover: Greenwillow. Paperback: Harper. 32 pages. Ages 3–8. PICTURE BOOK.

An old-fashioned steam train runs through the center of this remarkable story based on a real event. In 1914, when young Charlotte May Pierstorff traveled seventy-five miles by rail across Idaho to visit her grandmother, she went as a package. Her parents mailed her parcel post, classified as a baby chick, to save money. This fictionalized version of the story follows May on her trip in the mail car as the train rode over trestle bridges and through mountains to her grandmother's house. Splendid expansive watercolors portray the train and convey the personalities of May, her family, and the amused railroad workers.

Wood, Audrey. *Red Racer*. 1996. Hardcover: Simon & Schuster. Paperback: Aladdin. 40 pages. Ages 3–8. PICTURE BOOK.

When Nona sees the Deluxe Red Racer in a bike shop window, she sets her heart on it, but her parents object to the price. Then the girl has the "wicked thought" (which appears as a large green blob) to wreck her old bike so she'll need a new one. Just when she's about to succeed, she arrives home to find her parents ready to fix up her old bike. In the end, the three of them happily fix it up together. Wildly energetic, exaggerated pictures suit the spirit of the story.

Heap, Christine. *Big Book of Trains: Over 50 of the World's Most Amazing Trains*. 1998. Hardcover: DK. 32 pages. Ages 3 and up. NONFICTION.

Anyone with even the slightest interest in trains will love this huge book. Each double-page spread has several colorful photographs of trains from the oldest to the newest. In large print, one paragraph on each spread gives an overview, while captions supply more information about train parts and specific trains. One double-page opens out into two more pages, creating a very large spread on the Chunnel trains. The book closes with snow trains that clear tracks operating much like snowblowers. Attractive and informative.

Lord, Trevor. *Big Book of Cars*. 1999. Hardcover: DK. 32 pages. Ages 4 and up. NONFICTION.

Car enthusiasts will love the enormous color photographs of sleek, shiny cars from the Dodge Viper, capable of exceeding 170 mph, to the futuristic Renault Zoom and Peugeot Touareg. Two pages open out in the book's middle to show a pink stretch limo in a photograph that measures a yard long. Cars from movies such as the Batmobile and Chitty Chitty Bang Bang, sports cars like the Corvette and Lamborghini, and dragsters are among the other cars shown. A paragraph of text and long captions supply information. Sure to be a hit.

Lord, Trevor. *Amazing Bikes*. Photographs by Peter Downs. 1992. Paperback: Knopf. 32 pages. Ages 5–10. NONFICTION.

Children interested in bikes, motorbikes, and motorcycles will enjoy browsing through this attractive "Eyewitness Junior" book or reading it from cover to cover. Each double-page spread discusses one topic with a main paragraph, plus a large color photograph, many small ones, drawings, and informative captions. It begins with historical bicycles and motorcycles, goes on to sports associated with each, and then to unusual vehicles from the past and present. Photos show the longest motorcycles ever made, a solar-powered bike, a scooter with seventeen lights and twenty mirrors, and other oddities.

Moss, Marissa. *True Heart.* **Illustrated by C. F. Payne. 1999. Hardcover: Harcourt. 32 pages. Ages 5–10. PIC-TURE BOOK.**

This fictionalized tale of a sixteen-year-old girl who be-came a railroad engineer was inspired by a turn-of-the-century photograph of a ten-woman railroad work crew. Large, old-fashioned illustrations show a lanky girl in overalls who be-friends engineers and learns all she can, then seizes her chance to drive a train herself. Young history buffs will enjoy the train lore, the expansive sense of the West, and the determined heroine.

Otfinoski, Steve. *Wild on Wheels! Motorcycles Then and Now.* **1998. Hardcover: Benchmark Books. 32 pages. Ages 7–9. Of interest to younger children. NONFICTION.**

Many photographs of colorful motorcycles dominate this enthusiastic book whose large print and ample white space make the popular subject accessible to younger readers. A short history with a few intriguing black-and-white historical photographs opens the text, which quickly moves on to the kinds of motorcycles ridden today. Ten pages cover the topic of racing, with action-packed shots of racers doing wheelies and airborne jumps. One in the "Here We Go!" series that includes books on cars, bikes, trucks, fire trucks, and other vehicles.

Cleary, Beverly. *The Mouse and the Motorcycle.* **Illustrated by Louis Darling. 1965. Hardcover: Morrow. Paperback: Camelot. 172 pages. Ages 7–10. Of interest to younger children. FICTION.**

One day a boy named Keith checks into the old hotel where the mouse Ralph lives. Ralph can't resist trying out Keith's toy motorcycle and ends up in a wastebasket, where

Keith finds him. That begins their friendship, for "Two creatures who shared a love for motorcycles naturally spoke the same language." The motorcycle leads to exciting adventures for Ralph. Except for its dated depiction of women, this popular novel has a timeless quality and a keen understanding of what children like. Followed by *Runaway Ralph* and *Ralph S. Mouse.*

Napoli, Donna Jo. *Trouble on the Tracks*. 1996. Hardcover: Scholastic. 190 pages. Ages 9–12. FICTION.

When thirteen-year-old Zack and his ten-year-old sister, Eve, get on the famous Australian train "The Legendary Ghan," they have no reason to worry about taking the twenty-two-hour trip on their own. But Eve's interest in Australian birds leads her to track down a bird call she hears from the train, and suddenly the two American kids find themselves face-to-face with dangerous smugglers. The siblings have to draw on their courage and ingenuity to survive the encounter. Full of details about the train, this is an exhilarating trip on and off the tracks.

Bauer, Joan. *Rules of the Road*. 1998. Hardcover: Putnam. Paperback: Puffin. 200 pages. Ages 10–14. FICTION.

Sixteen-year-old Jenna is as smart and strong as she is funny, but it takes a strange road trip for her to appreciate her own strengths. In order to buy herself a car, she agrees to drive Mrs. Gladstone, an elderly businesswoman, from Chicago to Texas. Jenna has little experience driving a huge car like Mrs. Gladstone's, but she comes to enjoy her hundreds of miles behind the wheel. Along the way, she learns a lot about business and even corporate takeovers. In the end, Jenna surprises herself with her courage and endurance. A wonderfully funny and thoughtful road novel.

Murphy, Jim. *Across America on an Emigrant Train.* **1993. Hardcover: Clarion. 150 pages. Ages 10–14. NONFICTION.**

This excellent book takes the reader on a train journey across the United States in 1879 with writer Robert Louis Stevenson, using many quotes from his writings to add color and detail. Starting in New York City, Stevenson travels to California in trains filled with immigrants. The well-written text describes this and other trains, how they worked, accidents and problems, the building of the Transcontinental Railroad, and the effect the railroads had on the country-side and Native Americans. The abundant black-and-white photographs and etchings show the insides and outsides of many trains, the workers, countryside, and much more. Highly recommended for train and history buffs.

Wukovits, John F. *The Composite Guide to Auto Racing.* **1998. Hardcover: Chelsea House. 64 pages. Ages 10–14. Of interest to younger children. NONFICTION.**

Almost as soon as cars were invented, drivers started racing. This history of a popular sport reviews the early days of racing with black-and-white photographs and descriptions of the cars and events. It follows the sport in the United States and Europe as cars got faster and drivers more daring. Fans of Formula 1 Grand Prix racing, NASCAR's stock car racing, and CART's Indy Car races will enjoy stories about legendary drivers of the past and present, surprising facts, and lots of anecdotes about racing.

Young, Karen Romano. *The Beetle and Me: A Love Story.* **1999. Hardcover: Greenwillow. Paperback: Avon. 182 pages. Ages 11–14. FICTION.**

Fifteen-year-old Daisy wants her own car to work on and eventually drive. And not just any car: She wants her family's old broken down Volkswagen Beetle. Her Porsche-loving father, her aunt who's a mechanic, and her race-car driving uncle discourage her from the insurmountable task. Even when romance enters her life, the car plays a huge role. Readers who don't care about cars will come to understand Daisy's need, while car lovers will find a lot of space devoted to mechanical details. A refreshingly original novel.

Children's Magazines

American Girl

For ages 8 to 12. From the creators of the "American Girls" books, this bimonthly magazine aimed at girls includes historical and contemporary fiction and nonfiction. For more information, go to americangirl.com.

Appleseeds

For ages 7 to 9. From the creators of *Cobblestone*, a magazine for younger readers that has a theme for every issue, with strong articles, photographs, illustrations, and activities on a variety of subjects. For more information, go to cobblestone pub.com.

Archaeology's Dig

For ages 8 to 12. Published bimonthly by the Archaeological Institute of America. Uses well-written text, color photographs, and drawings to convey information about interesting topics related to archaeology. For more information, go to archaeology.org.

Calliope: World History for Young People
For ages 9 to 14. A forty-eight-page magazine issued five times a year; each issue focuses on a theme in history. For more information, go to cobblestonepub.com.

Chickadee
For ages 6 to 9. A Canadian nature and science magazine published ten times a year by the Young Naturalist Foundation. Has articles, activities, puzzles, drawings, stories, and color photos on nature and science. For more information, go to owl.on.ca.

Cicada
For ages 14 and up. A high-quality, bimonthly literary magazine with fiction and poetry for teenagers, written by well-known authors as well as teens. From the publishers of *Cricket*. For more information, go to cricketmag.com.

Click
For ages 3 to 7. A bimonthly magazine about science, nature, history and the arts from the publishers of *Cricket*; uses stories, characters, and photo-essays to convey information. Includes pull-out Parent's Companion with articles and book reviews. For more information, go to cricketmag.com.

Cobblestone: The History Magazine for Young People
For ages 9 to 14. A forty-eight-page magazine issued nine times a year, this contains high-quality articles focused on one aspect of American history, with photographs, games, activities, puzzles, and more. For more information, go to cobblestone pub.com.

Cricket: The Magazine for Children
For ages 9 to 14. Issued monthly. An unusually attractive general-interest magazine with stories, poems, and illustrations. For more information, go to cricketmag.com.

Faces: The Magazine about People
For ages 9 to 14. Published ten times a year in conjunction

with the American Museum of Natural History. Offers articles, projects, and photographs on natural history and anthropology. For more information, go to cobblestonepub.com.

Footsteps: African American History

For ages 8 to 14. Published five times a year, this magazine about the history and achievements of African Americans has a theme for every issue, with nonfiction articles, photographs, and activities. From the creators of *Cobblestone*. For more information, go to cobblestonepub.com.

Girls' Life

For girls 9 to 14. A glossy bimonthly magazine that includes feature articles about puberty, school issues, self-esteem, fashion, and beauty. For more information, go to girlslife.com.

Highlights for Children

For ages 2 to 12. Issued monthly. While not as high in quality as *Cricket* or *Spider*, this general-interest magazine continues to be popular. Offers puzzles, articles, stories, activities, and more for a wide age range. For more information, go to highlights.com.

Hopscotch

For ages 6 to 12. A bimonthly magazine that offers fiction, nonfiction, and poetry oriented toward an audience of girls. For more information, call 491-358-4610.

Kid City

For ages 6 to 10. Published ten times a year by the Children's Television Workshop. "For graduates of Sesame Street," this is a general-interest magazine on a variety of topics. Includes some advertisements. For more information, go to ctw.org.

Ladybug: The Magazine for Young Children

For ages 2 to 6. A companion magazine to *Cricket*, this also has unusually good stories, poems, and illustrations as well as songs and games. Also contains an insert for parents. Issued monthly. For more information, go to cricketmag.com.

Merlyn's Pen: The National Magazines of Student Writing

For ages 12 to 18. An annual magazine that consists of short stories, poems, essays, letters, and illustrations by middle and high school students. For more information, go to merlynspen.com.

Muse

For ages 8 to 14. Published bimonthly by the publishers of *Cricket,* in conjunction with *Smithsonian* magazine. A magazine of different aspects of science and the arts with good photography and well-written, up-to-date articles. Includes some advertising. For more information, go to cricketmag.com.

National Geographic

For ages 10 and up. Published monthly by the National Geographic Society. This well-established magazine with beautiful photographs and lively articles appeals to children as well as adults. For more information, go to nationalgeo graphic.com.

National Geographic World

For ages 8 to 14. Published monthly by the National Geographic Society. An attractive magazine with articles, stories, and color photographs about science, people, and places of interest to children. For more information, go to nationalgeo graphic.com/media/world.

New Moon: The Magazine for Girls and Their Dreams

For ages 8 to 14. This bimonthly, forty-eight-page magazine is by and about girls and women. It includes fiction, essays, artwork, columns, and more on topics of interest to girls. Emphasizes strong, self-sufficient images of girls. For more information, go to newmoon.org.

Odyssey: Adventures in Science

For ages 11 and up. Published monthly September through May. A fifty-two page magazine from the creators of *Cobblestone,* this has moved beyond covering only astronomy to themed issues on different aspects of science and scientists. For more information, go to cobblestonepub.com.

OWL: The Discovery Magazine for Children

For ages 8 to 12. A Canadian nature magazine published ten times a year by the Young Naturalist Foundation. Has articles, activities, puzzles, contests, stories, and color photos on nature, the environment, science, and technology. For more information, go to owl.on.ca.

Ranger Rick

For ages 7 to 12. A nature magazine published monthly by the National Wildlife Federation. Excellent color photographs, short articles, and columns about animals, plants, and other aspects of the natural world. For more information, go to nwf.org/rrick.

Sesame Street Magazine

For ages 2 to 6. Published ten times a year by the Children's Television Workshop. Stories and activities, some related to characters from the Sesame Street television show. Includes an insert for parents. For more information, go to ctw.org.

Skipping Stones: A Multicultural Magazine

For ages 8 to 15. Published bimonthly during the school year, this magazine focuses on multicultural issues with themes such as intercultural adoption, exchange students, and world religions and spirituality. For more information, call 541-342-4956.

Spider: The Magazine for Children

For ages 6 to 9. Published monthly. Another companion magazine to *Cricket*, with excellent stories, poems, articles, and illustrations, often by recognized children's writers and illustrators. For more information, go to cricketmag.com.

Sports Illustrated

For ages 12 and up. Weekly. Older children often prefer

this version to *Sports Illustrated for Kids*. For more information, go to sportsillustrated.com.

Sports Illustrated for Kids

For ages 7 to 13. Published monthly. A popular glossy magazine with articles and photographs about sports, including amateur and professional athletes. Includes many advertisements. For more information, go to sikids.com.

Stone Soup: The Magazine by Young Writers

For ages 6 to 13. A forty-eight-page magazine with stories, poetry, book reviews, and illustrations by children up to age thirteen. With an insert for teachers. For more information, go to stonesoup.com.

3–2–1 Contact

For ages 8 to 14. A science magazine published by the Children's Television Workshop ten times a year. With articles, activities, and color photographs on a central theme. For more information, go to ctw.org.

Your Big Backyard

For ages 3 to 6. A nature magazine published monthly by the National Wildlife Federation. Excellent color photographs, short articles with big typeface, and simple activities about animals, plants, and other aspects of the natural world. Includes several pages for adults. For more information, go to nwf.org/ybby.

A Basic
Reference Shelf
for Home

Ideally, every child should have access to a good dictionary, encyclopedia, and atlas at home. One of each is recommended below, although there are many other good choices in
each category. Other books for looking things up are less crucial but can appeal strongly to certain children. Those who
love facts will enjoy the almanacs, while those who are drawn
to the strange and superlative will love the Guinness book.
Children who have discovered the pleasures of writing letters
will welcome the *Kids' Address Book*. Field guides are a must
for nature lovers.

Ours is an information age, so children need to learn
where to find accurate information. They are starting to turn
first to the Internet for their answers, but unfortunately, assess-
ing the accuracy of information on the Internet is difficult for
most children. The amount of information produced through
a typical search engine can also overwhelm those who are
looking for a simple answer or some basic facts on a topic.

While books are not perfect, the books listed below are reliable sources of information for curious children that provide a good starting point for answering many questions.

Macmillan Dictionary for Children. Edited by Robert B. Costello. 1997. Macmillan. 864 pages. Ages 8–12.
An unusually accessible dictionary that includes several small color pictures on each page, frequent demonstrations of a word used in a sentence, easy-to-use pronunciations, and occasional sidebars with word histories. The introduction is clear and helpful.

World Book Encyclopedia. Published annually by World Book, Inc. Ages 9 and up.
This is an outstanding multivolume encyclopedia that covers a variety of topics about which children want to know for their own pleasure as well as for school assignments. It has well-written, well-organized articles with useful photographs and diagrams. The material is updated frequently (instead of simply reprinted from year to year). It is most accessible to children third grade and up, but a parent would also find it helpful for answering the questions of younger children. Although this may change, so far a good print encyclopedia provides more information than on-line encyclopedias like Encarta, which excels in graphics and provides a good supplement.

The Eyewitness Atlas of the World. 1994 Revised Edition. DK. 160 pages. Ages 8–12.
This is an attractive, affordable world atlas with more than a thousand diagrams, photographs, and other graphics. It is arranged by continent, then by regions within the continent. The text is useful and the pictures unusually good.

***World Almanac and Book of Facts*. Published annually by World Almanac. 1,024 pages. Ages 11 and up.**

The small print and overwhelming amount of information may intimidate children, but for those who love information, this is the best, most inexpensive compilation of facts available. Every home full of curious people should have a current copy. It answers an enormous number of quick questions from details on every country and state to birth dates of celebrities, from sports teams' addresses to the periodic table of elements to a reprint of the Declaration of Independence. A phenomenal resource.

***World Almanac for Kids*. Edited by Elaine Israel. 2000. World Almanac Education. 336 pages. Ages 9–12.**

This has a far more colorful look than the standard *World Almanac*, but offers far less information. It covers a range of topics including science, geography, history, sports, animals, and more, with lots of graphs and graphics.

***Guinness 2000 Book of Records*. Published annually by Guinness Media. Ages 10 and up. Of interest to younger children.**

Most children love this remarkable compilation of records. If possible, get a hardcover copy because the photographs are much better, allowing children to see the longest fingernails ever, the tallest person, and the like. The records vary from important to silly, including the most yo-yo loops in a row and the farthest distance hopped on a pogo stick. Sports fans will also love the *Guinness Book of Sports Records*, updated annually.

The New Way Things Work by David Macaulay. 1999 Revised Edition. Houghton. 400 pages. Ages 9 and up. Of interest to younger children.

This huge volume explains through words, clever pictures, and diagrams many different kinds of technology, machines, appliances, technical processes, telecommunications, and much more. This updated version includes a new section on "The Digital Domain" about computers and related topics.

Kids' Address Book. Edited by Michael Levine. 4th edition, 1999. Perigee. 304 pages. Ages 9–12.

This handy paperback is perfect for kids who have discovered the fun of letter-writing. With more than three thousand entries, including some e-mail addresses, it lists addresses for contacting actors, rock stars, athletes, useful organizations, businesses of interest to young consumers, and more.

Field Guides

These are wonderful books to have at home. The smaller, inexpensive guides, which include familiar animals and plants, are the best places to start and won't overwhelm beginning naturalists. Specific field guides are listed under the subject categories in this book, including "Birds," "Insects and Spiders," "Reptiles and Amphibians," and "Sea Animals." The Golden Book field guides and the Peterson guides aimed at younger children are unusually good for identifying natural objects, thanks to their detailed drawings. Although children often prefer photographs, pictures tend to be more informative and give details that facilitate identification.

Encouraging
Your Child to
Read

Creating a Life Rich
in Books

Research on children who are strong readers reveals that many come from homes where books, magazines, and newspapers are prominent. In these families, reading reaches far beyond school into many parts of their daily lives. The children frequently see their parents reading—a factor in turning children into readers because the parents are teaching by example. These children get the message that reading is important to adults, and because they want to be like the adults they love, they want to read, too. Not all children respond to a book-rich environment by becoming enthusiastic readers, but many do.

Parents who value reading can be creative about ways to tie

books and magazines into their child's interests. Columbia University professor Lucy Calkins, in her book *Raising Lifelong Learners*, recommends this kind of active promotion of books: "We (as parents) support reading by attaching books to everything our children love. One of my nephews collects baseball cards, so for his birthday, I gave him a collection of Alfred Slote and Matt Christopher books. If my child loved horses, we'd subscribe to horse magazines and own all of those wonderful horse books." Calkins describes how the family sought out books on different pets when they were deciding what kind of pet to buy and, later, when they sought advice on how to take care of the one they acquired. She recommends saturating everyday routines with books and other reading materials.

Parents who want their children to love reading might want to encourage favorite relatives to give books and magazine subscriptions as gifts. A book from an admired uncle, aunt, or older cousin can elevate reading into something special. If the choice has special meaning, like a book the relative loved as a child or a book on a topic of shared interest like a sport, so much the better. A magazine subscription from a distant friend or relative brings that person to mind when each issue arrives.

Making libraries and bookstores a part of a child's life is another avenue to encourage reading. Public libraries make it possible even for those without large incomes to fill their homes with books and magazines for their children and themselves. Getting children in the habit of using the public library (and, depending on the school, their school library) will help them become lifelong learners who know where to find the information they want. Libraries typically provide a wider range of informational books than bookstores do, plus hundreds of fine picture-story books and novels that are out of print and no longer available for purchase. Many public libraries offer magazines, videos, and audio books that can be checked out for free.

Finding a knowledgeable children's or young adult librarian to recommend books and other resources makes life easier for a reading family. Some bookstores have staff members who know a lot about books, but many don't. Similarly, on-line booksellers make recommendations that should be taken with a grain of salt, as the choices are often based less on book quality than on book sales (and sometimes on publishers paying for promotion).

Because they are free, libraries are a good place for children to explore lots of new topics through books. Children typically enjoy making their own choices. Let them sample topics in which they show an interest they haven't yet pursued. They can take out a lot of books on different subjects to see if they want to pursue those areas, or a lot of books on a subject they already know they like. Give children the freedom and opportunities to explore their interests, and you might be surprised at how excited they become about books.

Reading Aloud

Reading aloud is a gift to your child. Research shows that it is another key factor associated with children who become avid readers. But more important, in a difficult world, reading aloud together is a quiet time of shared enjoyment in a family. By creating the time to read, parents are communicating that they believe reading is important and they are creating a positive atmosphere around reading. By laughing or crying together over a good book, families grow closer and create memories that can last a lifetime. Many adults who were read to as children look back on those times as some of the happiest in their childhood.

At the same time, reading aloud introduces vocabulary and exemplary grammar to the listening child. Most children can listen to a much higher level of vocabulary than they could read on their own. Books tend to use even more complex vocabulary than occurs in conversation, so reading aloud introduces new words in context. Hearing a word that way makes it easier to decipher and understand when children later encounter it in print. Similarly, most books contain more complex sentence structure and better grammar than children hear in conversations. They will absorb some of this elegance in language through listening, the better to learn it later in school and perhaps use it in their own writing.

Picture-story books, which are so much fun to read aloud, introduce children to excellent artwork in lots of different media: watercolors, oils, collage, cut-paper illustrations, and much more. These short books also model simple story writing at its best, honed down to fit thirty-two pages yet still hold the attention of a child. Keep in mind that older children enjoy picture-story books, too, just as many adults do. Older children often enjoy returning to the comfort of earlier days through a picture book. But there are also more picture-story books written expressly for older children, an exciting trend in children's book publishing.

While many parents choose to read novels aloud and most children enjoy listening to them, the right nonfiction can also be a good read-aloud. Some children prefer information to stories, or a combination of the two, like a biography. Many children have informational interests that outstrip their reading ability; you can help satisfy their thirst for knowledge by reading them well-written nonfiction books. Parents who haven't seen children's nonfiction books recently will be dazzled by how attractive they are compared to the nonfiction of the past. Thanks to technological improvements, it is now far less expensive to print color photographs, so many striking photo-essays have been published on a range of subjects, another welcome development in publishing.

One benefit that reading aloud offers is the perfect chance to discuss values and opinions about issues raised in the books. Nonfiction that touches on topics like ecology, the treatment of minority groups and immigrants, and even good sportsmanship can provide topics for discussion. While reading fiction, you and your child will also encounter people and situations that open up areas of discussion about important questions and choices in life. You can find out your child's thoughts and reactions to fictional dilemmas, and voice your own. Not every book leads to talking, and many are better enjoyed without scrutiny, but now and then reading aloud can be the perfect opportunity to explore with your child issues that matter to you.

Whatever you choose to read, your main goal should be enjoyment. Never make it a chore or primarily a lesson. If the book doesn't hold your child's interest, switch to something else. Reading aloud should be a pleasure for both of you. It may very well become a cherished ritual and one of the best moments in your child's day—and yours. Have a good time together and as a result, books will mean something special and wonderful to your child.

Tips on Reading Aloud

Reading aloud well does not come naturally to everyone. Here are techniques you can practice until they come easily. *The Read-Aloud Handbook* by Jim Trelease (4th edition, Penguin, 1995) offers more ideas on how to go about it as well as numerous reasons that reading aloud is beneficial.

- If you haven't read the book already, scan it to get a sense of its content before you start reading aloud.
- Choose books you or your child are excited about. It is hard to read a book you don't enjoy, especially a long one.
- Read with expression. A monotone is hard to listen to. Children need to hear changes in your voice to indicate when you are reading dialogue. Vary your pace, too. Slow down to build up suspense and speed up during exciting scenes.
- Create voices for different characters if you enjoy it, but it isn't necessary for a good reading. A story can be read effectively in a straightforward manner as long as you have expression and enthusiasm.
- Read at a moderate pace, not too fast. Listening is a challenge for many children and you don't want to leave them behind as you speed ahead. Picture-story books require time for enjoying the illustrations.
- Feel free to stop and discuss the book if you and your listener want to. Answer questions as they come up. How much you want to stop and explain new words is up to you. If they can be understood in context, you may want just to keep reading. Stopping too often to explain can undermine the story's impact.
- Keep in mind that children can look bored or restless and

still be listening. Some children need to be moving around or fidgeting with something. The real question is, are they following the story? If so, let them squirm or even draw pictures as they listen.

- Sometimes a book will lead to conversations afterward, sometimes not. Play it by ear. Either way is fine.
- If your child wants to read to you sometimes, great. Beginning readers especially enjoy their new skills. You can trade off pages or chapters, or just sit back and listen.
- If your child is not enjoying a book, you are not obliged to finish it. This is most likely to occur with chapter books. You don't want to abandon a book quickly, but if it has not sparked interest after several sessions, try another one. If this is a pattern, you may want to switch to shorter books and build up to longer ones.
- Try reading just a few poems together at a time. Start with light verse if you are uncomfortable with poetry. You may be surprised at how much fun you and your child can have with poems.
- Reading aloud has a host of educational benefits, but it works best if it isn't approached as an educational exercise. Parents have been known to have children repeat each word after them as a device to teach reading. Such a tedious approach is more likely to dampen enthusiasm for books than to promote learning. Just enjoy the books together; the increased vocabulary, understanding of story structure, exposure to correct grammar, and other benefits will follow naturally.

Book Clubs

Book clubs bring children together to share excitement about books. Mother-daughter book clubs have made their mark in the past several years, encouraged by the publication of *The Mother-Daughter Book Club* by Shireen Dodson, a helpful guide with ideas on starting any type of book group with suggestions of books to read. The Multnomah County Library in Oregon has lots of ideas for starting and running kids' book clubs on its Web page, www.multnomah.lib.or.us/lib/talk/guidelines.html.

Some book clubs invite all members of the family to join. In such clubs, the parents may read the selected book aloud, enabling both younger and older children to form opinions for discussion. Schools, libraries, and bookstores may sponsor book groups for children and adolescents, sometimes called "Junior Critics." The club members will meet to talk analytically about books, with guidance from an adult. Such a group may produce a list with comments about the books they liked, to be distributed at the library or bookstore. The age range in such clubs can often span three or four grades.

Typically, book clubs meet once a month all year or during the school year, and discuss a book that all the members have read since the last meeting. Meeting styles vary from formal to casual. In some clubs, one member will give a presentation on the book or its author, or perhaps both. That person may have prepared questions to keep the discussion going, or a group leader, librarian, or other adult may take that role. In other clubs, the conversation is less directed. Another activity can be rating the book with a certain number of stars or compiling written evaluations. Lots of clubs keep a running list of what they've read and share it with other readers or new clubs.

Here are a handful of questions that can be asked about a wide range of fiction books, the usual club fare. Many groups like to set a positive tone by first focusing on what they liked about a book and turning to less positive comments later in the discussion.

- How did this book make you feel?
- What did you enjoy about this book?
- What parts did you like best?
- Did the book pull you in? How did the author make that happen?
- Who was your favorite character? What did you like about him or her?
- Did the characters seem believable? Did their actions and words seem real?
- Does this book relate to your own life in some way? How?
- Who, if anyone, would you recommend this book to?

Parents may occasionally want to use questions such as these at home to spark conversation about books they are reading aloud with their child. Novels with complex characters and plots will probably elicit the strongest responses, but even a simpler book will produce a favorite character and part. This provides a chance for parents to express their views, too, and share their values, as well as to tune into what their child is thinking. Not every book needs to lead to a meaningful discussion, of course, but questions *can* make a special book last longer by talking about it afterward.

Books, Field Trips, and Travel

Books can inspire field trips and travel, and field trips and travel can inspire reading. If your child likes reading about airplanes, why not visit a large or small local airport? Get excited about a trip to a planetarium by first reading about astronomy or to an aquarium by reading about sea life. A visit to the zoo can be enriched by reading before or afterward about the animals there. Read about the history of a sport before attending a professional or amateur sports event.

Some books lend themselves to music or art events. *Visiting the Art Museum* by Laurene Krasny Brown and her husband, Marc Brown, creator of the popular Arthur books, is the perfect introduction for younger children. Biographies of individual artists make good pre- or post-visit reading for older children already familiar with art. Similarly, older children might like to read about a composer before a classical music concert, while younger ones could learn a little about instruments first through an entertaining book like *Zin! Zin! Zin! A Violin.*

For natural history buffs, read about a natural habitat nearby, such as a pond or seashore, then visit it. Be sure to bring along a field guide. Or, if you are going on a trip, nothing is better for building up anticipation than reading about your destination with your child. Some books in this guide are specifically geared toward visiting certain places, such as *The National Civil Rights Museum Celebrates Everyday People*, for a trip to Memphis, Tennessee, and *Where to Find Dinosaurs Today* for sites all over the country. Historical sites like Ellis Island lend themselves to reading one of the many fine historical novels available on different places and times.

Taking books along on car or airplane trips can provide a welcome distraction. Audio books, discussed in the next section, make car trips seem short and enjoyable. Books of brain teasers and, for children who don't get carsick, visual puzzles can entertain for hours. A guide to card games, such as *Let's Play Cards: A First Book of Card Games*, can keep more than one child happily occupied. *While You're Waiting for the Food to Come*, an outstanding science experiment book, has science activities that can be done in restaurants.

The possibilities for combining books and field trips are limitless, depending on what your child enjoys and where you live or can travel to visit. Here are some specific books to read before the related activities; they are all annotated earlier in this guide.

- *Teddy Bears' Picnic* and *Teddy Bears' Picnic Cookbook*—planning a picnic (p. 202).
- *Katie Meets the Impressionists*—visiting an art museum (p. 70).
- *Onstage & Backstage at the Night Owl Theater*—attending a play (p. 84).
- *Let's Rodeo: Young Buckaroos and the World's Wildest Sport*—attending a rodeo (p. 154).
- *Roller Coasters, or I Had So Much Fun, I Almost Puked*—visiting an amusement park (p. 231).
- *Arms and Armor*—visting a museum with an armor collection (p. 165).
- *America's Greatest Game: The Real Story of Football and the NFL*—attending a football game or watching one on television (p. 310).
- *My Visit to the Zoo*—visiting the zoo (p. 63).

Audio Books

One of the great improvements in recent years has been the increased availability of audio books for children as well as adults. Many outstanding children's and young adult novels have been recorded in unabridged format, and can be checked out of public libraries and some school libraries. Some can also be rented from companies listed below. As soon as novels win important awards, they appear on tape, often with excellent readers who bring the story and characters to life.

Tapes, which can make a long car ride enjoyable, provide some of the same benefits to children as listening to books read aloud. They introduce new words in context, correctly pronounced and typically at a higher vocabulary level than most conversations. Later, when a child encounters that word in print for the first time, it may seem familiar thanks to having heard it before. Similarly, audio books expose children to good grammar with more complexity than most spoken conversations offer.

For children who are not strong readers, audio books give them access to books at their own emotional level. A middle school student reading below grade level can listen to books written for middle schoolers that address their concerns, instead of always being limited to books aimed at younger children. This opens up a world of literature otherwise accessible only when someone reads aloud to them.

Many strong readers enjoy audio books, too. I've known children who want to listen to a book even though they have already read the print version. Other kids find audio books too slow. They would rather read the book silently and get through it faster.

Be sure to check your public library and your child's school library for audio books. Here are a few sources for renting audio books:

Recorded Books
800-638-1304
www.recordedbooks.com
Offers more than 700 books for children.

Books on Tape
800-882-6657
www.booksontape.com
Has more than 250 unabridged children's books available for purchase, many of which are available for rental.

Blackstone Books
800-720-2665
www.blackstoneaudio.com
Offers a limited number of children's novels on tape, many of them old or new classics.

Creative Writing
and Making Books

Most children like to think of themselves as authors and enjoy the process of writing stories and making them into illustrated books. Even young children are often natural storytellers. Before they know how to read or print, it's great to let them dictate the story to an adult to write down. The child can then add pictures. Older children can set down a story by themselves, taking care with spelling for the final version. Many children like to type their stories on a computer and print them, taking advantage of special computer fonts and formats. These printed pages can also be illustrated and bound. For a special story, it's fun to bind the book in an attractive way, perhaps using handmade paper for the whole project if it is printed by hand.

One simple project is to create an alphabet book with a page and picture for each letter. A challenging variation on this idea is to choose a theme, such as animals or food, although it makes it more difficult to find words for certain letters. A collection of a child's favorite poems, either written by the child or by others, makes a good project to print, illustrate, and bind. Recounting a family trip or event is another possibility, especially for a child who prefers fact to fiction. Or they could try another nonfiction theme such as describing a favorite animal or place, describing a hobby or crafts project, compiling a cookbook, or writing about a person.

Tomorrow's Alphabet by George Shannon and other books in the "Visual Puzzles & Optical Illusions" chapter provide entertaining models for making books. Children can make their own versions of Shannon's book, Tana Hoban's *Look Book*, a collection of mazes, a riddle book, or another that inspires imitation.

Whatever type of book your child creates, don't forget the "About the Author" paragraph at the back, preferably with a self-portrait. It is always interesting to see how children choose to describe themselves. Look at children's books together for other book parts that can be included, like the "blurb" on the jacket flap that describes a book, the title page (your child may want to invent a publisher's name), endpapers (the decorated pages just inside the book's front and back covers), and even copyright information. Adding these features will alert children to look at those parts in the books they read.

For more writing ideas and advice, take a look at *Live Writing* by Ralph Fletcher, a particularly helpful book for older children who like to write. Children who enjoy composing poetry, and adults who want to help them, will find excellent guidance as well as many poems in *Knock at a Star* by X. J. Kennedy and Dorothy Kennedy (listed in the "Poetry" section). A wonderful look at a real author-illustrator at work is *From Picture to Words* by Janet Stevens, which uses a picture-story-book format to show how she plays with ideas to write a story and illustrate it, and shows some of her dealings with her publisher. Similarly, the short illustrated books *What Do Authors Do?* and *What Do Illustrators Do?* by Eileen Christelow reveal inside information about how children's books are created.

Bookworks: Making Books by Hand by Gwenyth Swain (listed in the "Crafts" section) explains how to make paper and a number of creative ways to bind books, with step-by-step directions. Some children will want to experiment with bindings like accordion books or in different shapes such as Swain describes.

Homemade books also make wonderful gifts, especially for the adults in a child's life. They often become treasured objects that parents, grandparents, and other relatives keep long after the child has grown.

Learning More About Authors and Illustrators

Sometimes a favorite author can be the spark that turns a child into an avid reader. If your child likes a particular author or illustrator, enrich the experience by helping him or her find out more about the person. Children are, in fact, often surprised to realize that books are written by real people, often people who are still alive. Parents and teachers can help instill this understanding, pointing out the biographical information on the book flap, where there is often a photograph, too. When a child likes a certain book, immediately look for others by the same author or illustrator to keep the excitement alive.

It's also increasingly easy to find information about children's authors and illustrators in books and on the Internet. Introducing this kind of research encourages enthusiasm about the writer, and will also come in handy for school projects.

More and more authors are writing autobiographies, a wonderful source of information and inspiration for their fans. Some are easily available, like Beverly Cleary's *A Girl from Yamhill* and *My Own Two Feet,* and Roald Dahl's *Boy: Tales of a Childhood,* all three written for older children. It may take more searching to find *In Flight with David McPhail* or *On the Bus with Joanna Cole: A Creative Autobiography,* both written at a level for younger readers who enjoy McPhail, the creator of Pig Pig, or Cole, the author of the "Magic School Bus" series.

Collective biographies, which cover more than one person, are other good sources of information. A large public library will probably carry *Something About the Author,* a reference set of more than a hundred books filled with profiles of children's authors and illustrators. On a much smaller scale, the three volumes in Pat Cummings's "Talking with Artists" series each have excellent interviews with about a dozen well-known children's book illustrators and samples of their work. A similar volume is Leonard Marcus's *Author Talk*, which has interviews with some of the best and most popular children's writers. A good children's librarian can help you find more information. Some public libraries have videos about children's writers, an entertaining way to meet a favorite author.

If your child wants to write to a favorite author or illustrator, sending the letter to the publisher of one of their most recent books is the best method. If the publisher's address isn't in the book, you can call a public library to get it or find it on the Internet. The publisher will forward the letter—though not always quickly—to the author. It's important for the child to understand that many authors do not have the time to reply to all their mail, even if they enjoy hearing from readers. Some do, of course, which can be exciting and inspiring.

The Internet offers hundreds of Web sites of widely varying quality that relate to children's authors. Jan Brett, for example, has a vibrant Web site with lots of information and activities about her and her books. Other sites give more limited, and sometimes dated, facts about an author. As always, if you want to be sure the information is accurate and up-to-date, check the authority of who put the Web site together and when it was last updated. Some are the author's own page, others are at a publisher's Web site, and still others are maintained by fans or students. Sometimes an author's site will allow a child to send e-mail to the author and, less often, the author will reply. Here are two excellent Web sites with links to Web pages about children's authors and illustrators;

the first Web site also provides links to many children's book publishers.

- Children's Literature WWW Guide, University of Calgary
  www.acs.calgary.ca/~dkbrown/
- Internet School Library Media Center—Index to Children's Authors and Illustrators
  http://falcon.jmu.edu/~ramseyil/biochildhome.htm

Movie Tie-ins to Books

In recent years, many movies have been made based on well-known or lesser-known children's books, among them *Harriet the Spy*, *Madeline*, and *The Witches*. Parents can use this trend to get their kids, especially reluctant readers, excited about the book that led to the movie. Studies have shown that children who have trouble picturing characters and digesting descriptions in a novel find that the movie supplies images for them. They feel more comfortable picking up a novel *after seeing the movie* and reading it with the characters and setting already clear in their minds. This isn't cheating! It is, in fact, a good learning technique for certain readers.

Other children prefer to read a book first so that their reactions to the book aren't influenced by the movie. They may then enjoy seeing the movie and making comparisons. Often the movie will diverge significantly from the book, for better or worse. A movie can add characters and change the plot somewhat, and still capture the spirit of the book; *The Whipping Boy* (movie title *Prince Brat and the Whipping Boy*) is a good example. In other cases, the movie changes the book so drastically that many readers will object to the movie version.

The following list consists mainly of novels and a few picture-story books that inspired major movies. (Many picture-story books have been translated faithfully into video by a company called Weston Woods, and can be found in some public libraries and video stores.) The list, which is just a sampling of what's available, gives the book title and author, then the title of the movie if it differs from the book.

Alias Mrs. Doubtfire by Anne Fine—The movie is called *Mrs. Doubtfire*.

Babe the Flying Pig by Dick King-Smith—The movie is called *Babe*.

The Borrowers by Mary Norton

Charlie and the Chocolate Factory by Roald Dahl—The movie is called *Willy Wonka and the Chocolate Factory*.

Charlotte's Web by E. B. White

Harriet the Spy by Louise Fitzhugh

James and the Giant Peach by Roald Dahl.

Jumanji by Chris Van Allsburg—A picture-story book expanded into a movie.

Madeline by Ludwig Bemelmans—Another picture-story book expanded into a movie.

Matilda by Roald Dahl

Stuart Little by E. B. White

The Whipping Boy by Sid Fleischman—The movie is called *Prince Brat and the Whipping Boy*.

The Witches by Roald Dahl

Television Tie-ins
to Books

Television is often considered the enemy of reading, but if used well, it can sometimes promote books. Some television producers have found a way to highlight good books or have based a television series on a high-quality book or series of books.

Parents can create their own tie-ins between television and books by following up on informational television shows with books that expand on the show's subject. For example, if your child has watched a nature show about a certain animal, stop by the library and pick up a few books on that subject. History shows also lend themselves to follow-up reading.

The public television show "Reading Rainbow," with host LeVar Burton, has been tremendously successful in connecting children with high-quality books. In each episode Burton leads viewers on an expedition that relates to the main book of the show and children recommend other books at the end. Thanks to the show's contagious enthusiasm, many children light up when they see that a book has a "Reading Rainbow" logo on it. (For a guide to past titles, see *Reading Rainbow Guide to Children's Books*. Liggett, Twila C. Carol Publishing, 1994.) Another PBS show that promotes good books is "Storytime."

The "Magic School Bus" shows, based on the high-quality series of science books written by Joanna Cole and illustrated by Bruce Degen, have been another huge success. In the books and on television, children take field trips with the incomparable Ms. Frizzle to learn more about an aspect of science. The television production has inspired many children to read the books, too.

Television has also turned Marc Brown's aardvark Arthur into a superstar. The series deals with the problems children face every day and has struck a chord with young viewers, leading many of them to read the Arthur books.

Miniseries occasionally do justice to a well-loved children's book or series. The *Anne of Green Gables* production on public television pleased many of those who already loved the character, and sent others to read the books. Videotapes of good miniseries can sometimes be found at libraries or video rental stores.

Adults and older children who love children's books might like to tune into the weekly interviews with children's writers and illustrators on "Children's TV" on C-SPAN 2's "Book TV" channel. To see the schedule, log on to www.booktv.org/children.

Here are some television shows based on children's books or series of books. Keep in mind that the shows sometimes switch networks or cable channels. They vary in quality but are worth checking out if you think it might spark your child's enthusiasm for books.

"Arthur" series by Marc Brown (PBS)
"Babar" series by Jean and Laurent de Brunhoff (HBO)
"Clifford" series by Norman Bridwell (PBS)
"Dear America" series by various authors (HBO)
"Dumb Bunnies" series by Dav Pilkey (CBS)
"Franklin" series by Paulette Bourgeois (CBS)
George Shrinks by William Joyce (PBS)
Kipper by Mick Inkpen (Nickelodeon)
Little Bear by Else Holmelund Minarik and Maurice Sendak (Nickelodeon)

"Little Bill" series by Bill Cosby (Nickelodeon)
"Madeline" series by Ludwig Bemelmans (Family Channel)
"Magic School Bus" series by Joanna Cole (PBS)
"Maisy" series by Lucy Cousins (Nickelodeon)
"Paddington" series by Michael Bond (HBO)
"Redwall" series by Brian Jacques (PBS)
Richard Scarry's Busytown (Nickelodeon)
Time Warp Trio by Jon Scieszka and Lane Smith (PBS)
Timothy Goes to School by Rosemary Wells (PBS)

Fiction in Series: A Suggested List

Series books offer many benefits that parents sometimes overlook. For children who do not yet feel comfortable with chapter books, a series can ease the transition from short books to novels. In a series, characters and often settings recur, so readers don't have to learn them from scratch, and instead can concentrate on plot and new language.

Even strong readers enjoy sharing the excitement of series books with other children. Kids trade books and talk about what comes next in the series. They ask for books as presents, and want to stop in bookstores to see if the next sequel is out yet. They may even meet new kids at school or camp and form a bond because they like the same popular series. These are all wonderful ways to get children more excited about reading. Loving a series may provide the first time a child identifies himself or herself as a reader.

Reading series books can turn children into faster, more fluent readers. Research shows that children who read more challenging novels also enjoy series books. Like many adults, these children are reading for more than one reason: to expand their minds, to enjoy themselves, to escape.

Parents who are worried about their child's attachment to series books that are not particularly well-written may like to introduce some of the good books in series listed below. Look for similar genres and age levels, and realize that the new suggestions will not necessarily replace the well-loved series but perhaps supplement it. And remember, your child will not continue to read the same popular series forever.

Reference Books

Reading in Series: A Selective Guide to Books for Children. Edited by Catherine Barr. Bowker, 1999.

Sequels for Readers 10 to 16: An Annotated Bibliography of Books in Succession. Edited by Vicki Anderson. 2nd edition. McFarland, 1998.

Sequels in Children's Literature: An Annotated Bibliography of Books in Succession or with Shared Themes and Characters, K-6. Edited by Vicki Anderson. McFarland, 1998.

Fiction in Series

The books are listed by the first book in the series.

The Adventures of Ali Baba Bernstein. Johanna Hurwitz. Morrow, 1985. Humorous. Ages 8–11.

The Agony of Alice. Phyllis Reynolds Naylor. Atheneum, 1985. Humorous. Ages 11–14.

Amber Brown Is Not a Crayon. Paula Danziger. Putnam, 1994. Contemporary. Ages 8–11.

Anastasia Krupnik. Lois Lowry. Houghton, 1979. Humorous. Ages 9–13.

A Bear Called Paddington. Michael Bond. Houghton, 1960. Fantasy. Ages 8–11.

The Beast in Ms. Rooney's Room. Patricia Reilly Giff. Dell, 1984. Humorous. Ages 6–9.

FICTION IN SERIES: A SUGGESTED LIST

Bunnicula: A Rabbit-Tale of Mystery. Deborah Howe and James Howe. Atheneum, 1979. Mystery. Ages 8–11.

The Burning Questions of Bingo Brown. Betsy Byars. Viking, 1988. Humorous. Ages 9–13.

Cam Jansen and the Mystery of the Stolen Diamonds. David A. Adler. Viking, 1980. Mystery. Ages 7–10.

A Case for Jenny Archer. Ellen Conford. Little, Brown, 1988. Humorous. Ages 7–10.

The Dark Stairs: A Herculeah Jones Mystery. Betsy Byars. Viking, 1994. Mystery. Ages 10–13.

Dealing with Dragons. Patricia C. Wrede. Harcourt, 1990. Fantasy. Ages 10–13.

Dinosaurs Before Dark. Mary Pope Osborne. Random House, 1992. Fantasy. Ages 6–9.

Dog Friday. Hilary McKay. Simon & Schuster, 1995. Humorous. Ages 9–12.

The Ghost Belonged to Me. Richard Peck. Viking, 1975. Ghost story. Ages 10–13.

Harry Potter and the Sorcerer's Stone. J. K. Rowling. Scholastic, 1998. Fantasy. Ages 9–13.

Hatchet. Gary Paulsen. Aladdin, 1999. Survival. Ages 10–14.

Help! I'm a Prisoner in the Library. Eth Clifford. Houghton, 1979. Adventure. Ages 8–11.

Henry and Mudge. Cynthia Rylant. Bradbury, 1987. Easy reader. Ages 3–8.

Herbie Jones. Suzy Kline. Putnam, 1985. Humorous. Ages 8–12.

Homecoming. Cynthia Voigt. Atheneum, 1981. Contemporary. Ages 10–14.

Horrible Harry in Room 2B. Suzy Kline. Viking, 1988. Humorous. Ages 7–10.

The House with a Clock in Its Walls. John Bellairs. Dial, 1973. Supernatural. Ages 9–13.

Junie B. Jones and the Stupid Smelly Bus. Barbara Park. Random House, 1992. Humorous. Ages 6–9.

Knights of the Kitchen Table. Jon Scieszka. Viking, 1991. Humorous. Ages 7–11.

The Lion, the Witch and the Wardrobe. C. S. Lewis. Harper, 1950. Fantasy. Ages 9–13.

Marvin Redpost: Kidnapped at Birth? Louis Sachar. Random House, 1992. Humorous. Ages 6–10.

Meg Mackintosh and the Case of the Missing Babe Ruth Baseball. Lucinda Landon. Secret Passage Press, 1986. Mystery. Ages 7–10.

The Mouse and the Motorcycle. Beverly Cleary. Morrow, 1965. Fantasy. Ages 7–10.

My Father's Dragon. Ruth Stiles Gannett. Random House, 1948. Fantasy. Ages 6–9.

My Teacher Is an Alien. Bruce Coville. Pocket, 1989. Fantasy. Ages 8–12.

Nate the Great. Marjorie Weinman Sharmat. Coward, 1972. Easy reader. Ages 3–8.

The Not-Just-Anybody Family. Betsy Byars. Delacorte, 1986. Humorous. Ages 8–13.

Over Sea, Under Stone. Susan Cooper. Harcourt, 1965. Fantasy. Ages 10–14.

Pinky and Rex. James Howe. Atheneum, 1990. Contemporary. Ages 6–9.

Ramona the Pest. Beverly Cleary. Morrow, 1968. Humorous. Ages 8–12.

Redwall. Brian Jacques. Philomel, 1986. Fantasy. Ages 9–14.

Soup. Robert Newton Peck. Knopf, 1974. Humorous. Ages 9–13.

The Stories Julian Tells. Ann Cameron. Pantheon, 1981. Contemporary. Ages 6–10.

A Toad for Tuesday. Russell E. Erickson. Lothrop, 1974. Fantasy. Ages 6–9.

Wild Magic. Tamora Pierce. Atheneum, 1992. Fantasy. Ages 11–14.

Witch Week. Diana Wynne Jones. Greenwillow, 1982. Fantasy. Ages 9–13.

A Wrinkle in Time. Madeleine L'Engle. Farrar, Straus & Giroux, 1962. Fantasy. Ages 10–13.

Yang the Youngest and His Terrible Ear. Lensey Namioka. Little, Brown, 1992. Sports. Ages 8–11.

Book-Related Parties

Why not bring books into a part of life that most children treasure: parties. Celebrations of all sorts provide great opportunities for including books in a child's life. For any party, books give ideas for activities, games, or crafts that can form the center of the entertainment. Cookbooks are a good place to start while planning refreshments and getting your child excited about what is to come. You are also modeling behavior you hope your child will imitate, using books as resources for enjoyment as well as information.

Some children's books or series are ready-made for parties because they offer so many details related to food, games, and even costumes. The "American Girl" series, which has several commercial tie-ins in the form of dolls and clothing, has inspired bookstores and libraries to put on "teas" based on the books. Parents can easily adopt this idea, which appeals especially to elementary school girls. Thanks to cookbooks and crafts guides about the "Chronicles of Narnia," *The Secret Garden*, *Little Women*, *Anne of Green Gables*, the "Little House" series, and Roald Dahl books, parties centered on these favorites are easy to plan.

Host a cozy "cocoa and books" party, perhaps a slumber party where each child brings a favorite picture-story book and shares it with the other children, before or after cocoa and cookies. Or have a pizza party for younger children and include some books, both about pizza making and stories about pizza. If your child is excited about the best-selling "Harry Potter" books, plan a party based on the series, with some of the many foods described in the books. Your child will undoubtedly come up with other magical touches such as dividing the guests into the four houses at Harry's school or perhaps inventing a board game based on Quidditch, the sport in the series.

For any of the parties, consider giving inexpensive paperbacks related to the theme as party favors, which will last longer than most small gifts sent home with the partygoers.

Here are some other ideas for parties around books in general or a specific book.

Book Character Party

Adapt this popular school idea of a "book character party" for a birthday party at home. Each child comes dressed as a character from a book. Classics like *The Wizard of Oz* and *Winnie the Pooh* make it easy to think of distinctive costumes, but lots of modern books work, too: Lilly with her red cowboy boots from *Chester's Way*, or *Nate the Great* in his detective clothes. For older children, Rudy from *Pool Party* carrying an inner tube or *Harriet the Spy* wearing a backpack are a few of the many characters with distinctive looks. Children who like books enjoy choosing a character and putting together a costume. Start the party with a game where children guess who each character is, giving clues if necessary. In the invitation, suggest that the children bring the related books to share.

Fairy-Tale Character Party

Model this kind of event on the Book Character Party, but with fairy-tale characters. Possible costumes are fairies and elves, fairy godmothers and wicked witches, kings and queens—the possibilities are endless. Plan crafts like making magic wands out of dowels and gold paper or castles out of colored cardboard. And, of course, read some fairy tales and have lots of beautifully illustrated books for the children to look at.

Mad Hatter Tea Party

Use this funny scene from *Alice's Adventures in Wonderland* to plan a party around decorating hats and having tea. Jazz up the room with different kinds of hats, borrowed if you don't own an assortment. Buy inexpensive felt hats and decorate them—with help from a crafts book. With older children, read aloud the scene from the Lewis Carroll book. It consists mainly of dialogue, with four roles; you can add a narrator for the parts that are not dialogue. Get together some shorter books about hats that other children can read aloud if they like, such as *The 500 Hats of Bartholomew Cubbins*, *Three-Hat Day*, and *Caps for Sale*.

A Teddy Bears' Picnic

Have the children invited to the picnic bring their favorite teddy bear and introduce the bear to the other children. Start by reading the book based on the song, *Teddy Bears' Picnic*, of which several versions are available. One of the versions comes with a cassette of a Dixieland rendition by Jerry Garcia and David Grisman. Many children will have heard the song before and can sing along.

Have on hand other books about teddy bears, like *Corduroy* by Don Freeman or *This Is the Bear* by Sarah Hayes.

Happy Birthday to a Favorite Author

Use the birthday of a favorite author as a reason to have a party and to celebrate the author's books. Dr. Seuss's birthday

399

(March 3) has become a national event, celebrated in classrooms across the country with readings of his books. Children can dress up as characters from his books such as Thing 1, Thing 2, Cat in the Hat, and many more. His shorter books lend themselves to impromptu skits as well.

Help your child learn more about the birthday author from books or Web sites (see the sections on the Internet and children's books, and on learning more about authors). Gather together the author's books from your own collection or the local library, and spend some time at the party reading and browsing. Sing "Happy Birthday" to the author, with a birthday cake for him or her. The Web site "Kathy Schrock's Home Page for Educators" (www.discoveryschool.com/schrockguide) lists many authors' birthdays.

Halloween

Halloween and books go hand in hand, whether for costume ideas or party plans. Look for craft books that give instructions for traditional costumes such as pirates, princesses, and monsters that usually require minimal sewing, if any. Directions for mask-making will be found in these books or in other craft books. Book lovers may want to model costumes on characters. For fresh ideas on carving pumpkins, look in the "Cooking" section of this guide for the wonderful book *Play with Your Pumpkins*.

Scary stories, the heart of many Halloween parties, are easily found in books that have tales for children of different ages. The same books may be tapped for slumber parties for older children, or scary tales around the family campfire. (See the chapter on "Ghosts, Aliens, and UFOs" for recommended scary tale collections.)

Cookbooks and Activity Guides Based on Novels

Not all of these books are still in print, so you may need to get them at a library.

Collins, Carolyn Strom, and Christina Wyss Eriksson.
The World of Little House. Harper, 1996.
The Little Women Treasury. Viking, 1996.
The Anne of Green Gables Treasury. Viking, 1997.
Recipes and directions for crafts and games, based on the books in the series.

Cotler, Amy. *The Secret Garden Cookbook: Recipes Inspired by Frances Hodgson Burnett's The Secret Garden.* Illustrated by Prudence See. Harper, 1999.

Fison, Josie, and Felicity Dahl, recipe compilers. *Roald Dahl's Revolting Recipes.* Photographs by Jan Baldwin and pictures by Quentin Blake. Viking, 1994.

Gresham, Douglass. *The Narnia Cookbook.* Illustrated by Pauline Baynes. Harper, 1998.

MacDonald, Kate. *The Anne of Green Gables Cookbook.* Illustrated by Barbara Dilella. Oxford University Press, 1987.

Walker, Barbara M. *The Little House Cookbook: Frontier Foods from Laura Ingalls Wilder's Classic Stories.* Illustrated by Garth Williams. Harper, 1995.

"American Girl" Books

There are related cookbooks and craft books based on each of the various "American Girl" series, set in different times in American history. Here are two examples:

Addy's Cook Book. Pleasant Company, 1994.
Recipes and historical information about cooking based on novels about a girl who, with her mother, escapes from slavery during the Civil War.

Felicity's Craft Book: A Look at Crafts from the Past with Projects You Can Make Today. Pleasant Company, 1994.
Step-by-step directions for crafts tied to the books about Felicity, a fictional girl who lived in Williamsburg in the 1800s.

More Resources and Tips for Parents

Locating the Recommended Books

Libraries

Public libraries are a great resource for parents. They are free, and typically offer a broader and deeper range of books than many bookstores do. Libraries are the best place to find books that are out of print, an important service because many children's books go out of print quickly. Libraries are also more likely than bookstores to carry books from smaller presses.

Good libraries are increasingly easy to use. Many have a Web site so you can check hours and program information. Some public library catalogs can be accessed from home, using a computer and modem. Many libraries are part of a branch system or a large cooperative system, so you can use your card at more than one library. In such cases you can usually return books to the library closest to you, even if you checked them out elsewhere. Most libraries have bookdrops so that you can return books when the library is closed.

Computerized catalogs may intimidate some first-time library users, but most people get accustomed to them quickly. Like the traditional card catalog, the computerized catalog shows you whether your library or your specific branch owns a book, with the added feature of indicating if it is on the shelf or checked out. Often, computerized catalogs also show whether a nearby branch or another library has the book, which you could then borrow through interlibrary loan.

Interlibrary loan (ILL) is a convenient way to get access to many more books than your local library has in its collection. In many libraries, there is no cost to borrow a book through ILL, although some public libraries charge a small fee per book. Some computerized catalogs allow you to input your library card number if you want to request a book from another library. Your local library will call you or send a notice when it arrives, often in a few days.

While you are signing out books, find out what other programs and services your local library offers. You may discover storytimes for younger children, summer reading programs for a wide range of ages, junior critic clubs for older children, programs on parenting, and more. Many libraries also carry audio books and videos.

School libraries come in all sizes, and the large ones will probably have many of the books in this guide. Some school libraries are open during the summer, although most are not. Whether parents can sign out books depends on the school.

Bookstores and Catalogs

Bookstores vary enormously in their selections of children's books. Some offer a wide array of books, usually with an emphasis on paperbacks. Others have only a small selection, or carry mostly books in popular series. Some cities have bookstores devoted just to children's books, a treat for children's book lovers.

It is important to know that most bookstores will order a book for you for no charge if the bookstore doesn't carry it but can get it easily from another source. If you don't see the book you want, ask about placing such a special order. Bookstores are increasing the services they offer families, adding storytimes, author book signings, and other programs.

On-line bookstores such as amazon.com and barnesandnoble.com are increasingly popular. They are especially helpful for getting obscure books that a local store might not carry, or for people who don't live near a bookstore. Their Web sites offer an easy way to survey what books an author has written and if they are available for purchase. They may also offer an out-of-print service to get books that a publisher no longer supplies. It is discouraging how many children's books go out of print quickly, as you can easily see on these Web sites.

Take the recommendations of on-line bookstores and the information they provide with caution. While some of the recommendations come from knowledgeable staff, others seem to stem from sales rather than quality. "Subject" searches on amazon.com, for example, to find books on a certain topic like pirates or whales in no way sort the books for excellence. Worse, a search for fiction on a subject most often turns up nonfiction as well and results in a huge number of series books rather than a few well-chosen novels.

Most catalogs and book clubs typically offer a small selection of good children's books. One exception is Chinaberry Books, an outstanding catalog of more than five hundred children's books, with thoughtful descriptions of each title. It covers toddlers through adolescents, with a section on parenting books and a small selection of novels for adults. *Chinaberry Books, 2780 Via Orange Way, Suite B, Spring Valley, CA 91978. 800-776-2242.*

More Resources About Children's Books

The children's books listed in this guide make up a carefully chosen but small percentage of what's available. If you and your child want to find more good books on a topic, try the resource books listed below. When possible, first ask a good children's librarian or knowledgeable teacher who can advise you. If you are on your own in the library and looking for nonfiction, consult the list of Dewey Decimal numbers that follows this resource book list.

Here are three excellent reference books that most large- and medium-sized public libraries carry. They recommend thousands of good children's books and are arranged and indexed by subject.

- *Best Books for Children: Preschool through Grade 6.* Edited by John T. Gillespie and Corinne J. Naden. 6th Edition. Bowker, 1998.
- *Children's Catalog.* H.W. Wilson. 17th Edition. 1996 plus annual supplements.
- *Elementary School Library Collection.* Edited by Linda L. Homa. 22nd Edition. Brodart, 2000.

To find thousands of picture-story books indexed by subject, check your library for A to Zoo: Subject Access to Children's Picture Books. Compiled by Carolyn W. and John A. Lima. 5th Edition. Bowker, 1998.

If you are looking for the next book in a series that your

child likes and cannot figure out the series order, check your library for these useful guides:

- Anderson, Vicki. *Sequels in Children's Literature: An Annotated Bibliography of Books in Succession or with Shared Themes and Characters, K-6.* McFarland, 1998.
- Anderson, Vicki. *Sequels for Reader 10 to 16: An Annotated Bibliography of Books in Succession.* 2nd Edition. McFarland, 1998.

Here are several other helpful books about children's literature, all available in paperback:

- Horning, Kathleen T. *From Cover to Cover: Evaluating and Reviewing Children's Books.* Paperback: Harper, 1997. This outstanding guide to evaluating children's books explains clearly what elements make a good children's book.
- Kobrin, Beverly. *Eyeopeners II.* Scholastic, 1995. An enthusiastic guide that describes children's nonfiction, arranged by subject.
- Rand, Donna, Toni Trent Parker, and Sheila Foster. *Black Books Galore: Guide to Great African American Children's Books.* Wiley, 1998. An excellent resource for finding books with positive African-American characters, for babies through ninth-graders.
- Odean, Kathleen. *Great Books for Girls: More than 600 Books to Inspire Today's Girls and Tomorrow's Women.* Ballantine, 1997. A 420–page annotated guide to books with strong female characters for children ages 2 to 14.
- Odean, Kathleen. *Great Books for Boys: More than 600 Books for Boys 2 to 14.* Ballantine, 1998. An annotated guide to recommended picture books, novels, biographies, informational books, folklore, and poetry.

Finding Nonfiction
Books in the Library

If your child wants to look at a lot of books on a certain topic, the nonfiction section in a sizable public or school library is a good place to start. Here are some numbers for high-interest subjects in the Dewey Decimal system, the numbering system most public and school libraries use. Not all books on a topic will be at the number given, since many books fit into more than one category. For instance, a book on the *Titanic* could be under history, ships, or archaeology. But this will give you and your child a good place to start for finding nonfiction books on popular subjects.

Spooky Topics
UFOs & Aliens (001.9)
Monsters (001.9)
Dragons (398.4)
Scary Stories (398.2)
Pirates (910.4)
Titanic & Buried Treasure (910.4)

Hobbies and Fun
Codes & Secret Languages (652)
Origami (736)
Drawing (741.2 and 743)
Crafts (745)
Paper Airplanes (745.592)

Ballet (792.8)
Riddles & Brain Teasers (793.73)
Visual Fun (793.8 and 152.1)
Magic Tricks (793.8)
Team Sports (796)
Gymnastics (796.44)
Martial Arts (796.8)

Nature and Technology

Disasters (551 and 620)
Dinosaurs (567.9)
Snakes & Other Reptiles (597.9)
Wolves (599.74)
Airplanes (629.13 and 629.133)
Household Pets (636)
Horses and Horseback Riding (636.1 and 798.2)

Serious Subjects

Death (155.9)
Divorce (306.89)
Child Abuse (362.7)
Sex Education (612.6 and 613.9)
Holocaust and Hidden Children (940.53)

Keeping Up with What's New in Children's Books

If you are interested in keeping up with what's new in children's books, here are some recommended magazines, review journals, and Web sites. Also check your local newspaper, which may have regular or occasional articles on new children's books. Many libraries provide booklists that highlight recent recommended books. For example, each year the American Library Association publishes an annotated list of approximately seventy-five Notable Children's Books, a useful resource available in most libraries and on the American Library Association Web site, listed below.

The Horn Book Magazine is a well-established, bimonthly journal about children's books. It prints insightful reviews of recommended books and well-written articles about children's literature. Available at bookstores and libraries, and by subscription.
800-325-1170
www.hbook.com

Book Links is an attractive, useful magazine of great interest to children's librarians and educators, published by the American Library Association six times a year. It highlights books on selected topics and authors, geared toward curriculum needs. Available by subscription and in many libraries.
888-350-0950
www.ala.org/BookLinks/

BOOK: The Magazine for the Reading Life is a glossy bi-monthly magazine aimed at the general public that carries a column and a limited number of reviews of children's books, both written by Kathleen Odean.
800-317-2665
bookmagazine.com

The *Children's Literature Web Guide from the University of Calgary* is an outstanding site that provides information as well as links to many other good sites.
www.acs.calgary.ca/~dkbrown/

The *Fairrosa Cyber Library of Children's Literature* Web site is an enthusiastic collection of information, links, and booklists.
www.dalton.org/libraries/fairrosa/

The American Library Association Web site provides links to ALA journals, Web site picks for families, booklists, award information, and a limited number of book reviews.
www.ala.org

Useful Books on Serious Subjects

Books can often help children and parents cope with difficult issues. Here are some suggestions of informational books on divorce, death, and sexual abuse that parents may want to share with their children or, in a few cases, give to them to read on their own. The sexual abuse books address prevention and describe some fictional situations of abuse and how to handle them. Several of the books about human sexuality, listed in the "Human Body" section, also discuss sexual abuse.

Many novels involve deaths of humans or pets, divorce, and abuse. A good children's librarian can help you find novels that will suit your child as well as picture-story books on death and divorce.

Death

Brown, Laurie Krasny, and Marc Brown. *When Dinosaurs Die: A Guide to Understanding Death*. Little, Brown, 1996. 32 pages. Ages 3–8.

Bright illustrations from the creator of the Arthur books are combined with sensible advice.

Romaine, Trevor. *What on Earth Do You Do When Someone Dies?* Free Spirit, 1999. Ages 8–12.

This simple, small book covers many questions children have about death, different memorial customs, and ways to cope with feelings about death.

Grollman, Earl A. *Straight Talk About Death for Teenagers: How to Cope with Losing Someone You Love.* Beacon, 1993. 144 pages. Ages 13 and up.

A poetic, effective approach to dealing with the pain and emotions from the death of a close relative or friend.

Divorce

Rogers, Fred. *Let's Talk About It: Divorce.* Putnam, 1996. 32 pages. Ages 3–7.

Rogers, Fred. *Let's Talk About It: Stepfamilies.* Putnam, 1997. 32 pages. Ages 3–7.

Both books use bright photographs and minimal text to advise children gently about these changes in their lives.

Stern, Zoe, and Evan Stern. *Divorce Is Not the End of the World: Zoe's and Evan's Coping Guide for Kids.* Tricycle, 1997. 96 pages. Ages 9–14.

A sister and brother whose parents divorced offer realistic thoughts and useful suggestions in a conversational tone, sometimes disagreeing with each other.

Swan-Jackson, Alys. *When Your Parents Split Up: How to Keep Yourself Together.* Price Stern Sloan, 1997. 90 pages. Ages 9–14.

This helpful book consists largely of a wide range of questions from adolescents about divorce followed by down-to-earth answers.

Sexual Abuse

Spelman, Cornelia. *Your Body Belongs to You.* Illustrated by Teri Weidner. Albert Whitman, 1997. 24 pages. Ages 2–5.

A very simple text illustrated by large watercolors emphasizes a young child's option to refuse unwanted hugs and kisses, and defines and discusses "private parts."

Girard, Linda Walvoord. *My Body Is Private.* Illustrated by Rodney Pate. Albert Whitman, 1984. 32 pages. Ages 4–8.

A girl named Julie talks about privacy, her right to say "no" to being touched, and the importance of talking to her supportive parents if anyone bothers her.

Wachter, Oralee. *No More Secrets for Me.* Illustrated by Jane Aaron. Little, Brown, 1983. 46 pages. Ages 6–9.

Each of the four chapters describes a fictional situation in which a child encounters unwanted touching from an adult, ranging from an insensitive baby-sitter to incest by a stepfather. The children all tell adults who help them.

Terkel, Susan N., and Janice E. Rench. *Feeling Safe, Feeling Strong: How to Avoid Sexual Abuse and What to Do If It Happens to You.* Lerner, 1984. 68 pages. Ages 9–13.

Six scenarios describe children who deal with unwanted touching from relatives, pornographic photo sessions with a neighbor, an incident with an exhibitionist, incest, obscene phone calls, and attempted rape. Each scene is followed by advice on preventing and coping with such abuse.

Author Index

AUTHOR INDEX

AUTHOR INDEX

Title Index

TITLE INDEX

Subject Index

spoonbills, 5
Stetson, John, 151
stock market, 274
string games, 231
subways, construction of, 345
surfing, 321
survival stories. *See* adventure and survival
    stories
swamps, 5
swimming, 322, 326

tamarinds, golden lion, 67
Tarzan, 65
teddy bears, 202, 227, 333, 399
telescopes, 285
television, 249, 388–390
Texas, 48, 122, 152, 155, 192, 339, 352
Thanksgiving, 214
theater, 82–88, 176, 220
Titanic (ship), 254, 255
tongue twisters, 199
tornadoes, 250
trains, 176, 215, 347, 349, 351, 352, 353
trolls, 120
trucks, 347, 348
turtles, 50

UFOs (unidentified flying objects), 127,
    130
Uganda, 64
Underground Railroad, 149
underwater exploration, 55, 57, 60
unicorns, 104
Utah, 22

vampires, 110
Venezuela, 291
Vermont, 46, 276
veterinarians, 47
video games, 245
Vietnam War, 196
virtual reality, 247, 248
visual puzzles, 200, 239–242
volcanoes, 252
volleyball, 324

wars
    Bosnian war, 195
    Civil War, 194, 195, 196
    Revolutionary War, 169, 192, 193

Vietnam War, 196
    World War I, 194
    World War II, 193, 194, 196, 238, 335
Washington (state), 252
Washington, D.C., 146
weapons, 161–166, 189
Weatherspoon, Teresa, 287
West (U.S.), 32, 122, 123, 144, 150–155,
    190, 210–211, 351
westward expansion, 143–145, 148, 159,
    173, 176, 178
whales, 57, 61
whaling, 146
wildfires, 250, 254, 260
wildlife rescue, 57–59, 67–68, 259,
    261–262
witches, 103, 105, 107–110
wizards, 106–111
wolves, 67, 261
women archaeologists, 138
women athletes, 289, 297, 298, 314, 324,
    331
women civil rights activists, 144, 146,
women dancers, 87,
women photographers, 75
women pilots, 334, 336
women pioneers, 144
women rulers, 171, 172,
women scientists, 56, 236, 259
women spies, 195
women, strong
    in fiction, 32, 185, 190, 352
    in folklore collections, 115
    in picture books, 4, 31, 89, 91, 105, 156,
        173, 174, 192, 289
woodworking, 228, 230
World War I, 194
World War II, 193, 194, 196, 238, 335
Wounded Knee Creek, 182
wrestling, 326
Wright, Wilbur and Orville, 339
Wyoming, 26, 33, 155, 182

Yellowstone National Park, 260, 261
yoga, 321
Yom Kippur, 216
yo-yos, 234

zoos, 63, 68

About the Author

KATHLEEN ODEAN has been a children's librarian for seventeen years in schools and public libraries. She is chair of the 2002 Newbery Award Committee and previously served on the Caldecott Award Committee and the American Library Association's Notable Children's Books Committee. She is also a contributing editor for *Book: The Magazine for the Reading Life*. Her two other guides to children's books are *Great Books for Girls: More than 600 Books to Inspire Today's Girls and Tomorrow's Women* and *Great Books for Boys: More than 600 Books for Boys 2 to 14*.